Come with me through
MARK

David Pawson

Terra Nova Publications

This revised edition is published in Great Britain by
Terra Nova Publications International Ltd.
Orders and enquiries: PO Box 2400 Bradford on Avon BA15 2YN UK
Registered Office (not for trade): 21 St.Thomas Street, Bristol BS1 6JS UK

ISBN 978 1901949 88 9

Printed in USA by Createspace.com

Come with me through
MARK

Contents

	Introduction		7
1	Book and Baptism	*1:1 – 13*	9
2	Disciples and Demons	*1:14 – 45*	23
3	Hostility and Authority	*2:1 – 3:6*	41
4	Friends and Foes	*3:7 – 35*	61
5	Parables and Pointers	*4:1 – 34*	79
6	Fear and Faith	*4:35 – 5:43*	97
7	Actions and Reactions	*6:1 – 56*	113
8	Places and People	*7:1 – 8:26*	129
9	Testing and Transfiguration	*8:27 – 9:13*	145
10	Lessons and Life	*9:14 – 50*	163
11	Tough and Tender	*10:1 – 52*	179
12	Colt and Crowd	*11:1 – 11*	197
13	Jesus and Jews	*11:12 – 12:12*	209
14	Cut and Thrust	*12:13 – 44*	227
15	Tragedy and Triumph	*13:1 – 37*	249
16	Anointing and Betrayal	*14:1 – 11*	267
17	Indoors and Outdoors	*14:12 – 52*	277
18	Trial and Execution	*14:53 – 15:47*	287
19	Resurrection and Ascension	*16:1 – 20*	303
	Note on Mark's 'Lost ending'		309
	Appendix: Study Guide		311

INTRODUCTION

I was sitting with the then Archbishop of Canterbury in the little Mermaid Theatre on the bank of the Thames. Curiosity had taken us both to see a unique phenomenon on a London stage. There were no costumes, no scenery and no 'props', except for a small table and chair. A cast of one, by name Alec McGowan, was simply reciting from memory an ancient piece of literature. Yet he held the attention of the packed audience for over two hours. So successful was the performance that it was transferred to a large theatre in the West End, where it ran for months.

As a boy, Alec's grandfather had made him kneel on the carpet, laid hands on his head, and predicted that one day he would 'take the gospel to thousands of people'. But he had become an actor, not a preacher. Now the prophecy was being fulfilled in an unexpected way — for he was narrating a book in the Bible, the Gospel of Mark, written by the man whose mortal remains were brought from Egypt to lie in the Cathedral of St Mark in Venice.

It is an extraordinary story. An unknown young man of thirty abandons his job in the building trade and launches into a new career as travelling preacher and healer. Immensely popular with the general public, he quickly falls foul of the religious leaders of his day and then the political authorities. Just three years later he was dead, executed as a dangerous criminal. End of story? Just the opposite! Three days later, his body had disappeared from his grave. That was only the beginning of the story of which you, the reader, are now part. Read on . . . .

David Pawson

1

BOOK AND BAPTISM
Mark 1:1 – 13

Mark was the first to write down the things that Jesus did, providing an account of his life, death and resurrection, yet this is the Gospel which is most often neglected. It seems that Matthew and Luke both used Mark's details when they wrote their Gospels, adding what they had found out from other sources. John Mark was a friend of both Peter and Paul, and it seems likely that in his home was the upper room where the Last Supper was held and a number of other important events took place. Certainly, there is one very unusual little story in this Gospel about a young man having to run away in the middle of the night without any clothes. It is such an inconsequential detail that many have felt this is Mark's way of saying 'I was there', for there is no obvious point in including that story unless he is referring, humbly and indirectly, to himself. What looks certain is that Mark got most of his details from Peter. This is the one Gospel of the four that constantly brings Simon Peter down a peg or two. One would think that this would not have happened unless Simon Peter himself had passed on these details and wanted someone to tell others that he, Simon Peter, was a simple sinner like everyone else.

This is the shortest Gospel, and you could read it through

quite quickly in one sitting. (Actually, I ask you to do so. If you want to get the most benefit from this study, it would be a great help to you; and preferably read it in a translation with which you are not familiar, then you will be able to get a new flavour of it.) If you add up everything that Jesus says in this Gospel, it only comes to twenty minutes of speech. If you add up all the events portrayed in this Gospel they only come to three weeks. Mark is letting us know that if you just have twenty minutes of what Jesus said, and three weeks of what he did, then you have enough to go on to become a Christian, and to have your life changed completely. Is there anyone else of whom you could say that?

Mark's Gospel is not only the earliest and the shortest, it is easily the liveliest. If you want a narrative with tremendous pace, read Mark's Gospel. He has a favourite word — every preacher has them, and you have them as well, and Mark's is *immediately*, which occurs forty-one times in the first few chapters. Somebody has said that Mark's Gospel is like an express train. That is true: you rush from one thing to the next. 'Immediately' the boat is at the other side. How it got there so quickly, nobody knows! Mark conveys a tremendous sense of events happening *straightway*, *immediately* — it is the same word in Greek. But I would say that Mark's Gospel is like an express train slowing up and finally coming to a grinding halt. In the first few chapters we race through months in a few sentences. Then we begin to slow down and we look at weeks, then we slow down more and begin to look at days, then we begin to reduce speed further and look at hours, until finally we are left at a standstill on a hill outside the city of Jerusalem, as if the whole thing was leading us to that platform, as if the brakes were trying to slow us up and bring us to an utter standstill before the cross and make us look at it. It is very cleverly done, and I am sure the Holy Spirit was guiding Mark to write this way.

He was probably writing for the Romans, who were very practical, down-to-earth people. They loved an exciting drama and they wanted action — they were not usually interested in mystical philosophy. Mark offered history that was full of action and excitement. As he wrote it down, his pen kept writing that word *immediately*. So it is the shortest, the earliest, and the liveliest of the four Gospels.

What is Mark's Gospel about? Let me underline that it is not a biography. Sometimes I have heard people say that Matthew, Mark, Luke and John wrote biographies of Jesus. But this Gospel would be a very curious biography! It only mentions three out of Jesus' thirty-three years, with nothing about his birth, his boyhood or eighteen years spent working as a carpenter. Furthermore, a third of this book is spent on his death. Some Victorian writing emphasised deathbed scenes — but a third? This would be going a bit too far, surely, in any biography. Had Mark been giving us a biography he would not have spent a third of the book on Jesus' death. So it is not meant to be a story, or a biography, it is a *Gospel*.

What does this word 'Gospel' mean? In English it means the story of God. It goes back to two Anglo-Saxon words, *God* and *spell*, and *spell* means a story, so 'God-spell' or 'Gospel' means 'God's story'. But that is not the meaning of the Greek word that Mark used. What was the meaning? It is exciting. Very often in the Roman empire there was a big war going on at some distant boundary, and the people waited, breathless, in the city of Rome, for news of the battle, to hear whether it had been won or lost. If it had been won, the messenger would come running into Rome, shouting, 'Gospel, gospel, gospel!' And he meant victory. Good news: the battle is over and it has been won. That is what the word *gospel* means. It does not just mean something nice to hear or a good story, or even the story of God, it means this: a battle has been fought and we can now announce the victory — peace can be ours.

That puts the word 'Gospel' into a really exciting context. It is my job as a preacher to be a preacher of the *gospel*. When I was ordained a minister I was told to preach the gospel, to tell people the war is over and they can have peace because the victory has been won.

What war was going on here? One might say it looks like a war between Jesus and the Jews — that comes out again and again. If that is the war, then Jesus won. We do not realise that until the last page, but don't read that first because it spoils it! But that is not the warfare Mark is writing about. One might say that here is a war between good and evil. There is a truth in that too, because we see in Jesus goodness personified, and we see in some of the other people — Herod, Pilate and others — evil personified, and we see a battle between the two. So we could say that good wins, as in so many nice stories — but it is more than that. In the very first part of the Gospel, the battle is shown to be between God and Satan. That is the warfare. That battle was engaged two thousand years ago, and the victory has been won by God — the beginning of the Gospel, the good news of victory. How did it all take place? Where was the warfare engaged? The answer is: in a man called Jesus Christ, who was also the Son of God.

So the real question about this book is not '*What* is it

about?' but, '*Who* is it about?' It is about a man called Jesus — a historical human being. But if that was all you could say about him it would not be a Gospel. I have met people who believe that Jesus was a great man, a great healer, a great teacher, a great leader, but they believe no more than that. The simple result is they have no *gospel* to preach, they have no good news to offer people. They can only say, 'Well, try and copy him; try to live as he would have you live.'

They have no victory to announce because they only have Jesus as a human being. But Mark tells us that his gospel is *the gospel about Jesus Christ.* (See Mark 1:1, *NIV.*) The word translated *Christ* has tremendous meaning. Its significance went back in the history of this people of God called Israel, to the days when they first got a king. It refers to one who was anointed with oil. When Queen Elizabeth II was crowned in Westminster Abbey, her forehead was anointed with oil. That act was called the 'Chrism' — it means being anointed to be king or queen. A 'Gospel' is what it is because it is not just about a human being called Jesus, it is about someone who is an anointed *king.* That is what the word Christ means. But if you believe that Jesus was a human being and you also believe that he was the King of the Jews, their Christ, you still have not got a *gospel.* Of what possible interest is it to us Gentiles in the twenty-first century that there was a man called Jesus who was anointed King of the Jews? No interest at all, unless you are interested in history.

Why, then, is this a gospel for today? Because this was not only a human called Jesus, and not only a Jewish king, the Christ, but *the Son of God.* Here was no ordinary human being, here was God's own Son on earth — that is what makes it a *Gospel.* Because for the first time God was in the battle; for the first time the warfare was being fought by God and not just by men, and God's own Son was fighting it, and got the victory, so that it is *the beginning of the gospel of Jesus Christ, the Son of God*. Now we have some good news; now we have a Gospel to look at.

This, then, is an account of how our religion began, of how Christianity started. And from the very beginning one could write this in large, golden letters: *Christianity is Christ*. We are not preaching opinions, we do not have a new philosophy, we do not have a new system or even a way of life, we have a person to preach about — *Jesus Christ, the Son of God*. It is his story. I once put up on a church notice board this saying: 'History is *his-story*'. I had people ask me what it meant, and it gave me a grand opportunity to tell them. He split history into AD and BC. This is his story, and the only bit of history everyone really needs to know is this part. If they do not know this, they are lost; if they do know this and believe in the person who is described here, they are being saved.

Look at John the man, first of all. Here is a most interesting person. Consider the place where he lived. It is not very large — about thirty miles long and fifteen miles across — but I have never seen anything so horrible, so utterly desolate. Death broods in its valleys. It is in the rain shadow, so no grass grows there and it is barren and dead. It is a sloping piece of land between the top of the Judean hills and the Dead Sea many thousands of feet below.

John did not have any food to speak of, so he lived off locusts and wild honey. He did not have any decent clothes. He had an old camel's hair coat around him and a leather belt, and that was it. And John was getting a congregation of thousands. There was something about him that was different. What was it?

John was both a *fulfilment* of prophecy and a *revival* of prophecy. Many centuries earlier, God had made certain predictions which were promises: one day he would send to them a 'Messiah' (Christ), but God revealed that he would first send someone to prepare the way. There must be a highway, a straight, level road, because the king was going to come. Isaiah taught this about six hundred years before Jesus came. Around four hundred years before Jesus came, Malachi, the very last prophet of the Old Testament, said that, when he came, the people would have to be cleaned up with soap. (You can read about this in Malachi chapter three.) John the Baptist was that messenger. He was one of those great men whose work is to play second fiddle to someone else. He was a humble man, and he could do it. He was a *fulfilment* of prophecy.

But more than that, John was a *revival of prophecy*. Do you realise what it must be like to wait for four centuries before God speaks to you? The people of Israel had been waiting that long for a man to say just four words: *Thus says the Lord*. After all the prophets, from Moses to Malachi, this was a terrible loss. In our Bibles there is a gap of four hundred years between Malachi and Matthew, because nobody spoke from God. No wonder the people went out from all Judea and Jerusalem to see John — they had waited so long! Prophecy was revived again. Once again there was a man who could say: this is what God is saying to you now — and they dashed out to hear. Then they noticed that he was wearing the same type of clothing as Elijah. The crowds got the message. God was speaking again.

What then was John's mission? He came preaching. I have been at conferences where it has been suggested that the church should stop preaching. It has been said that preaching is a waste of time and it is just talk, that we must feed the hungry and clothe the naked and care for the immigrants, and this is mission and this is what God is telling us to do. There is a place for these things, and they ought to be done. But what is the first thing we are told to do? I can put it another way: what is the biggest need of men and women today? Food for their bodies? No. Freedom for their minds? No. *Forgiveness of sin* is still the greatest need of men and women, and I know of no other way to meet that apart from preaching the gospel.

The forgiveness of sins is at the heart of Christian preaching. It is the greatest blessing you can be offered, and it is your fundamental need. To live with a guilty conscience is the worst thing that you can go through, and the forgiveness of sins is the loveliest thing to experience. Two things were needed to express forgiveness of sins: repentance and *baptism*. This message goes straight through into the rest of the New Testament. If you are in need of forgiveness of sins, the two things I must say to you are: repent, and be baptised. What is repentance? It is not just feeling sorry — that could be remorse or regret. Repentance is more than the emotions, it is the *mind* saying: it is wrong and I do not want to do it again. But, above all, it is the *will* saying: I turn away from it and I turn to God. Repentance may be accompanied by feelings, it will certainly involve thoughts, but if it is real it will issue in an act.

Baptism is also an act. The word means to dip or to plunge or to drench. So John was given a nickname: the 'dipper', or the 'plunger' or the 'drencher', or the 'baptiser', whichever word you use. The word is better translated or used as 'plunge' or 'dip'. Why did John plunge them? He was communicating to people: do you want to be clean from head to toe? — then this is how to show it; wash yourselves, and express your appeal to God for a clean conscience this way. It always did mean that, but the significant thing is that, until John came, no Jew had ever been baptised, only Gentiles. This was because, to the Jew, it was the Gentile who was unclean and who needed to wash himself; it was the Gentile who needed to get his past washed away, and so the Jew was quite happy to baptise Gentiles when they came to the synagogue, but he would not baptise a Jew. After all, if you were a Jew you had been circumcised when you were a baby, you had been through all the ceremonies, you belonged. The most startling thing about John the Baptist is that he is saying to people who have been through all the religious ceremonies, who outwardly belong to the people of God, 'Repent and be baptised for the forgiveness of your sins.' I must say that, however offensive it may seem to some, I care not what religious ceremonies you went through as a baby, and whether your name is on a membership roll of a church or not, my message is repent and be baptised for the forgiveness of sins. This is what John was saying to the people, and it was offensive to them. They had been circumcised. Jesus had been circumcised, and had been dedicated as a baby, yet he came at the age of thirty and asked to be baptised, and he approved John's ministry in so doing.

This was John's mission, and I underline it because I think it is important that John's appeal was not to babies but to believers. You cannot tell a baby to repent and be baptised.

COME WITH ME THROUGH MARK

It was to mature, morally responsible people who were guilty and needed cleansing. I believe that what the world needs more than anything else today is an appeal to mature, morally responsible adults to repent and be baptised for the forgiveness of their sins, and not to rely on any connection outwardly or physically by heredity with the people of God.

John declared, *"After me will come one more powerful than I, the thongs of whose sandals I am not worthy to stoop down and untie"* (Mark 1:7, *NIV*). I find here a most interesting little insight. In the order of slaves — and they had a grading system whereby each slave had certain duties — the job of the second from the bottom was to untie shoes. After that slave had untied the shoes, the bottom one had to wash the feet. Does that speak to you about the humility of Jesus? So John was indicating that he was not even fit to be the second from the bottom, but when Jesus came he came to be the bottom one. Then John said something else. This mighty one who was coming after John was needed by men because he could give a baptism that John could not give. John said, *"I baptise you with water, but he will baptise you with the Holy Spirit"* (Mark 1:8, *NIV*). This was a baptism they would need as well. Here are two baptisms mentioned at the beginning of the Gospel itself. One is a physical one, the other is spiritual; one is an outward thing, the other is an inward thing; one deals with your past, the other deals with your future; one is connected with pardon, and the other is connected with power. John is indicating that he can only help to a certain point; you will need the one he says is coming after him, and you will need the Holy Spirit.

John's work was to connect people to God. He was baptising them and getting hold of them. But now the other thing that John needed was to get hold of this Christ. How was he going to do this? If John was going to connect Israel with Israel's king, he needed to be in contact with both, and so far he had only contacted Israel.

On one particular day John saw his cousin Jesus coming along the river bank and, to John's astonishment, Jesus asked to be baptised. We know from the other Gospels why John thought he should not be, and why Jesus thought he should be. I am not going to dwell on that because it is not here. The simple fact is that Jesus was baptised, and if Jesus was, and calls me to be, can I refuse? There were, however, three unique features of Jesus' baptism.

First, Jesus saw heaven being torn open (Mark 1:10), which means that the clouds parted, and suddenly, they saw right up through the heavens to the deepest blue of the sky, and way down through the gap in the clouds there came a white dove — not the symbol of peace as we often think it is, but the symbol of God's power: the dove that brooded over the chaos in Genesis 1:3 and brought the order of the universe out of the chaos; the dove that brings order and power; the Holy Spirit was coming. Jesus did not preach a single sermon or perform a single miracle before this moment. Why not? Because, being a real human being as well as the Son of God, he could not do it without the Spirit's power. Jesus needed an anointing of the Holy Spirit with power, to do what he did. As the great American evangelist D. L. Moody once said: 'If the Holy Spirit, who came down on Jesus and enabled him to do what he did, is available to a man today, what could that man not do with that same Spirit?' Then he wrote in his diary that night, 'I intend to be that man', and that day Moody began his great work.

If the power of the same Holy Spirit who came down on Jesus at the Jordan river is available to us, then the truth of what Jesus later said can be seen clearly: *". . . anyone who has faith in me will do what I have been doing."* [I wonder if any Christian has ever had faith to believe that Jesus meant what he said.] He continued, *"He will do even greater things than these."* (See John 14:12, *NIV*.) Lord, we believe, remove our unbelief! That was the vision, and it should encourage every Christian today to seek the Holy Spirit's anointing with power.

Second, there was a voice, obviously God speaking. Notice that God quotes the Old Testament twice—but then he is only quoting himself, because it was his word originally.

What God said is most interesting. It comes from Psalm 2:7 and Isaiah 42:1, and it refers to two things that he had said hundreds of years earlier. One was *"You are my Son"* which in the context of Psalm 2 is a coronation service for a sovereign. But in Isaiah 42:1 the words *"in whom I delight"* refer not to a sovereign but to a servant. Here is the amazing thing. Psalm 2:7 concerns the highest place that man can have, a sovereign ("You are my Son"), but Isaiah 42 ("in whom I delight") concerns the lowest. When Jesus was baptised, we see that the Father wanted him to combine the highest and the lowest — greatest sovereign and humblest servant — in his ministry. That is what his baptism meant to Jesus. It meant taking the responsibility of being King of kings and Servant of servants. How do you combine the two? I only know that when I look at the life of Jesus Christ I see the highest and the lowest perfectly combined. I see someone who can wash feet and wear a crown with equal dignity. I see someone who fits anywhere in the social scale. I see someone who is equally at home with the highest and the lowest in the land—with the religious and political leaders, and with women of the streets.

A vigil followed. I have read elsewhere that Jesus was alone for forty days after his baptism, but don't you believe it, he was anything but alone. I know there were no human beings, but it was a pretty crowded scene in the wilderness. The Spirit led him into the wilderness, so the Spirit was with him; Satan met him there, so Satan was with him; he was with the wild beasts — they prowled around him — and the angels came and ministered to Jesus. If you have no other human beings near you, that does not mean you are alone. Sometimes when you are sitting by yourself, with nobody in sight, the room seems crowded. We need to remember that the angels worship with us when we are in church. Jesus was not alone in the wilderness, the battle had begun. On the one side the Spirit and Jesus and the angels; on the other, the wild beasts and the devil. Natural and supernatural forces were engaged. It is significant that it was *after* the high moment of Jesus' baptism that this battle took place. There is a spiritual battle on, and we are fools if we think we can just have nice times in church without engaging in this warfare. But Jesus went into it, and he came out in the power of the Holy Spirit, and the first round was won. Following that victory he began to preach and liberate the victims of Satan in Galilee — the first public episode in his ministry, which we look at in the next chapter.

2

DISCIPLES AND DEMONS
Mark 1:14–45

One of the most amazing things about the life of Jesus, which is nowhere mentioned in the Bible or anywhere else, is the fact that he spent eighteen years in a village carpenter's workshop and only three doing what God had called him to do. Eighteen years stuck in that little place making doors, chairs, window frames and tables, and then just three years healing people and travelling around doing a public work. It should encourage a lot of other people who feel that their life is circumscribed and that they are limited in their opportunities. Those eighteen years in a village working with a hammer and chisel and saw are over by the time Mark's Gospel begins, and our Lord has now come right out into the centre of the stage and is going to begin his public work. In the public three years we find the deepest meaning of what he came to do.

He began his ministry when John was put in prison. John and Jesus were not rivals. Some people tried to set them off one against the other, and they came to John the Baptist one day and pointed out that Jesus was getting a bigger congregation. The devil loves to set the people of God against each other like this. But John's reply to such talk was along the lines of: that doesn't matter, I came to get ready for him and if I get smaller and he gets bigger that's as it should be;

if I become less and he becomes greater, that is right and proper. What a big man it takes to say that. John was thrown into prison. He had done all he could to get people ready, so now Jesus must start.

It is interesting to notice not only the time when Jesus began but the place, Galilee. I can see a lot of interesting things in that, but I shall give you only two. One is this: it was where he *lived*. It is comparatively easy to go and preach somewhere else, but in front of people who know you, that is not always the case. I remember the first time I had to preach in front of all my family and relatives. I would much rather have gone and preached in front of a million in America than preach in front of those few. Jesus began to preach in Galilee, where he had been a carpenter and everybody knew he was the man down the street if you wanted a table mended.

The other interesting thing is this: Judea is on the road to nowhere; Galilee is on the road to everywhere. I have no doubt that he chose to start his ministry there because it was at the centre of the world. Imagine a map of the region. There is a road that goes from Europe down through to Arabia and ultimately to the East. There is another road that comes from Asia through Mesopotamia, through Damascus, down through the middle to Egypt and to Africa, so that those three continents were linked by a gigantic crossroads, and the junction was about three miles from Nazareth in Galilee, at a place called Megiddo. It always has been the crossroads of the world, with Nazareth just above the crossroads — so it was called Galilee of the nations, Galilee of the Gentiles — and everybody came through Galilee one way or another. One of the places on that main road was a fishing town called

Capernaum. Jesus was choosing to begin his ministry at the very point where news of it could go to every part of the world, and perhaps that is why he began in Galilee.

There are three features of his wonderful ministry that come out in these verses. The first is the remarkable *pattern* of his ministry. What did he actually do? The answer is very simple: in his grace and power he met the threefold needs of men — physical, mental and spiritual. The ministry of our Lord was to the *whole* of man, and it was for the *whole* world. We find this balance: he preached to meet all three kinds of needs.

Take first the *preaching*. Jesus believed in preaching. This was the fundamental priority of his ministry. He did not begin with healing, he began with preaching. And the church, in the days when it spread so rapidly in its first three hundred years, always had this priority: there was healing and there was teaching, but they *began* with preaching. They did not begin by opening a school or a hospital, they began with preaching and the other things followed. This is the emphasis of our Lord's ministry because this is the way in which God meets the deepest needs of men. As we saw earlier concerning the ministry of John, the deepest need of every man and woman on earth is the need of forgiveness. Why did Jesus begin with preaching? Because the world is in the grip of Satan, and Jesus came to set men free from that grip. The world was full of vice and crime, disease and death, pain and suffering; but all these things were caused by one thing only, and that was the grip of evil. Therefore, Jesus was going to tackle that. He came preaching about this, and he came saying certain things. I want to single out seven key words.

Gospel is the first key word: he came preaching the gospel, and that means the good news of freedom to those who have been bound by an enemy.

Secondly, Jesus came to preach the gospel of *God*. He was teaching that *God* is doing something for you: he has come to set you free. When you read the Old Testament you find that people recognised that the world was not good, it was full of things that were evil and enemies of men, and for century after century the people had been waiting and longing for God to do something — and they prayed for him to come and set them free from these things.

Time is key word number three: the *time* is fulfilled. In other words, the things that you have been waiting for are *now*; the timetable of God is here; the things that people have longed for for centuries are now coming true. When you study the social and political history of that period, you realise that Jesus was born at the crucial time. If he had been a hundred years earlier or a hundred years later it would have been the wrong time. Everything was just right for God to do something about the plight of men.

Key word number four is *kingdom*. This is a word that is most misleading, especially to us who live in the United Kingdom. We think of a political or a geographical region. But I learned what the word 'kingdom' means by living in Arabia for three years. I found that on the map of Arabia, which is an oblong shape sticking out into the Indian Ocean, the boundaries are straight dotted lines, and when you go and look for them all you can see is sand dunes. I travelled many hundreds of miles by Land Rover over nothing but desert, rock and sand. You could not tell where one kingdom began and where another ended, it all looked the same. But there were kingdoms there, and they called them sheikhdoms. If you were under the power of a particular sheikh then you were in his kingdom. If he could reach you and force you to do something, then you were counted as in his kingdom. You could not put that on a map, you could only put a dotted line. That is what the word means in the Bible, it does not mean a political or a geographical area, but the reach of power.

The next point is that this kingdom was *at hand*. Jesus said, *"My kingdom is not of this world"* (John 18:36, *NIV*). What does it mean? It means this: wherever God's power reaches out and controls, that is the kingdom of God. Jesus said, *". . . if I drive out demons by the Spirit of God, then the kingdom of God has come upon you"* (Matthew 12:28, *NIV*). Wherever a life is being touched by the power of God, there is the kingdom. If we would like to live in the kingdom of God we do not need to move house or change jobs, we do not need to get a boat or a plane. You can live in the kingdom of God at this very moment if you allow God's power to take hold of and control your life. This is tremendous because: God has power over disease; God has power over death; God has power over fear; God has power over all the things to which we are prey. Therefore, if I allow the power of God to enter my life then I am in the kingdom. I shall see these things under his control, and he will control these things within my own life because I shall be within the reach of his power. This world is *not* the kingdom of God — according to Jesus it is the kingdom of Satan. That is why our newspapers are full of lust and cruelty, bloodshed, suspicion and hatred, because this world is not the kingdom of God. But wherever someone comes under the power of God, and the evil things are put out of his life by God's power, that person has entered the kingdom and is living within the reign of God — God is reigning over his life. The good news that Jesus preached was that the kingdom of God is breaking into this world *now*; it is very near *now*; you enter it *now*; you can live under God's power *now*; you can have God's power conquering the enemies in your life *now*. That is good news, tremendous news — it is a *gospel*. So Jesus came preaching the gospel of the kingdom of God which was *at hand*.

The next key word is *repent*. How can we hope to be in the kingdom of God and ask God to deal with our enemies if we do not want him to deal with our sins? How can I ask God to get disease out of my life if I am unwilling for him to get envy out of my life? How can I expect God to give me the victory over death if I do not want the victory over bad temper? In other words, you cannot have God in bits and pieces, you cannot have God help you with one enemy if you want to hang on to another enemy. All the enemies of God and all the enemies of men must be dealt with at the same time. While I may feel that my sickness is an enemy that God should help me to conquer and should banish from my life, I must also realise that gossip and worry are just as much enemies of God as illness and disease.

How then do I get ready for the power of God to break into my life and give me the victory? The answer is: I repent. In calling people to repent, Jesus was saying just what John said before him. In other words, when God comes, he comes to put everything right, not just what we want put right. So the need is to repent, which is to change our minds and to hate the things we have done that were wrong. Let me underline this. Most of us are sorry when we have done wrong if the wrong catches up with us and we suffer for it. The real test of whether we have repented is whether we feel sorry about the things we did that were wrong that nobody knows about and that have not cost us anything. If we do, we are repentant. A man who was asked by a magistrate, 'Are you sorry about this?' replied, 'Yes.' The magistrate continued, 'What are you sorry about?' and he answered, 'I'm sorry I was caught.' The criminal was being absolutely honest, and he had plenty of remorse, which he expressed in that court, but he was not repenting. Cain never repented of the murder of Abel; he may have been terribly sorry he did it because it cost him so much, but he was never sorry about the thing he did. The repentant person will say, 'Lord, I have asked you to get me out of this trouble, I have asked you to banish this enemy, but I am sorry about all the other things now and I am asking you to put all of it right,' and then believe the good news.

Believe is the final key word. Believing is the opposite of seeing. Do not believe those who say seeing is believing. I would say that seeing is not believing, because once you have seen, there is no more need to believe. The kingdom of God is an invisible kingdom — the power of God is invisible. You must believe that it is breaking through, you must believe that it is at hand and that God can give you the power to conquer. Repent and believe. This was Jesus' preaching to the soul.

So Jesus' teaching was for the *spirit*. It was also to the *mind*. One of man's greatest needs is to get the truth, to know the difference between true and false, right and wrong — he needs teaching.

The synagogue was the place of teaching in Israel. There

was one synagogue to every ten families and it was the place where many received education. Within the synagogues there were scribes, and their job was to teach what was right and what was wrong, what was true and false. But they did it in a peculiar way. They did not do it by saying, 'This is right and that is wrong,' they did it by saying, 'One of our ancient scholars said this is right,' quoting what some great rabbi had said. They were always quoting somebody else. Maybe you have heard preachers like that, who are always quoting great men and flinging out quotations by the yard — that is how the scribes did it. They always quoted the authorities, the scholars, the experts. But when Jesus got up one day in the synagogue to teach we are told that the congregation was absolutely astonished because he did not quote anybody else, he just told them what was right and what was wrong on his own authority. He taught them as *one having authority*. That can mean one of two things. We might say of someone that he is an authority in his subject, and what we mean by that is don't argue with him, he knows, he has the expertise, he has the knowledge so you cannot argue with what he says. But it can also mean something much deeper. When Jesus taught, he not only taught as having the authority of one who knew, who did not need to look up the books or to quote others, he spoke and things happened. This is a unique authority. One kind of authority is that of the expert to whom you go with a problem and ask what should be done; the expert sits behind a desk and tells you the right thing to do. The other kind is when the man behind the desk presses a button on the desk and another man comes in, and the man behind the desk tells him about the problem and orders him to get it sorted out, and it is. That is the authority of power, as well as the authority of knowledge. Jesus had both. He had the authority of knowledge — it was not possible to beat Jesus in an argument because he *knew*, but he had the authority of power as well. The people knew this because in the middle of the synagogue service (this does not often happen in a service, and it is pretty disturbing when it does) somebody challenged him. It was a man who was possessed by a demon who got up, and yelled: *'What do you want with us, Jesus of Nazareth? Have you come to destroy us? I know who you are — the Holy One of God!'* (Mark 1:24, NIV) Can you imagine somebody shouting that in the middle of a service? And Jesus said, *"Be quiet! Come out of him!"* The man fell down in a faint, then came round and was perfectly normal. This was authority; it is not just saying from a pulpit, 'This is it', it is being able to say, 'Do this' and it is done. They were amazed; they had never had any teaching like this.

The third area of Jesus' ministry was healing for the body. All of us face sickness sooner or later. We find that whatever sickness Jesus encountered — sometimes acute conditions such as fevers; sometimes chronic sickness; sometimes illnesses which in those days were incurable — Jesus was able to deal with it. Usually he did something physical — he might touch the sufferer. There was no situation beyond his control. Just imagine what would happen if a man arrived in your town who could cure every known disease. Supposing you heard that he was at the bus station and he was curing every known disease without a failure yet. What queues there would be! People say that health is everything, but it is not, the Bible does not say it is. Those who think health is everything would do all within their power to get near a man like this, and people flocked to him. So the pattern of our Lord's ministry is wonderfully balanced. All the needs of mankind — physical, mental and spiritual — come within his reach. Therefore our ministry, following his, must be balanced and must seek to meet all the needs of men—in his name.

Jesus had partners in his ministry. I remember hearing about a fine Christian man who was a Sunday school superintendent and evangelist. He did so much good. But somebody said this about him to me: 'He can only work on a committee of one.' I know what was meant. Although he did a great deal of good, it was always by himself. You could never say this about Jesus. He was a unique individual, but never an individualist. We shall think about his human and divine partners.

Let us consider his human partners first. To extend his ministry, he called other people to share it. This would mean extending it in space while he was still on earth, and extending it also in time after he left earth. So he called men to be his disciples and apostles. I do not know whether you realise the excitement of this, but when you read the story of how he walked along the shores of Galilee and called four fishermen, it was the beginning of the church. That was the beginning of a human society which would last two thousand years and more. Every group of believers calling themselves a church began on the morning Jesus walked along that shore and said to four fishermen, *"Come, follow me."* So simple a beginning, so utterly sublime. It is remarkable that the church should have started in that way, not with a committee, not with a great assembly, not with a procession, not with a lot of hullabaloo, not with a lot of different vestments, not with a lot of paraphernalia; just four fishermen and Jesus walking along the seashore. Maybe the church would be more effective today if it had managed to retain that simplicity.

They had met Jesus before, when they had been with John the Baptist down by the Jordan river. Now we notice two things: first of all, what they were (or, rather, what they were not); and, secondly, what Jesus said to them. First, what they were. They were young, so they were not very experienced or mature. Most of them were probably in their teen years or early twenties. They had not had much education such as all of us have had in this country. They were ordinary people who worked with their hands. From the world's point of view they were nobodies. And God chooses nobodies. He does not choose people for what they are but for what they are not. This is the story of the Bible; this has been the story for two thousand years. He takes a cobbler in Northamptonshire and turns him into a William Carey. He takes a parlourmaid from London and makes a Gladys Aylward of her. Thank God he chooses nobodies! If God had said that he needed a church of rich people, clever people and good people then there would be no hope for most or all of us. But he did not start that way, he started with a group of ordinary, young, working men and said, *"Follow me"*. In other words, everything that they would be was because of him. They would therefore give glory to God and not to themselves. They were nothing. Of course, as fishermen they would be tough, they would be brave, they would be patient, but they were just fishermen. They were certainly not very religious people.

In 1948, the Dead Sea Scrolls were discovered. I have been down to the caves where they were found and saw the ruins of the Qumran community — a company of monastic

Jews called the Essenes who were there in the time of our Lord, or just before. And there were monasteries of holy Jewish people who had given their whole lives to prayer, fasting and studying the scriptures, and who lived all over Judea at the time of Jesus. We did not know this until the Dead Sea Scrolls were discovered. The interesting thing is that Jesus did not go to the monasteries for his disciples; he did not go to the religious people for them. A man once said to me, 'Ah well, you're religious and I'm not.' But I was not religious when God called me, I was milking cows! Amos could say: I was a vinedresser; I was looking after a market garden and God touched me. It has been like this ever since. The tragedy is that although the church started with a group of working men like this, it is the one group that you cannot find in the church today in any great number. Jesus chose them for what they were not, rather than for what they were — ordinary, practical, down-to-earth, uneducated men; he told them to follow him, and he would make them fishers of men.

Notice he made a demand and an offer simultaneously. He never makes a demand without making an offer, or an offer without making a demand — the two go together. The demand was 'follow me' — unconditional. He did not lay down any terms. He did not say, 'Is there a shop steward of the fishermen's union that I'll have to negotiate with? What wages will you require? How many hours will you work for me?' He said, *"Come, follow me."* Only the Son of God has the right to tell a man to do that. Unconditional! It was going to be a kind of slavery and yet perfect freedom. So Jesus made the demand with no conditions, no terms — and they did follow him, leaving immediately. It meant giving up a good job; and, in some cases, leaving their relatives. Simon had to leave a wife, presumably. Zebedee the father was left by James and John. It meant, ultimately, leaving their life, because only one of those original disciples died of old age in bed; the others were martyred, yet they had followed him immediately. When Jesus calls you to follow him, you cannot make conditions or terms, you cannot say, 'Well, Lord, I will follow you if . . .', or, 'I will follow you but . . .' There are cases in the Gospels of people who have tried to do this, but there can be no 'buts', we are simply to follow.

The offer was a wonderful one. If they followed him, he would make them fishers of men. They were pretty good at handling those nets, but he was going to help them handle people. Maybe one of the greatest things that Jesus can say to a man or woman today is, 'You may be very clever with things but I am going to make you wise with people, I am going to help you to help others.' Notice he did not call them to an easy life. He did not say: follow me and I will make you happy; follow me and I will make you contented; follow me and I will make you peaceful; follow me and I will make you prosperous. The message was: follow me and I will make *you* work; follow me and you won't get out of fishing — your fishing will be more demanding; follow me and I will make you able to do things. He does not call us to a life of ease, but if they followed him they could do a job that they had not been doing before. From cobbling shoes William Carey went to mend lives in India; from cleaning a home in the middle of London Gladys Aylward went to cleaning lives in China. If those he called followed him he would make them skilful in handling others, bringing them to God and helping them. That was the offer. So these were the human partners in his ministry.

We turn now to the divine partner. It is very easy to get so involved with people that you lose touch with your divine partner — Jesus never did. Prayer was more important to him than sleep, so he would get up very early in the morning, and he would get alone with the Father, who was his other partner. He had human partners and he had a divine partner. He was down-to-earth with the men he chose, and he was up to heaven with the Father he loved. Jesus was not a mystic shut away, he was right in the middle of human society, and he would get up before daybreak and pray. This is the secret of ministry: to get right in among ordinary folk and love them as he loved them, and to get right away from them and love God. It is this combination of getting into society and out of it again that marks the life of Jesus. Once again, I am impressed with the balance of our Lord's ministry. As far as the pattern goes, he balanced their physical, mental and spiritual needs; as far as the partners went, he balanced the divine and the human, the earthly and the heavenly — what a balance there was in his life. And I am more impressed the older I get with the fact that most of us find it difficult to balance. It is so much easier to get unbalanced in ministry, to go for one of men's needs instead of all of them, to spend too much time helping people at the expense of prayer, or too much time alone at the expense of people, but Jesus kept everything in balance.

This comes out in the third thing that we need to look at: his problems. I find it a comfort to know that in his ministry Jesus had big problems. The interesting thing is that every time it is mentioned that Jesus prayed we find it is because he had a big problem on his hands and he did not know what to do about it. That is a time to pray. Let us look at the problem. What crisis is mentioned here? The clue lies in the fact that three times in this short passage he told people to shut up. That is a literal translation of what he said; our polite Bibles translate it as 'Be quiet.' Why should he have said that? Each time he told them to stop talking about himself, when surely he wanted the world to know. Didn't Jesus want us to talk about him? Isn't it true that he wants us to talk about him everywhere we can? Yes, he does. Then why did he tell them to be quiet? There are two interlinked problems here —one supernatural, the other natural. One was concerned with demons, the other with disease, and on both occasions Jesus told them to shut up. Let us see why.

First of all, take the demon-possessed. I have heard a great deal of nonsense spoken concerning these demon-possessed people in the Gospels, as if they were mentally ill, as if they were schizophrenic, and that this was a way of describing mental illness. I believe it firmly, on the authority of the Bible and confirmed by experience: demon-possession and mental illness are two quite different things and must never be confused. Demon possession is a spiritual problem and it comes to those who have dabbled in spiritism, astrology, and other things, and who have laid themselves open to it. Mental illness is quite a different thing, and requires different treatment. One of the symptoms that distinguishes between the two (there are about ten major symptoms that enable us to distinguish) is that a possessed person is clairvoyant and knows things that could not possibly otherwise be known, whereas a mentally ill person is not.

Here was Jesus, up against a clairvoyant in the synagogue. This man said, *"I know who you are — the Holy One of*

God!" (Mark 1:24, *NIV*). Nobody had told him, but the demons knew of course: the spirits knew who Jesus was. And Jesus told them to shut up. He said, *"Come out of him!"* Why? The Holy One of God was the promised King of the Jews and it would have been devastating and dangerous if this had come out at this stage. His friends would have wanted to crown him straight away and wanted him to be a political king, and his enemies would have wanted to kill him straight away. Furthermore, it is not right for such things to come from demons; such things have to be told us by the Holy Ghost, not by evil spirits. And even if demons say the right thing, we must not listen to them; our knowledge should not come that way, as they are trying to get hold of us. So Jesus commanded silence. And all through the three years he had the problem that the demons *knew* who he was, and he did not want people to know — before the right time.

The other problem was concerned with disease, and this was the danger of men's physical needs dominating their spiritual need. As I have said, if a man who could cure any disease came to your town he would have a full-time job and would have no time to do anything else at all. Jesus had only been in Capernaum a day and a half and the main street was packed with sick people. Our Lord could have spent the rest of his life doing nothing but healing people, and this was his problem. So, before the sun rose, he climbed up the hills behind Capernaum and prayed, and he asked the Father what he should do. There were all those sick people, and the street was going to be full of them the following day. The Father told him that he must preach, so he must go somewhere else and leave those sick people. The disciples found him up on the hills, and they told him that everybody was looking for him. But he told them that they were going to go to other towns to preach.

This is the constant battle Christians have had ever since, and which the church is having today to a greater degree than ever before, now we are so aware of the physical needs of mankind. With the food needed here and there, the medicine needed, the doctors and nurses and hospitals required, we could be completely overwhelmed with the physical needs of men. People say health is the most important thing in life but we forget that there is one thing that is more important, and it is holiness.

Jesus, facing this crisis, realised that he had to decide now that preaching was going to come first and healing must follow. So they left Capernaum, and left a street full of sick people, and Jesus went on to preach.

The tragedy was that he met a leper. It is the most tragic story in this chapter. Right in the middle of a country lane they met the leper. Why was he not in the town? Because he was not allowed there, he had to live outside it. He had heard what was going on in the town, wondered how he could reach Jesus — and there he was, coming along the road! No wonder he ran up.

This man who was condemned to a living death said with astounding faith, *"If you are willing, you can make me clean"* (Mark 1:40, *NIV*). What faith — in one who had an incurable disease! Jesus had compassion on him and touched him and said, *"I am willing. Be clean!"* and he was.

But now comes the tragedy. This man's need was obvious, his faith is obvious, and the next thing that is obvious is his disobedience. Jesus said, *"See that you don't tell this to anyone."* He gave him this order because he was trying to preach. He told him to go to Jerusalem, where he would be inspected, get a medical certificate and go back into society. But the man went rushing down the road, and to everybody he met he said that he had been healed by Jesus. Jesus could not even get into the towns, he had to keep away from them, so that he might preach where only the fit could reach him. We see the problem and, again, the wonderful balance in his ministry. While he had deep compassion for people in physical pain and suffering, he had a deeper compassion for people in sin — people who were facing a suffering in the next world that those living in this world never dreamed of — so he went on preaching.

Here, then, is the ministry of Jesus: perfectly balanced between physical, mental and spiritual needs, perfectly balanced between heaven and earth, yet terribly visible. All we have considered occupies three days out of those three years, and that is just the beginning of a ministry that continues to this day. In the next chapter we shall continue the story and see how opposition began to arise.

3

HOSTILITY AND AUTHORITY
Mark 2:1 – 3:6

Many centuries before Jesus' ministry on earth, Socrates, a philosopher who had obviously thought about human nature and the world in which we live, said: 'If ever a perfectly good man appears on earth he will be murdered.' Nevertheless, it comes as a shock to us that when Jesus went about doing good, almost immediately somebody began to plot his assassination. It seems quite extraordinary that the hands that had done only good, within three years would be pierced by nails as Jesus was hung on a cross. One of the most puzzling things that has to be explained is how this lovely life came to such a terrible end so quickly. Mark's Gospel gives us the answer to this conundrum. This passage tells us when that opposition came, who started it, how they opposed him, and most important of all, why — because for the very same reasons people are still opposing Jesus Christ.

The answer to the question 'When?' appears right at the beginning of his ministry. Within days, or certainly weeks, of his beginning to help people, there were others who began to hate him. That is not too strong a word because Jesus told us: they hated me; they will hate you. It is a very strong word. There were three particular occasions on which Jesus helped people who were in need, and yet these three very occasions were the points of the beginning of this terrible plot. Let us just look at them in brief.

The first was the man who was paralysed. I am not going to go through the story as we have heard this since childhood. We know the details; you may have drawn pictures in Sunday school of the hole in the roof, maybe imagining the damage and wondering how it was put right afterwards. We are very familiar with the details: the vivid picture of a crowded house, a crowded street, people digging through what was probably brushwood and clay, and letting a man down on a stretcher. But there are two key words in the story. One is *faith* and we notice what faith is from this story — it is not just accepting a creed, it is being absolutely determined to find Jesus, and it is being utterly confident that he is the one to help us.

But the other key word here is *forgiveness*. Why did Jesus deal with the sins of the paralytic rather than just his sickness? Was it just a case of seeing another need that the man was not aware of and simply doing the whole job at once? Was he just saying that as well as this paralysis you have got something else so we'll just clear this up first, then tackle the main thing? No, there is something much deeper.

This is not true in every case, but I believe in this man's case his suffering and his sin were directly related — that is why Jesus dealt with it. He did not deal with others in the same way. Psychologists will now tell us there is nothing difficult in imagining that paralysis can be brought on by wrongdoing and by guilt. Jesus could always diagnose perfectly — that is what makes him a good doctor of people. He saw straight through to the cause of this difficulty in this man's case, and he dealt with the cause, not the symptoms. He dealt with it straight away and said to this man, *"Son, your sins are forgiven"* (Mark 2:5, *NIV*). Then to prove that this was the real trouble and to show them that he had dealt with the problem, Jesus released him from the consequences of the cause, saying, *"I tell you, get up, take your mat and go home"* (Mark 2:11, *NIV*), and he did. The key factor here that caused the opposition was not the fact that he healed a paralysed man but the fact that he dealt with sins. In other words, if only Jesus had stayed with physical diseases he would have been perfectly alright. If he had gone round the world just helping sick people to be better, the cross would never have happened. Why then did he not just remain on earth as a physician as he could heal people? Surely that is a wonderful mission in life; surely to heal sick people is one of the noblest things you could do. Why did he prejudice, indeed jeopardise, the ministry of healing most by doing other things as well? Could he not just have left the religious side alone? No, because Jesus came not to save people from sickness primarily but to save them from sin. That is why he had the name he had, and he had to deal with this at whatever cost to himself. And he was claiming a divine prerogative — to forgive sins!

The second occasion when he helped a man and was hated for doing so concerned a crooked tax officer whom he straightened out, getting the man's life upright and honest. Why should a man be hated for doing that? I know that tax collectors will always be unpopular, even if they are honest, upright people, and if you are known as having no friends but tax collectors it may not help your public relations! But that is not the difficulty here. (The word 'publican', in older translations, is even more misleading because that now means something quite different.) What was a tax collector? I want you to imagine that the Germans had won the Second World War, that Britain was now occupied by German troops, and that they were doing here the kind of thing they did in Holland, Belgium, France, Denmark and Norway, and that in fact they imposed very heavy taxation to pay for their army and their empire, and to pay for Berlin and the Reichstag and its activities there. Then suppose that they insisted those taxes be collected not by Germans but by British people, and that anyone who would sell his soul sufficiently to do this for them would be given a plush office and allowed, moreover, to line his own pockets. In other words, provided the Germans got what they wanted they would not ask how much he took from the people. Now you begin to see the picture. These people were collaborators. Can you understand what it was like to make a friend of one of them? Imagine what it was like to be such a person — to be a social outcast, and for the sake of money to have cut yourself off from your people. Jesus straightened out a man like that, and he became unpopular as soon as he did so. But he called this man, who from collecting taxes became a man who collected stories about Jesus, and ultimately we got the Gospel of Matthew!

Apart from the tax collectors and his friends within the trade there was another group of people who tended to mix with them for the same reason — they were social outcasts. The word 'sinner' is a peculiar word in the Gospel. Aren't we all sinners? Yes. But the word as they used it meant people who were in a state of excommunication from their local synagogue. They were people who were not allowed to go into the congregation — they had broken the laws of God, whether knowingly or otherwise. They could not or would not live up to the religious standards imposed by the preachers of the day, so were simply untouchable. Here were two groups of people who had difficulty in mixing in ordinary society and were out on the fringe. Because they were outcasts they tended to mix together. Matthew (Levi) threw a party for them; he invited them along, and Jesus was right in the middle of the party. The thing that upset others was that Jesus would mix with religious outcasts. The first problem, as we saw with the paralytic, was that Jesus would bother about sins. If only he had stuck to healing he would have been alright, there would never have been a cross. The other problem was that he would bother with sinners. If only he had left them alone as everybody else did there would have been no cross. But Jesus came to deal with sinners and he came to deal with sins.

The third thing that seems to have brought this to a head, and led to the direct plotting of Jesus' death within months of his beginning his ministry, was his encounter with the man with the withered hand. Once again, there was nothing wrong with his healing. It was the time and the place that he did it. For the religious leaders this was the wrong time and the wrong place. They were not disagreeing about his healing activity. Whether they were glad that the man with the withered hand was now able to use it again, I do not know. I would imagine they were not even glad because they probably did not notice it, or if they did they had no feelings for him. But the point is that in their view this was the wrong time and the wrong place.

What was wrong about it? Simply that they had developed

a kind of attitude that I am tempted to call the 'Sabbath Day Observance Society'. I remember speaking to a group of masters and boys at a Roman Catholic school. I had a grand time talking with them about what I believed. They wanted to know what made me different from them, and I was very happy to tell them. Apparently, they had recently had a Jewish rabbi speaking to them and they had been absolutely shattered, and I got the backwash from this. They had been told not to switch on electric light switches on the Sabbath; they had been told not to cook meals on the Sabbath; they had been told this, that and the other. Mind you, they were awe-inspired by a man who would switch on all his lights on Friday afternoon so that they would be on all day Saturday and ready for use, so that he would not be involved in the work of doing that! They had not realised that there were still people who took their religion so seriously that the matter of switching on a light entered into it and became a wrong thing to do.

That is not the religion of the Old Testament that God taught the people at Sinai, it is a perversion of it. The trouble is that Jesus' 'religion' and that one did not mix. One of their cardinal rules was this: you must not do anything on the Sabbath that you can do the day before or the day after. If a man is dying you can do something for him because that cannot wait. But a man with a withered hand who must have had it for years was a different matter. It could have been dealt with on the Friday, or waited until the Sunday, but not on the Sabbath, and Jesus went right ahead and did it. In other words, he was challenging something that was central to their religion, and they did not like it one bit.

This passage tells us that because Jesus did things with

sin, and because he did things with sinners, and because he did things with the Sabbath, that inevitably meant that people hated him to the point of wanting to kill him. Isn't it extraordinary that men can be so perverse that three occasions on which people were being helped became occasions for planning a judicial murder? It is a comment on our human nature that such things are possible.

Now who were these people who did it? Who were the ones who had this reaction? Three groups are described and I want to outline them here because I want us to say as we look at them, 'Lord, is it I? Can I see myself in the mirror here?'

The first group were the scribes. They were a group of professional religious people, rather like a mixture of solicitors, magistrates and teachers with a few others rolled in. Their job was to give detailed guidance to people as to how they were to apply the laws of God. The trouble is that there is always a market for such guidance. It is much easier to be told exactly what to do than to have to work it out for yourself. It is much easier to have a book of rules and just look up paragraph 395 sub section (a) to find out if you ought to do this, or ought not to do that, than to walk with God in that kind of relationship where you must come to a decision about an issue which the Bible does not mention directly — for example, birth control.

People would go to a scribe in those days and ask what they must do about this or that. The most ludicrous kind of question could be asked, maybe something like: 'May I use a safety pin on my clothes on the Sabbath?' 'No,' the scribe might say, 'that's ploughing something.' I remember going to Israel and seeing a kibbutz, and around it at suitable intervals there were tall poles, about fifteen feet high with a wire stretched round the top of them, and I thought: 'Well, that's a mighty big washing line!' So I asked, 'What is it?' The guide replied, 'Oh, this is an Orthodox kibbutz and that marks the limit of the Sabbath day's journey. They may walk out to the wire, but not an inch beyond it.' This is not the religion of God; it is not the religion of Jesus Christ, equally clearly. The scribes were those who gave out these pieces of guidance, these little rules and regulations — they tried to apply it all. But the problem was that the one thing a scribe could not deal with was a man who came and said, 'But I've broken it.' He could tell you what not to do, but he could not do anything himself about you when you had not done it or when you had done it. This was the problem: the scribe could deal out righteousness by the barrel load, but he could not deal out forgiveness at all. Indeed, he thought no-one could except God, which is true: I cannot forgive you for your sins against God; you cannot forgive me, only God can. So the scribes were men who stood for this: we will tell you what to do, but sorry, if you don't do it, don't come to us. Jesus stepped into that atmosphere before the eyes of the scribes, and showed people that he could deal with the wrong things that they did. He expressed concern with people's failures. He knew that people had not done what they knew was right. He was able to tell them that their sins were forgiven. The contrast between the scribes and Jesus was partly that they told people what was right, and he could deal with what was wrong. And since all of us have done wrong, Jesus can do more for us than any scribe.

The second group that I want to mention are the Pharisees. They were a denomination or sect of the Jews. They are not representatives of the Old Testament religion, and our Lord never once to my knowledge contradicted anything in the Old Testament or undid anything. He came to fulfil not to destroy the Law and the Prophets, and he said, *". . . until heaven and earth disappear, not the smallest letter, not the least stroke of a pen, will by any means disappear from the Law until everything is accomplished"* (Matthew 5:18, *NIV*). The Pharisees' religion was a perversion of the Old Testament.

It began with the best will in the world. In the days of the Greeks and others who overran the country, there were those who brought in things which Jews had never done: like nude sports and lewd theatre. Other things came in, and Jewish young people were being led astray into activities that horrified their parents and grandparents, and the Pharisees began as a reaction to the growing worldliness of the people of God. Now that was a right reaction in the beginning. They said that this was not the way for the people of God to be behaving. And the word 'Pharisee' means separator or separatist, one who stands apart. In the beginning these men must have started as a good group of those who said, 'It is wrong to be doing this; we shouldn't be mixed up in it, we should step outside it.' But, alas, as with so many such protests, the pendulum swung too far, and it went to the extreme where they got too far out altogether, and religion for them became so many 'thou-shalt-nots' that it became external, no longer an internal thing of life and joy and peace. It became more and more exclusive, and more legalistic, until the Pharisees were literally as far out as you could get the other way, which is equally unbalanced. The more I see of life, the more I feel it is so easy to get right *into* the world and it is so easy to get right *out* of it, but to be in the world yet not of it is one of the most difficult balances for a Christian to strike. The Pharisees got right out of it, and it is almost incredible what they did. Their righteousness therefore became self-righteousness, and that is a very offensive thing to God and to man.

Just as the scribes could not do anything about *sin* — and Jesus came right in and did something about it — the Pharisees could not do anything about *sinners*, because they did not know them, they never had them in their homes, they never mixed with them, they never met them and they would certainly never have eaten a meal with them. You cannot do anything about sinners if you are not prepared to talk to them, meet them, have a meal with them, get to know them — how can you? So the Pharisees, respected as they were at a distance, were just not in touch with the very people who needed most help. Jesus again showed them up by just going in and having a meal, because he was invited with a company of people who were religious outcasts. The Pharisees would not touch them, but Jesus did. Just as in the last chapter we saw that Jesus would touch a leper, he will touch a spiritual leper too.

The next group that comes in here is an interesting one. It is a group of politicians. And the only reason they are brought into it is that the Pharisees and the scribes, having decided to do away with Jesus, had no power to do it. They could not do anything about sin, they could not do anything about sinners, they could not do anything about Jesus the Saviour either, so they had to get some political power, and the obvious people to make for were the Herodians. Without going into a lot of history and geography, the land was divided up into regions, and over Galilee — the area which we are now concerned with — there reigned a man who came from one of the worst family trees you could imagine, a man called Herod. Like his father and grandfather, Herod was a man who was morally weak. It was the other Herod who had killed the babies in Bethlehem, and this line can be traced right back to no less a person than Esau, and Herod was not a Jew, he was an Edomite. He was a puppet king the Romans had put in, hoping that he would keep the peace for them, and because of the position they gave him he tried to do it. But he could not stand two things. He could not stand rivals — naturally, he was to keep the peace, and here was a popular leader in his own territory. Nor could he stand preachers. And down under his feet in the basement of his castle was a preacher called John the Baptist, who was there because he had criticised the moral relationships of Herod within his family. Every time that man sat down to a meal, underneath his feet was a preacher whom he dare not let loose.

It is interesting that the Pharisees made for the Herodians. The most amazing coalitions form when hatred is in people's hearts. It was so utterly contrary to their religion. They would not touch the sinners, they would not touch the tax collectors, and here they are touching Herodians. Actually, when it came to the push, as we shall see, it was not the Pharisees and the Herodians who finally caused the cross, it was the Sadducees and the Romans. Here are religious and political groups getting together, collaborating against Jesus Christ, and it was not the last time this would happen.

Now I come to the third question. How did their opposition show itself? There is a progression of the opposition. It began in thought; it moved to word, and finally it became deed. Jesus teaches that sin begins in the heart with thoughts, it will come out of the mouth in words, and then it becomes deeds. Sin covers all three; crime only covers the third — or possibly, in some cases of libel and slander, the second. I can never be hauled into the court, into the dock, for my thoughts, but I could be for my words, and I certainly could be for my deeds. However, I go to the court for crime, not for sin. Sin is something that starts deep down inside. Jesus taught that if you have ever wished anybody dead, or if you have ever lost your temper with somebody, you are a murderer in God's sight. You may never have committed adultery, but have you ever looked lustfully? If so, you are an adulterer in God's sight — the sin has begun. It may never have become word, though it may have become word in the form of a dirty joke or an angry word at somebody. But even if it never got as far as deed, it has started. This is exactly how the hatred toward Jesus began. The first time, they murmured in their hearts. They did not say a thing, but Jesus knew what people thought. He knows what you are thinking now; he knows what I am thinking. They asked him questions they never ought to have asked. Then it moved to words, and they began to complain. They spoke first to his disciples. Notice that they tried to come around the back door in this way. Finally they challenged him, and then they went out to plot his murder. So we see a progression of thought. The warning is that if our thoughts are ever set against Jesus this is likely to come out in our words and ultimately to become deeds. There is a dangerous beginning when we allow wrong thoughts to find a home. There is nothing wrong in being tempted, it is when we harbour the temptation. A wrong picture may present itself to our minds but we need to cut it off and not hang it on the walls of our imagination — that is when the temptation becomes sin. As soon as we allow that to happen, sooner or later something will slip out in our speech that we never thought we could say, and sooner or later the word can become deed. We notice the progression through these various stories. They began murmuring, they finished murdering; they began complaining, they finished by condemning the Son of God to death.

Now we come to the fourth and last question. Why did they hate Jesus? You have to hate a man greatly to want to kill him. The answer is two-fold.

First, he challenged their authority. When you have been put in charge of something it is not very nice to have somebody come along and try to run it for you. This is one of the commonest irritations that happen. It is behind many of our disagreements in life. One lady once said to me, 'I'm never going back to that church. I've always run the flower stall at the church fête and look what they did this year.' When you have been put in charge of something, and then somebody else comes along and just quietly takes over, it is not very easy to accept it graciously. John the Baptist did. He had said, *"After me will come one more powerful than I, the thongs of whose sandals I am not worthy to stoop down and untie"* (Mark 1:7, *NIV*), but not many of us are big enough to say that. The Pharisees realised that they were now being told what to do. They who had always up to this point told others what to do saw their authority vanishing with the morning mist. Here was a man who was telling people different things, and these were things that would not mix with their own religion. Furthermore, when they challenged him he always gave them such a *clever* answer

53

that they could not say a thing. He used scripture against them by quoting Abiathar, a case you will find in the Old Testament. He used logic against them. And what would you say if somebody said, *"It is not the healthy who need a doctor, but the sick"* (Mark 1:17, *NIV*)? There is no answer. It is like replying to, 'Have you stopped beating your wife?' What can you say? If you say yes or no you are wrong both times. These were brilliant answers. They were logical and they were unanswerable.

Jesus not only used the Old Testament scripture and logic against them, he used conscience against them too. He said, *"Which is lawful on the Sabbath: to do good or to do evil, to save life or to kill?"* (Mark 3:4, *NIV*). He used demonstration against them, and healed the man with the shrivelled hand in front of them. When you are up against a man who can tie you in knots and answer your challenge with a statement that you just cannot criticise or answer yourself, you are in real trouble. They realised that he would destroy their religion, and that was absolutely true.

Let us be quite clear that Jesus expected us to fast. It is part of the Christian life. Jesus tells his followers that when they give they are not to let their right hand know what their left hand does, when you pray not to let anyone see, and when you fast don't let anyone know. He did not say *if* you fast or *if* you pray, or *if* you give, he said *when* you do these things. But having said that, he did not fast, nor did his disciples, just because there was a public or official fast on. The time came when everybody else was fasting and they were not. So people came along and pointed out that they were not toeing the line and fitting in with contemporary religious practice. Nowadays, we might be told, 'It's Lent, you should be doing without chocolates.' Jesus teaches that fasting has to be real; it has to correspond with inner thoughts and feelings. Jesus was quoting their own rules against them, because one of the scribal rules was that if you had just married, or if you were a guest at a wedding, then you need not fast. Jesus said: *"How can the guests of the bridegroom fast while he is with them? They cannot, so long as they have him with them. But the time will come when the bridegroom will be taken from them, and on that day they will fast"* (Mark 2:19f., *NIV*). The disciples felt as though they were at a wedding because they had Jesus with them in person. They were excited, they were happy, they were joyful, they had everything to live for, so they should have been feasting, not fasting. It would have been most inappropriate for them to fast. There would come occasions when they should fast, and they would do so, but not at this time. In other words, religion is no longer a matter of imposed rules from the outside but expressed intention from the inside. People are not going to be told, 'You must fast from now to next week,' what is being said is that there are experiences and circumstances in which you and I should fast. There are spiritual needs that we have for guidance, for strength, for making decisions, which will require us to fast. There are problems in other people's lives which will not be dealt with except by fasting and praying. But this is something that comes out of the need; it does not get imposed from the outside, it is real because it is inside.

Jesus was showing them that their religion would not mix with his teaching. He could hardly have made it plainer that if anybody accepted his teaching they would have to leave that of the scribes and Pharisees. As always, he used two very homely illustrations. By the way, it is possible to tell a lot about the background of Jesus' home from his incidental speech. It was a home in which they had to patch clothes frequently. He said, *"No-one sews a patch of unshrunk cloth on an old garment. If he does, the new piece will pull away from the old, making the tear worse"* (Mark 3:21, *NIV*). Likewise, he used an illustration of new wine in old wineskins. They could not just add what he was teaching onto what the scribes and Pharisees taught. That is something that we need to remember. We all have our traditions, we all grow up with things that we have always done. There are two reasons for not doing anything that a minister suggests in a church: one is that we've done it before and it didn't work; the other is: we've never done it before and it won't work! We are all creatures of the old wineskin; we have all developed ways of doing things. 'Ah well, we Baptists do it this way, you know,' and so on. We have all got our old wineskins, we have our shrunken cloth, and sometimes Jesus comes to us saying that he has got something new and dynamic that will break open our form of worship. It will not be at 11 a.m. or 6:30 p.m., it might not be in a Gothic building — it might be something quite new. You cannot go on adding his religion to yours, his words to your traditions. It is all or nothing. We follow him and drop the rest. They did not like that, it challenged their authority.

The other reason why they hated this man was his claim to his *own* authority. By what authority did a man who did not even have 'reverend' — 'rabbi', to them — in front of his name, a man who had not been qualified theologically, a man from nowhere, a carpenter from Nazareth, a working man, come and tell them that he was starting a new teaching that would not work with theirs? The answer was *by his own authority*. Jesus refers to himself in five ways, any one of which is astonishing.

First of all, Jesus claimed to be the forgiver of sins. They came within an inch of the truth. They said, *"Who can forgive sins but God alone?"* Why could the teachers of the law not have just stepped another inch and said, 'It must be God standing there'? Why did they come so near and yet fall so far short of the truth? They said that only God could do it, and Jesus proved to them that he had done it by telling the paralytic, *"get up, take your mat and go home"* and the man doing just this. Why could their minds not understand that the next logical step was to believe that God was in Christ? But he did it in his own name because he was God, and they said that this was blasphemy. For a man to call himself God is blasphemy, and according to God's own law the punishment for blasphemy was capital punishment and he had to die. It was the worst crime in the book. This is the question still facing us. You cannot have Jesus just as a great man. You cannot have him as a preacher or a teacher and a healer and say, 'He was a good man, follow him' — because either he was the greatest blasphemer in history or he was God. You must either decide he was wrong and deserved to die as a blasphemer or he was right and he was God. You cannot have it both ways and there is no other way.

Jesus spoke as the forgiver of sin and he implied also that he was the physician of sinners. 'Physician' may mean to you a medical doctor, but to those people who heard him the word meant something else. *"It is not the healthy who need a doctor, but the sick"* — Jesus is quoting the prophet Jeremiah who, looking out on a nation full of evil, disobedient people, had said, *"Is there no balm in Gilead?*

Is there no physician there? Why then is there no healing for the wound of my people?" (Jeremiah 8:22, *NIV*). When Jesus said that it is not the healthy who need a physician he was claiming far more than to be a doctor, he was saying he was God's physician, sent to put you right.

The third thing Jesus called himself was the bridegroom. He said that they do not fast because he is the bridegroom. What is he saying? Is he just using a picture of a wedding? No, much more. All through the Old Testament, God says that he is the bridegroom of Israel, and Israel is the bride, and here is Jesus saying they have the bridegroom now. What a claim! This is now the third time he is claiming to be on the heavenward side of reality.

In saying, *"The Sabbath was made for man, not man for the Sabbath"*, Jesus is declaring that he made the Sabbath laws, he can remake them; he can override them and he will do so. The only person who can override laws is the one who makes them. When Jesus says, *"So the Son of Man is Lord even of the Sabbath"* he is claiming to be the one who gave the Sabbath law at Sinai.

'Son of Man' is a delightfully ambiguous title, but to those who have faith and look at it closely they see far more than just a human being in it, they see a divine being.

'Son of Man' is used throughout the Old Testament, particularly in the book of Ezekiel as simply a phrase for 'human being':

> *What is man that you are mindful of him,*
> *the son of man that you care for him?*
> *You made him a little lower than the heavenly beings*
> *and crowned him with glory and honour.*
> (Psalm 8:4, *NIV*).

We know it means a human being, but there is one passage in the book of Daniel where Daniel looks into the future, and he sees someone coming down with the clouds from heaven to have an everlasting dominion and kingdom, and he says, *"In my vision at night I looked, and there before me was one like a son of man, coming with the clouds of heaven"* (Daniel 7:13, *NIV*). By the time Jesus came, the words 'Son of Man' had this double meaning. Some, at any rate, saw in it the one who was coming from heaven to rule over the kingdoms of the earth.

Five times in just these incidents Jesus is letting people know that he is God —they needed eyes to see; they needed to open their understanding; they needed to believe. He is the one who forgives sins and who heals sinners; he is the one who is the Bridegroom of Israel, the Lord of all the laws that God gave, the Son of Man coming in the clouds of heaven. With those five things, Jesus signed his death warrant. And the reason why the symbol of Christianity is not a stretcher or a red cross on a white background, but broken bread and poured out wine, is simply that Jesus was a Saviour and not just a healer. It is because he knew that he ought to die; it is because from the very beginning of his ministry he realised perfectly well that if he did what the Father had told him to do he would finish on a cross. It is because of that he was able ultimately to help sinners with their sins today. If Jesus had not gone to the cross, if he had just lived out his life in Israel preaching and teaching and healing, wandering the dusty lanes of Galilee helping people, then he could not be helping me, and he could not be helping you, today.

So you come to him as a sinner needing a physician, and as the bride of Christ — as the bride who comes to a bridegroom, looking forward to the wedding reception which we shall enjoy in heaven. Come to the one who is Son of Man. The bread of communion represents his body, and the wine represents his blood — real body, real blood — yet he is the Son of Man who is going to come again with the clouds of heaven, and we shall see him and we shall recognise him by the nail prints in his hands. He is Lord of the Sabbath; Lord of all the laws that were ever made; Lord of your Sunday, Lord of your Monday, Lord of your Tuesday; the Lord who is to govern and to rule your life. So come to him realising that your greatest need is to have someone say, 'Son/daughter, your sins are forgiven.'

4

FRIENDS AND FOES
Mark 3:7–35

I have found myself wondering from time to time what difference it would make to my daily life and to the kind of things I plan to do if a doctor told me I had one year to live. It is a very healthy exercise to ask yourself this because if that news were given to you and you knew that your time was very limited it would be a very revealing thing as to whether you would change your plans or carry on doing what you were already doing. If you are already doing what is right and what God intended you to do, you will make very little change.

We have seen that within months of beginning his public ministry at the age of thirty people began to plot the death of Jesus, and he knew it. He knew perfectly well that his days were numbered, and he was in fact only going to have just under three years in which to do all that the Father wanted him to do. Did this alter him in any way? Well, the answer is yes and no. He certainly took certain steps and changed his plans somewhat, mainly to gain enough time to do the Father's will. But on the other hand, it impresses me very deeply that, although Jesus died at the age of thirty-three and knew that he was going to die, there is an unhurried, quiet approach in all he does; there is no panic, there is no feverish activity, there is no sense of, 'Oh, I must got on with this and I must hurry to do that before it's too late', but with deliberate and quiet pace he moves among people to do what he has been sent to do.

In this short section there are five groups of people with whom he comes in contact, and each one of them sees Jesus in quite a different way. Some of them are right and some of them are wrong, some of them are part of the truth and some of them are the whole truth and some of them are not true at all. But it is very interesting that when Jesus strides among men they look at him through their own eyes and not through his, so they see different things.

The first group is a vast crowd travelling on foot up to one hundred miles to see Jesus. There is no doubt about it that at the beginning of his ministry our Lord was very popular. It just had to be whispered that Jesus was coming to a certain place and people would set off up to five days before, and they would hike and trek to that village to meet him. At the first stage of his ministry he had to take practical steps to avoid being crushed by the mobs. What he did was to arrange for one of his fishermen followers to have a boat standing by. It is striking that Jesus could have walked on the water (as he did later, so we know he had the amazing power to do so), but he preferred to use a boat. He chose a natural, normal way of avoiding a danger. This tells me a great deal about Jesus. He did not abuse his power. He did not use it as a substitute for practical, sensible action, like the man praying for rain because his house was on fire. Jesus was a very balanced person and it comes out so clearly in this arrangement to have a boat handy. But there were two groups of people who came in this crowd who were an embarrassment and a problem to him.

The first problem group were those who came with diseases. He had the power to heal, he had compassion for sick people, so why should it be a problem that sick people came in such numbers? Well, apart from the fact that they were desperate, and so desperate that they wanted to touch him before he touched them, and therefore were in danger of killing him just by sheer numbers, it was the old problem that people put physical needs before anything else. We say in popular proverbial speech that health is the most important thing in life, but it is not — there are some things even more important. We have heard it said so frequently, but it is a half-truth with a real element of truth in it, that you must not preach to a starving man until you have fed him; that the greatest need of the world is for food. Others would say the greatest need of the world is for freedom. But, as I have said before and underline again, the greatest need of the world today is forgiveness, whether the world realises it or not. And the great tension in our Lord's early ministry was that people wanted him for the physical blessings he could bring and not for the spiritual. He knew perfectly well that if he went on healing people all his ministry he would not have done the thing that God sent him to do for them. While it was part of his service to heal those who were sick, it was not the prime thing. So his problem was that they were so keen to have the miracles of healing that they came for little else. We notice that they walked a hundred miles from Idumea, from Tyre and Sidon, not because of what they heard that he had said but because of what he had done. They did not come to listen to him, they came to see him and they came to be healed physically. But our Lord had fought this battle out alone; he had been six weeks without food. He had been desperately hungry, and the devil had said: turn these stones into bread. Invited to use his power to meet physical need, his answer to the devil was, "Man shall not live by bread alone." If we say that the greatest need of the human race today is food then we are saying that human beings are no more than animals. But people are more than animals; they live longer than animals, they live for eternity. This world is not the limit of their being; birth may be the beginning of their life but death is not the end, and they have needs beyond the grave that must be met this side of the grave. So our Lord was in this tension, looking around the crowd that had come to see him. So many of the sick were not interested in the preaching; they wanted healing and they were pressing him to the edge of the sea to get it.

The other side of the problem was that in the crowd he also spotted certain people suffering from demonic possession. Now I want to stress again that demonic possession and mental illness are two completely different and separate things and must never be confused. They need separate diagnosis and separate treatment. You will never understand the Gospel story until you realise that when Jesus came preaching the kingdom of God he was invading the territory of another kingdom, and that the real battle in our Lord's life was not between him and the Pharisees it was between Jesus and Satan. You may laugh at this preacher, this poor obscurantist in the pulpit who still believes in a personal devil, and you may have accepted so many modern interpretations that say that they called mental illness demon-possession in those days because they had no psychiatrists. But I still say we are not discussing mental illness at all, we are discussing demonic possession. Call them fallen angels, call them evil spirits, call them what you like, but I just hope and pray you never come in contact with this because it is a most terrifying and horrible thing.

It is not surprising that in the crowd that Jesus preached to there were people who were possessed by demons, whose bodies were no longer their own, whose mouths were no longer their own, whose minds were no longer their own, they were just the shell, and inhabiting that shell was an evil spirit. And it is no coincidence that they came in the crowd, because Jesus threatened their very existence. I would like to bring this home to you by mentioning a gentleman I know who was a minister, who was called to a farm where the farmer's son was in a terrible state. The poor farmer who was nearly beside himself had tried doctors first and then psychiatrists, but nothing could help. The minister went and, as soon as he entered and began to pray, the boy went berserk and the minister recognised that this was not physical illness nor mental — he was fighting not the boy but a spirit inside the boy. For some hours they fought with that evil spirit who addressed them through the boy's mouth using all kinds of language and saying all kinds of things, and they fought together until finally the victory was won. The demons pleaded with the minister, 'Send us into someone else, let us go into someone else,' but the minister would not. He said, 'You go where the Lord Jesus tells you to go, and in his name I tell you to get out.' The boy fell as one dead, then recovered and sat up and has been normal ever since and became a pastor of a church and a very fine minister. But, as the boy recovered, there was a noise outside in the farmyard such as they had never heard before. They went out, and the farmer's herd of twenty or thirty pigs were killing each other out in the yard. Finally the farmer had to get his gun and shoot the lot. That is not the Gospel story, that is not the Gospel according to St Mark, but it will remind you of something in that story. Jesus was up against something real.

The evil spirits knew long before men who Jesus was. Of course they did, they recognised here the one who could turn them out of their kingdom. Jesus taught that this world is not the kingdom of God but the kingdom of Satan, that Satan is the prince who reigns over it. If you want to know why there is evil in the world, if you want to know why there is disease in the world, if you want to know why there is death, if you want to know why your newspapers are full of these things, the answer is that this world is not the kingdom of God. And when Jesus came preaching the kingdom of God he was saying: *I* have invaded *your* territory; I have come to bring the power of God to liberate the victims. It was 'D-Day' when Jesus came. So the demons fought back. There they were in the crowd, and they shouted out using the mouths of their victims, *"You are the Son of God"* — and that was not only a personal danger to Jesus because it could have finished him there and then, it was a distraction, it was the wrong time for this to be said, it could have ruined his ministry if this had come out at this stage. And certainly these things must not come from demons, they must be realised by men. There would have to come a day when Jesus would say to men without evil spirits around, *"Who do you say I am?"* Then by the Holy Spirit a man was going to say, *"You are the Christ."* So Jesus rebuked these demons and he would not let them speak, and they shut up as soon as he said it, for Jesus has power over such things.

Here is Jesus, famous, popular, hundreds coming from

all over the place, yet within that crowd are two groups of people who have the wrong idea of him. There are the diseased and the demon-possessed, and the tension is there very clearly. Both of these groups see Jesus as supernatural. They see him on the one hand as a miracle worker and only that, someone you can get health from by miraculous power, and the demon-possessed see him as the supernatural Son of God, but Jesus must be seen to be human before they realise his divinity. Jesus must come as the Son of Man before they say he is the Son of God, and so he must have time.

The second group we meet in this passage are his followers. He is now taking steps to ensure the future and to extend his own ministry in time and space. How does one do that? The answer is that you train someone else. If you want to double your work, get hold of someone else and train them to do it with you and for you — alongside you first and then without you. So we come to the remarkable step that Jesus took when he chose twelve disciples and ensured in this way that there would be a church near where you live two thousand years later. For we are now reading of the beginning of the church, and it happened so ordinarily and so wonderfully. There are three questions that I want to ask: Why did Jesus choose the twelve? Why did Jesus choose *twelve*? And why did Jesus choose *these* twelve?

There are two reasons, and they are reasons why he chose you, too: firstly, that they might be with him and have *communion* with him; secondly, that he might send them away from him and *commission* them to do his work. Here is the balance of the Christian life, and if you and I do not get it right we shall be very ineffective disciples of Christ, and his work will come to an end as far as we are concerned. I must spend time with Jesus. I must go away from the world, out of it and into Jesus, and get to know him better and better. But I must not stay there. I must then take what I have learned and what I have received, and go out and share it with other people.

Here are two caricatures of the Christian life, neither of which is proper Christianity: one is those who shut themselves up in some cloistered cell, who lock themselves up in a private (or even a church) devotional life, who shut themselves up in six church meetings a week, who shut themselves up in Christian fellowship and who have nothing but communion, and who never get out where it is all needed. Salt is no use in the salt cellar. That is one side, and an unbalanced side. But equally unbalanced are those who say, 'Close down all this devotional life. Close down your private devotions and your public devotions — real Christianity is getting out and helping people.' That is only half the truth as well, and if they have no communion and no quiet fellowship together with Christ they will not be able to help people. It is getting this balance right: coming into Christ and into fellowship and into devotions, and then getting out where you belong in the world, getting out into the factory, getting out into those other activities and communities. How difficult it is to get these two right.

He called *these* twelve — why? That they should come in and go out. To put it in biblical language: that they should become disciples and then become apostles. The word 'apostle' means someone who is sent out. It passed into our language via the Latin root word *mittere* (to send) to our word 'missionary'. For his work to be extended and continued, it demanded people who would come and learn from him, and go out and tell someone else. One of the quickest ways of benefiting from a service is to go straight from that service to someone who could not be there and tell them about it. To come in and learn about Jesus, and then go out and tell someone else, is the surest way of keeping your blessing. But the surest way of losing it would be to enjoy the service and not share anything of it with anyone, and come back next Sunday for more. You can get indigestion. I remember one dear man telling me, 'If we don't get some outlet soon, our boilers will burst.' You cannot go on getting steam up forever within the church and within fellowship, you need to keep coming in and going out.

To us twelve is just a convenient number, a nice-sized group for training. But to the Jews it would mean much more. To them, twelve was almost a sacred number. It was written into their past. Way back, there was once a man with twelve sons, and that was the beginning of the people of God. They became twelve families and then twelve tribes, and the twelve tribes were the nation of God. Jesus could hardly have said in a clearer way that the old leaders had let God down; new people were needed.

The solemn lesson I apply to myself (and you can apply to yourself) is this: 'Lest having preached to others I should be cast away' — God can do without me and can call someone else. May it never happen to us that God chooses other disciples to do his work because we let him down.

Why did Jesus choose *these* twelve? Was it their temperament? We are all so different in temperament, and, when you look at the twelve disciples, you could not have had a more mixed group. Was it because you have to be particularly spiritual or religious in temperament to be a disciple? Nonsense! You do not have to have a special temperament to be a disciple. Was it a matter of politics? Far from it. Some imply that you have to have a particular political outlook to be a Christian — not true! Among the twelve was Matthew, a collaborator who had sold himself to the occupying powers, and Simon, a leader of the underground resistance movement. In following Jesus they were going to live together, eat together and follow him together. It had nothing whatever to do with their politics. Had it anything to do with their education? Somebody said to me cynically, 'I think we are emptying the church by degrees!' (Maybe that was a dig at ministers!) The twelve men were unlearned, so it was not a matter of education. Was it a matter of occupation? Of this group, some of them worked with their hands and some of them worked with their heads, and it did not matter at all — Jesus called them. There are no such distinctions in his band of disciples. Was it a matter of background? Well, eleven of them came from the north but one came from the south. It was not that. Was it a matter of blood relations? It may interest you to know that five out of the twelve disciples were related by blood to Jesus. But the other seven were not, so I do not think it was a case of that either. So what did these twelve men have that others did not have? The answer is: absolutely nothing. They were ordinary folk, they were mixed folk, they were folk such as you and I, and yet he called them and he made them what they were, and if he could do it for them he can do it for me, and he can do it for you, and he can do it for anyone. So he chose people not because of what they were but because of what they were not, and he called this 'mixed bag' together. May I put it like this: they were neither somebodies nor nobodies, they were anybodies and everybodies. That is how the disciples were called. The important thing was that the choice was his, not theirs. He called to him those whom he desired, and there comes a day — it came in my life at seventeen years of age — when the call comes, 'Follow me.' And if I am anything at all, it is because he kept his promise, 'Follow me, and I will make you. . . .' The call may come to you in different ways. It could come in a service, when you suddenly realise it is not just the preacher talking, somebody else is saying, 'This means you,' and he promises to 'make' you, too.

Now we come to another group in this brief passage: his friends — meaning his friends from his earlier life. Their opinion was different again. The crowd saw him as a miracle-worker; the disciples saw him as a master, one they would gladly surrender their lives to, but his friends saw him as a maniac. They said, *"He is out of his mind."* They may have seen him in the carpenter's shop and taken their chairs to him to be repaired, and suddenly here he is with thousands of people around him, doing all sorts of strange things. They honestly thought that the pressure of the crowds, the multitude that came, had been too much for him, and they came to have him quietly put away, thinking that it would be for his own good.

Why should they think he was mad? First, he was neglecting his health; he did not even have time for proper meals. Second, he was ignoring his trade and doing no work — there was no security, no livelihood in what he was doing. Third, he was surely forgetting his station; he was just a carpenter, not the leader of a nation. Fourth, he was disturbing the people and causing a frightful potential situation to arise. But most of all he was risking his life — they knew it.

I wonder if I could apply it like this. I have noticed that as soon as religion gets as big as life other people say, 'mania'. Provided your religion is a department, that is seen as normal. Provided you keep your religion strictly to Sunday, or strictly to a group, that is fine, but when your religion begins to extend a bit you will stand out. One British prime minister went to hear a preacher many years ago and came out muttering, 'Well, I don't know what things are coming to when religion begins to interfere with a man's private life.' He was quite happy to keep religion in a compartment, to do his duty, to show himself at the church. But when religion begins to interfere with a man's private life, when religion begins to affect his business, when religion begins to get bigger and bigger until everything is connected with this religion, that is thought to be 'mania', madness.

When a man called Saul of Tarsus threw up a promising career, a noble position, and went off into the unknown as a missionary it was not long before someone said, *"Your great learning is driving you insane."* Paul's reply included the words, *"I pray to God that not only you but all who are listening to me today may become what I am, except for these chains"* (Acts 26:29, *NIV*). It is madness to the world when religion takes over life.

So the 'friends' of Jesus came, as they thought for his own good, to try to shut him up.

Now look at Jesus' foes. His enemies went one step further than his friends. They did not say it was mental illness, but that he had evil powers. They thought he was only able to control demons, spirits, because he had the power of the greatest evil spirit in him and over them —the power of Satan. Only God and Satan have power over evil spirits, so if you can control demons you have either the power of God or the power of Satan in you. They thought it could not be the work of God so it must be Satan. They began to ask each other whether they had seen him tell that demon to shut up and seen him cast it out. How was he able to do that? They thought it was because the boss of the demons was in his heart. They called him Beelzebub in those days. They said, *"He is possessed by Beelzebub! By the prince of demons he is driving out demons"* (Mark 3:22, *NIV*). Nevertheless, they would not say this to Jesus' face, they were saying it to the edge of the crowd. Jesus called them to him. He then told them two parables and showed them, firstly, that they were utterly illogical and unreasonable. He showed them secondly that they were in terrible spiritual danger.

First of all, logically. He told them that if they were right, if by the power of Satan he was dealing with demons, then it would mean there was civil war in the enemy camp. Could they not see that really he was doing things against Satan? Were they so blind to what is good that they could not see Jesus was releasing the victims of Satan, setting them free? What was Satan doing if he was letting people loose? He has never been known to do such a thing in all of history. Satan has never willingly let go a single one of the people in his grip. That is why when you meet someone in the grip of Satan's power it is a battle to get them out. Perhaps you have known this battle with other people, and maybe in yourself. Jesus said, *". . . if Satan opposes himself and is divided, he cannot stand; his end has come"* (Mark 3:26, *NIV*). Jesus was showing them that, if they were right, Satan would collapse if he went on attacking himself like that!

Then Jesus warned them that it is not only blindness to what is good. Here he used a word that he rarely used, but when he did it meant something very important. From time to time, he said 'truly'. In his language it was the word 'amen', and it means 'absolutely', 'certainly', 'surely'. He said, *"I tell you the truth, all the sins and blasphemies of men will be forgiven them. But whoever blasphemes against the Holy Spirit will never be forgiven; he is guilty of an eternal sin"* (Mark 3:28–29, *NIV*). When his foes claimed that he was doing Satan's work they were in danger of committing the only sin that can never be forgiven. There is one thing that a man could do that could never be forgiven. Let us get it straight, it has nothing to do with sex, though many people have felt it was. It has nothing whatever to do with any physical desire or appetite. What is the sin that could never be forgiven? It is to call black white and evil good and light darkness, and to brainwash yourself until you cannot see the difference. Why can it never be forgiven? Because a man can never admit it is wrong once he has brainwashed himself. A man could never repent of this and he is therefore unforgivable; he could never receive the gift of pardon. It is a man who can look at something that God is doing and say, 'Satan is doing that.' It is a man who can look at something that Satan is doing and say, 'God is doing that.' It is a man who can look at a horrible sin and say, 'That's virtue', and can look at a virtue and say, 'That's vice.' It is a man who goes on doing that until he has so obliterated the boundary between good and evil, light and darkness, that there is no boundary in his thinking anymore. And because only the Holy Spirit can convince us of sin and righteousness, of what is bad and what is good, to say that good is bad and bad is good is to blaspheme against the Holy Spirit. Who else could ever tell you that you have done wrong? If, by your own wilful obstinacy, you shut yourself off from the only person who can teach you these two things, then who can help you?

Jesus was warning these Pharisees that in saying that he was of the devil they were in danger of putting themselves in a position where they could never find what is good and right and true. For your comfort may I add that we can therefore say that if any person is ever worried that they may have committed the unforgivable sin, we can say absolutely certainly that they have not, because if they had they would not be worried about it. It is a rare thing. I have only once or twice in decades of ministry come across cases where I have felt that a man or a woman was getting near this point. Thank God it is rare. But if you can look at something that Jesus is doing and say it is of Satan you are in mortal danger. What some were saying about Jesus was not only untrue, it was a most dangerous thing to say.

Finally, we come to Jesus' family. Joseph is dead, Mary and his half brothers and half sisters come, there is a huge crowd and they cannot get through, and word passes through the crowd that his family has come. Can you hear the chatter? 'Fancy being a brother or sister to such a famous man as this! Fancy being his mother!' 'Let's see his family.' Occasionally one sees a photograph in a newspaper of a dear, simple couple who happen to be the mother and father of a famous pop star and are being dragged into all the glory and publicity. Why did Jesus' family come? I do not know. To share his fame? I do not know. To see if he would still own them? I do not know. To persuade him to return to Nazareth, to go back to the carpentry business? I do not know. I only know that when the word got through to Jesus, he said to the crowd around him one of the most extraordinary things he ever said: *"Here are my mother and my brothers! Whoever does God's will is my brother and sister and mother"* (Mark 3:34–35, *NIV*). Anybody can belong to his family. Jesus values relationships rather than relatives. Do you realise there are people in our churches who are Jesus' brothers and sisters? Who is Jesus' family? People who by natural birth happen to have similar blood or chromosomes? No. So who is his family? Whoever does the will of God is his brother and sister. Real relationships, the deep relationships of life, are not flesh and blood ones, deep though those are. The deepest relationships of all are with those who know God and love him and do his will. I am so happy to say that Jesus did not use this as an excuse to evade the ties of flesh and blood — even when he was dying he was making provision for his earthly mother. But I am more thrilled to be able to tell you that on the day of Pentecost, when the Holy Spirit came down in tongues of fire and the sound of wind, and they began to speak in other languages, among the 120 was Jesus' mother, and among the 120 were Jesus' half brothers and his half sisters, and we are told this. That was when they really became his family, that was when they really belonged to him, not just for time but for eternity; and one of his brothers, James, became the leader of the church in Jerusalem.

May I apply that. There are many tragedies of broken families, families that are tied together with flesh and blood but are not yet fully related to Jesus Christ. They will never know what relationships really are until they are. It is one of the hardest things in life to be a believer and married to an unbeliever. Corresponding to the awful difficulty of that relationship is the terrific joy and peace of both being together in the Lord. The only partners that can look forward to being continued after death are those that do the will of God, because sex does not pass through death — in heaven we are neither married nor given in marriage — but a husband and wife who have had a flesh and blood relationship on earth can look forward to an even closer brother and sister relationship in heaven, because they have become one family in Christ. These were the relationships that Jesus came to bring us, not just to make the physical relationships better, though he does that, but to introduce new and deeper relationships. Who is my family? The answer is we in the church are his family, if we keep his commandments and believe in his name; we are his brothers and sisters, and that family circle can never be broken.

What a variety of attitudes they had toward Jesus. Some of them thought he was a magician, some a miracle-worker, some a maniac, some just saw him as a human being, a man from Nazareth. They had so many different attitudes, and people today have different attitudes. But you can divide them all into two: those who were right and those who were wrong; those who were for him and those who were against him. In the last analysis, whatever we think of Jesus Christ will boil down to this issue: are we for him or against him? Is he for us or against us? Do we see in him the Son of God who became man that we might become sons of God within the family of a heavenly Father? This is the big issue. The test to 'try all your plans and your schemes is: what do you think of Christ? You cannot be right in the rest unless you think rightly of him'.

5

PARABLES AND POINTERS
Mark 4:1 – 34

Jesus was a unique teacher. He had none of the things that a teacher today would consider necessary — no special buildings, no visual aids, no whiteboards, no special equipment, no systematic curriculum, no timetable, no libraries. Yet when you study him you find that here is the greatest teacher the world has known, and anyone engaged in the calling of teaching ought to analyse our Lord's teaching methods and then apply them, because they are still as up to date as they ever were.

One of the unusual things he used in his teaching was this thing we call a parable. I have met so many hazy and woolly ideas as to what a parable is that I am going to define it first. I have heard many definitions, and I shall mention some of them below. But in his hands the tool of the parable was perfected. His parables have gone down into history and will be remembered long after you and I are forgotten. Think of the parables of the prodigal son and the good Samaritan. No matter where you go in the world, you will be able to use those parables with great effect.

What is a parable? Firstly, it may be very short, it may be very simple, but it is a *story*, and all the world loves a story, especially if it is interesting and well told — if it is recognisable, if it is part of our life and if it is real and relevant. Our Lord could tell a story better than anyone else. But that is not all. If you think of parables just as stories you have missed the point.

Are they, secondly, *stories with a moral*? There was one child in Sunday school who said, 'I like our vicar, he has no morals'! Of course what she meant to say was that he did not tell a story and then bang the nail home at the end with a nice moral to it. There is much more to a parable than that. It is certainly true that they are stories with a *meaning*, for the very word 'parable' signifies a comparison. If ever you say, 'Well, such and such a thing is like so and so', then you have actually used a parable. If you can put that comparison into a story, then you have used the form of message that Jesus used.

One of the popular definitions that I was brought up on in school and in Sunday school was 'an earthly story with a heavenly meaning'. Fair enough, but I do not think it goes far enough. It is a good definition to begin with — not that we must press all the details of the story and find a meaning. We must always remember that the parables were spoken and not written, and that you would not remember all the details. The meaning is not in every detail but in the main thrust of the story. So when we read a parable the first question is: what is the main meaning of this story? What is it saying *altogether* as a story? If you get bogged down in the details you may miss the wood for the trees.

Another definition is one of my own, but it is going a little deeper still: not just a story with a moral, not just a story with a meaning, it is *a story with a mirror in it*. That is why they are not quite so nice. Mirrors are not the best of friends. When Jesus told a parable he invariably used it as a mirror, either so people might see God more clearly, by holding the mirror at forty-five degrees as it were, and letting them see up into heaven, or, much more frequently, holding a mirror in front of them so that they could see what they were like. The parable of the prodigal son is an outstanding example. It is not only about the prodigal son, the parable is also about the elder brother, and the 'elder brother' was standing there in front of Jesus while he told the parable. But if you read the parable as a mirror you would notice the elder brother's attitude as well. When we read the parables we find that Jesus was using them in a sense as a weapon to attack people and to defend himself, and to show them themselves and attack their complacency and their conscience, challenging them to think again.

But I am going to go even deeper. A parable is not just a story with a moral, though there are plenty of morals in them; not just a story with a meaning, though they are full of messages; not just a story with a mirror to show people themselves; a parable is *a story with a mystery in it*. What do I mean by that? Jesus used the word — it is translated as 'secret' in the NIV. He said to the disciples, *"The secret of the kingdom of God has been given to you. But to those on the outside everything is said in parables so that, 'they may be ever seeing but never perceiving, and ever hearing but never understanding; otherwise they might turn and be forgiven!'"* (Mark 4:11–12, *NIV*). This is one of the most extraordinary sayings of Jesus. It seems to suggest that our Lord deliberately used parables to hide the truth from people; not to make it plain but to make it obscure; not to make it clearer and bring them light, but to increase their darkness. You will never understand the parables until you understand why Jesus said this.

What do we mean by the word 'mystery'? It is the same in English as in Greek. If you say about somebody, 'Well, it's a complete mystery to me where he gets all his money from,' what do you mean? You mean that as far as you are concerned you just do not understand where it all comes from. If somebody removed the mystery by explaining that he had a wealthy aunt who left it all to him you would then be 'in the know' and it would no longer be a mystery. The mystery has been revealed to you, but it is a mystery to everybody else until they have been given the clue. Jesus told these stories but the disciples found them a complete mystery. They wanted to know what they were all about because they did not understand. Why did he just tell the crowd that nice little story? Jesus told his disciples that they had been given the mystery. He would explain it to them, but to the others he would not explain it; to these others it must come in parables so that seeing they may see and not perceive, that hearing they may hear and not understand. This is a riddle isn't it? And you may be feeling at this moment that you are seeing but not perceiving, and hearing but not understanding. Let me tell you a little more.

Jesus was presenting truth in such a way that it would be revealed to the right people and hidden from the wrong people. The parable is a very brilliant device for doing this. A man who is seeking after the truth, a man who is desperately wanting to be right with God, a man who is really wanting to go further with what Christ was saying — to him the parables would make sense. But a man who had no intention of altering his life, who did not want to know the truth about himself and who did not want to know about God but was just curious, the truth would be hidden by the parable, and he would go away and say, 'I don't know what he was on about; telling silly little stories for children. I couldn't understand a word of it.'

The same happens with preaching the Word of God today. A man or a woman who is really concerned with getting to know God, who is prepared to make changes in their life as God reveals the need, a person who is utterly sincere when they listen to the Word of God, will get more truth, but others will find it a complete mystery. Our Lord chose the parable because it sorted people out into those who wanted to go further and those who did not. The reason was that he had a very mixed congregation, and people were there for all kinds of reasons. Some were there merely because they had heard that he did miracles, and they wanted to see what they thought was magic. Others were there because a crowd always draws a crowd, and if you hear that everybody is going to hear someone, you want to go and hear him yourself. Others came because they wanted God. How was he going to sort out this congregation without standing at the door and saying, '*You* can come in and *you* must stay outside'? There was no door to say that, because Jesus was in a boat and his hearers were on the bank. He sorted them out by using parables, until finally the crowd began to give up — perhaps using words similar to those some disciples are reported as having used in John: *"This is a hard teaching. Who can accept it?"* (John 6:60, *NIV*). The parables were used to hide the truth as well as to reveal it. As we study these parables the same sorting out will occur. Either you will say, 'A load of rubbish, it doesn't mean a thing, not helpful. What's it all about? What's he getting at?' —or you will say, 'I can see and understand things now that I've never seen before.'

The other thing to note about the parables, before we look at them, is this: our Lord did not have a pile of old sermons which he produced, one by one, regularly. What he had was a mind filled with the wisdom of God from which he brought truths relevant to every situation. Therefore, the first thing to ask when you look at any parable is: what was happening around him at the time? Why did he tell it there and then? What was the situation? And the situation was that Jesus was besieged by people from all over who wanted health, and who wanted to see something, and who wanted to have miracles from him — and Jesus desperately wanted to preach. We have seen this tension building up through the first three chapters. The crowd wanted one thing, Jesus wanted to give them another. And this is the biggest problem of the preacher: to give people what they need rather than what they want. This is where the crowd so often failed to meet Jesus. The people want one thing and Jesus knows they need another. They wanted health and nothing but health — they were not interested in the rest; they wanted to touch him, and they had got it all out of balance.

I mentioned above that we live in a day when people no longer believe preaching is of much use. Sir Edward Maufe, who designed Guildford Cathedral, went on record as saying that he thought the day was coming when sermons would disappear and preaching would be a thing of the past, so he was going to design his cathedral not for preaching but for liturgy, for worship, for things you could see rather than things you heard. The people had come to see things from

Jesus, but he is now going to hold up a mirror before them so that they might look at themselves and question why they are not willing to hear, and why it is just healing that they want rather than preaching. According to our Lord, if you want to talk about preaching and put it in a mental picture, it is like sowing. What a preacher does is to try to sow and scatter good seed, planting something in every heart. So Jesus tells three parables.

There are three main criticisms made of preaching. First, some say that it has no *permanent* effect. People may be moved at the time but it fritters away and it goes, so why preach? I have had that said to me many times. I have been challenged to get hold of my congregation a week later and ask them how many remember a thing about what was said the previous Sunday. I have hopes that a little more is remembered than the critics would allow, but I know perfectly well that a lot is forgotten!

The second criticism is that it has no *visible* effect. Somebody could stand in church and watch the congregation while I preached and say, 'Well, what is happening? They are all sitting there looking very polite, and not quite so comfortable, but very determined to sit through it, yet nothing visible is happening.'

The third criticism against preaching is that it has no *great* effect. It might affect one or two here and there, but as far as the world goes and as far as world problems and the human race are concerned there is not any great effect from preachers, so why not give up preaching and get into something useful? Go back to literal sowing! Well, when I was doing that I could say I had effects, and it was a great joy to see a field that you have sown coming through and then to harvest it later — you can see where you have been. And by and large when I have some time off I like to do something practical, such as wallpapering; it is a healthy antidote to see where I have been and to see some permanent, visible effect. But what about preaching?

Jesus' teaching deals with the first criticism, that there is no lasting effect. It is interesting that it is made of almost every preacher by the crowd. It was occasionally said of Billy Graham, for example. People make a response and then they go, and that is it, it is there for a month or a week or six months, and then it is frittered away. But Jesus' preaching is defended. The point of the parable of the sower is twofold. Message number one: the fault does not lie with the preacher but with the congregation. The fault is not in the seed but in the soil. If Billy Graham preached his heart out and no-one was converted, if he had preached the Word of God the fault would be in the soil not in the seed. That is the first main message. If preaching is not having a permanent effect then one major reason is that the fault lies in the soil. When the seed is perfectly good it should be scattered as widely as possible. That is how they do sow in the Middle East, not through drills in rows as we do in Britain, but by throwing it out everywhere. That tells me I have to preach anywhere I can go, anywhere I get a chance to preach, whether I think the ground is ripe or not, whether the congregation is sitting quietly or (as I have encountered at a university) answering back. I must go and scatter the seed. The failure is due to the reception given to the seed by the soil and there are three particular groups of people, (types of soil) where a permanent effect from preaching is not seen.

The first is the wayside (the hardened). In the Middle

East there are patches of land belonging to different people and in between is the pathway which gets trodden pretty hard. The limestone soil becomes hard, like concrete, with people walking to and fro on it. If you scatter the seed about, some of it will go onto that hard ground. I remember one preacher coming back to me from a particular church and saying, 'It's just like preaching at a brick wall there.' It may be inside a church, it may be outside, but you can get so hard that the seed cannot get in. Hardness of heart, maybe because of pride; hardness of mind, because of prejudice, but just hard. There are some that are so hard that you can preach till doomsday and the seed never gets in, it never penetrates, and therefore it just falls off or it is picked up and it is gone. Jesus' words teach us that some people may listen to a sermon but they will have forgotten it before they get home because Satan will have taken it away from them. It is lying on the top, it never got in, and if it is lying on the top he can pick it off again, he can reach it there, so it needs to go much deeper.

The second type of ground is the rocky ground. I used to imagine the kind of garden I once had with stones everywhere, but that is not what he means. Rocky ground is where the soil is terribly thin, too thin to plough or dig. The seed lands on the top and it springs up fairly quickly, but there is not enough moisture and not enough nourishment down below, and therefore its roots cannot go down. It is shallow, it is superficial. There will be a response but it will be a very temporary response — a quick one, over as quickly as it came. We have all known response to the preaching of the gospel of this kind — people who flit about, from one friend to another, one job to another, and pick up Christianity in the same superficial, shallow way in which they pick up everything and everyone else, and they drop it in the same way in which they drop everything and everyone else. This kind of response is not permanent, and it is not because there is anything wrong with the Word of God, it is because the soil is too shallow; it does not get deeply into them.

Thirdly: the thorny ground. This is good thick soil but it is the result of something rather lazy. In the Middle East the thorns are really tricky things. They are terribly big — I have seen some of them five or six feet high. They send horrible roots down into the ground. If you are a lazy farmer, once a year you chop the tops off but the roots remain. Therefore, when the seed goes in, the soil looks clean, but there are still too many other things in it and they are not rooted out. What happens? The plants come up but the weeds grow more quickly than anything you sow. Have you noticed that? Weeds come up, the thorns come up, too many things are already there, and the mixture is too much. And because there are so many interests, so many other cares, other affections and so many wrong things, this new faith just gets choked for air. There are many people like this. You can fill your life with good things and choke your faith; you can also fill your life with bad things and choke your faith. Make no mistake about it, you cannot do everything. I would say if there is one thing that holds back some young people from full commitment to the Lord Jesus Christ today it is the desire not to miss anything, the feeling that if I get too committed to this, I might not be able to do that; the feeling that if I engage in some lifelong service for the Lord I am going to miss out on a whole lot of other things that others do. If I follow Jesus, I cannot follow others, and if I concentrate on serving him there are some things I will just have to cut out. You cannot do everything in life — or it chokes.

All this is a bit miserable isn't it? The farmer sows his seed, and this seed falls on the hard ground, and that seed falls on the shallow ground, and some seed falls on the thorny ground. Why preach, if that is the result? Every time I preach the Word of God I know this is going to happen in some cases, as does any preacher. So why do we go on preaching? Why have I given sixty years of my life to preaching the Word? And why will I give another twenty if God spares me? I will tell you why. I have been a farmer; I have seen people in the Middle East sowing seed — and the simple truth is (and here comes the main point in the parable) that the good ground makes it all worthwhile. It may be that only one seed drops on good ground for twenty seeds that fall on the other kinds of ground, but that one seed will produce thirty more, sixty more, a hundred more. In other words, that makes it successful. The farmer would not bother to sow if he did not get his returns. There is a harvest, and here we have a wonderful change of emphasis. From the seed that gets into good ground you get far more back than all that you lose from the other kinds of ground, and that is what makes preaching so worthwhile. Let me give you one or two illustrations.

I think of a lad in his late teens who came to know the Lord Jesus. That boy went on to have meeting with him every Sunday sixty boys he had led to the Lord through playing football with them. Whenever I met that lad my heart just thrilled. It would have been worth it if he had been the only person who came to Christ in that place because he had got sixty-fold. Just a boy playing football!

Take another example. Willy Mullin, the Irish boy who slept rough and lived rough and became the leader of a group of criminals, and then, by chance apparently, found himself one night listening to a preacher who was conducting a three week mission in an Irish town. That night, as Willy later said, the preacher planted a little seed of God's Word in his heart and he took it away with him. He thought no more about it until one night most dramatically, when he was planning a robbery for his gang, that seed germinated in his heart and he was converted. He did not meet that preacher until years later, when they found themselves on the same platform at a Christian convention. The man said to Willy Mullin, 'I don't think I know you,' and Willy replied, 'Well you ought to, you are my spiritual father.' The man said, 'How come?' Willy asked him whether he remembered a three-week mission in such and such a town. He told him, 'I was converted as a result of hearing you that one night.' And the preacher said, 'Do you know, I thought that crusade was a complete failure because I preached three weeks and didn't see a single conversion — not one.' But Willy Mullin has led literally thousands of people to Christ. Years later, when he visited that preacher, the dying preacher said, 'Willy, looking back now, that mission was the best I ever had.'

Sixty-fold, a hundred-fold, a thousand-fold; I could give you so many more examples. Let me give you one more. I was told when I visited Ethiopia about an incident that happened there just before Mussolini took it over and made it into Abyssinia. A missionary who had been labouring hard in a little village in that country for a long time led one blind beggar to Christ. Then Mussolini came in with his mustard gas and his troops, and took over the country, and all the missionaries were thrown out and sent home. The missionary was in Britain until the late 1940s. The missionary went back and discovered that one blind beggar had led three thousand Ethiopians to Christ and there was a massive church in that area, waiting for somebody to come and teach and lead them. It is all about sowing a seed. We may not be privileged to see thousands converted, but if one person is converted it has been worthwhile because that seed has power to reproduce itself.

The second charge against preaching is that it has no visible effect, it is just talk and you cannot see anything happening. It is true to say that people much prefer to see things happening. That is why they wanted miracles from Jesus. They liked to see him, but he wanted them to hear, and that is not so spectacular. Again, the answer comes from a farmer, and I am so glad that I had farming experience because it helps me to understand the Bible. There are two things a farmer needs to have. He has to have patience. Businessmen, generally speaking, make bad farmers. They buy a farm in the country and think how nice it is to be a farmer; but the farm does not run quite as quickly as other businesses; you plant something in the spring and you just have to sit and wait. You might be able to feed pigs with pills to increase their metabolic rate and get pork one month earlier (and this is one of the things that is being done to speed up farming), but when you work on the land you have to develop a certain patience — you cannot get quick returns. You also have to wait for God, you have to wait for life, you have to wait for germination.

The other thing you develop is confidence. When you sow a field and you are putting the seed in with a drill or anything else (and I have done it both ways, by scattering it or drilling it), you never doubt that it will turn green, that it will grow until it is knee-high, that it will begin to form other seeds; you have utter confidence in what you are putting in the soil. These two attributes — patience and confidence — are due to two facts about the seed. Jesus told a parable about the seed and he said that the seed is active of itself. From the Greek word translated 'of itself' we get our word 'automatic'. If you put the seed in, you do not need to do another thing — the conditions are there for that seed to grow. I never cease to be amazed when I look at seeds, which are dry little wrinkled things, and one thinks of the life that is in them. There is life in a seed like that which can crack concrete. You look at the dandelions coming through your tarmac; you look at the little tree roots in your backyard getting near that section of paving you put down! The life, the power, the activity right there!

The Word has the power to produce life in people. It may be some time before you see it, but it is germinating in their hearts and they cannot get rid of it. It is producing life and it is challenging them, and it is going to bring them through to faith.

The other thing about a seed is this: it not only has the power to live, it has the power to reproduce itself. The most glorious thing about one person coming to Christ is that now they are in a position to lead someone else to Christ. This is what makes a harvest possible, and this is why we have the patience and the confidence. 'First, the blade, then the ear, then the full corn shall appear.' And every person converted will one day be perfect because of the seed that has been sown in their hearts. That is very thrilling. Paul wrote to the Corinthians, *I planted the seed, Apollos watered it, but God made it grow* (1 Corinthians 3:6, *NIV*). You have to be patient and let God do the work. God gives life; God gives the increase, and every preacher is content, whether he sees results in his own lifetime or not, to go on sowing.

The third criticism of preaching is that there is no great effect. Even those who are converted, how perilously few they are. I remember going to see the Garden Tomb in Jerusalem. It is a lovely garden just below the hill of Golgotha. Somebody pointed out to me a very old tree about ten or eleven feet high. They said that it was a mustard tree, so I made straight for it. It had the pods on, so I shook a pod into my hand, and there in my hand were mustard seeds. A few tiny black things that I had to bend my head down to see, little specks of dust, and from just one such seed had come that tree. It is the most amazing thing: the smallest seed that they used in the Middle East became one of the largest trees in their garden. The birds love it for the seeds and the pods. Jesus said, *"What shall we say the kingdom of God is like, or what parable shall we use to describe it?"* (Mark 4:30, *NIV*). So the kingdom of heaven may have tiny beginnings, but look at the end product. The 'mustard seed' that Christianity began from was twelve men (and one of them a failure, so eleven men) and that is a tiny seed, so small on the surface of the earth. In relation to history it seems too small to do anything. Yet the church of Jesus Christ now numbers millions, and every minute there are some fifteen more Christians in the world, even allowing for deaths. Mustard seed? Yes! A young person is converted in your town or city. Just a mustard seed? Yes! An old person converted? Mustard seed? Yes! What is one among the millions massing around? He is lost in a football match crowd. But from these mustard seeds is coming the greatest kingdom the world has ever seen — the kingdom of Christ.

We can go even further because we know from the Bible that in those days they used the picture of a tree with branches and birds as a parable of an empire, the tree being the empire, the branches the different countries in it, and the birds the different peoples that come into the empire. Ezekiel likens the empire of Assyria to a tree with branches and the birds coming into it. The Roman empire was also called a tree with branches, different countries and nations coming into it like birds. From the seed Jesus sowed there will come a kingdom to which all the nations of the world will come; all the birds will fly into this tree. The glorious thing is that when you get to heaven you will see a multitude that you have never seen before; it will be a multitude that no-one can number, stretching as far as the eye can see. In that multitude you will see every kindred and every tribe and every tongue and every nation. It all began with the mustard seed that Jesus sowed in the hearts of a few fishermen.

Why preach? No permanent effect? If there is not, then the fault is in the soil. There is a permanent effect in the good ground and it outweighs all the loss. No visible effect? Who cares? If you have sown the seed in the heart of a man it will germinate, it will grow. Be patient, be confident — God will give the increase. No great effect? The kingdom of Christ is the greatest kingdom already, and it is a kingdom that spans heaven and earth and goes on growing.

The parables reflected Jesus' own ministry, his approach to things, his own desire to put preaching first and then add all other things to that. As if to emphasise the double effect it would have on people of telling them this kind of thing, in just a few verses that I have not commented on, he lays down two principles. First, light must be revealed. If you have the truth you must share it. What is the point of my finding the truth and then not preaching about it, not sharing it, keeping it to myself on my library shelf? Who buys a lamp and puts it under a bed? Why do we preach? Because light must be revealed and if you have seen the light you must tell others. The other truth he gives is that truth must be *received*. If you do not receive any truth when you listen to preaching then you will lose part of what you have. But if you receive, more will be given. This is true in other realms of life, why would it not be true here? It is true of study. If I am a student at a university, the more I give myself to study the more I learn, but if I do not, I lose what knowledge I have.

We hear that memorable phrase Jesus uses: *"He who has ears to hear, let him hear."* Some people do not have trouble with their hearing but with their listening. Some hear the words of the preacher, but they do not go deep down where they can germinate — they were not planted. But others open their hearts and say, 'Lord, are you talking to me now? Is my heart hard? Is my heart shallow? Is my heart too crowded with many other things so that my faith can't grow? Is that me, Lord? Lord, I want to be good ground. I want not only to receive this seed, I want to reproduce it, I want to win others; I want to tell the truth to them. I want to help to sow these little mustard seeds wherever I live, wherever I work, to sow the seed of truth.' Do you feel excited at the possibility? Do you wonder that I was thrilled to the core of my being when God said, 'I want you to preach; I want you to give your life to sowing — not seeds in a field, but seeds in the field of people's hearts'? I shall do that as long as he gives me breath.

6

FEAR AND FAITH
Mark 4:35 – 5:43

The first part of chapter four in Mark's Gospel is concerned with parables, and now this section is concerned with miracles. These are two main features of our Lord's life: his parables and his miracles; his words and his works — what he said and what he did. If you are going to have a full and balanced picture of Jesus you need to take both, because he said certain things and he did certain things, and both had a profound meaning. Just as it is the case that unless you study the parables closely they will hide the truth from you, so the miracles will do the same. In both cases there is a deep hidden meaning for those with ears to hear and eyes to see.

We look now at the miracles, and we take four which demonstrate the unique control of Jesus of every situation. There is no need known to man which Jesus cannot meet. And the four singled out here are four pretty serious troubles. Danger — danger of dying, real physical danger. Secondly, demon possession, a rare but terrible condition. Thirdly, a disease of twelve years standing about which the doctors can do nothing. Fourthly, death itself, which happens to us all. Jesus faces these four things almost accidentally as he travels around, and when he meets them it is not Jesus who gives way, it is they who give way. I have used a phrase or label to indicate human reactions to each of these things. There are only two basic reactions to the kind of crisis that we have here: either you react in fear or you react in faith. We find in each of these four stories a different kind of reaction. The first story begins with fear and it ends with fear; the second begins with fear but it ends with faith; the third begins with faith but ends in fear, and the fourth begins and ends with faith. You see a wonderful development here, and these stories are chosen, I think, by Mark under the Holy Spirit, to give you the whole picture, all the mixtures.

From this point on, our Lord's life was a constant quest for privacy which he rarely seemed able to have. From now on he was always trying to get away from the crowds, trying to get alone with his disciples, trying to get alone by himself and somehow he never really achieves it. He needed it not only for rest (so did the disciples, incidentally), he needed it to train them. He wanted to get alone with the twelve and share his heart with them. So he is now in a boat crossing the sea, and the picture is so well known I am not going to retell the story, except to point out that the sleep of Jesus tells us a great deal. There is not a word wasted in this account, and when it tells us that Jesus was asleep, that is there for a purpose. Why? Two things. First of all, it tells us that he was human enough to be very tired indeed. It was not quite dark and yet here he is fast asleep in the boat. It is said of some people they can sleep anywhere, and Jesus could. The second thing it tells us is that our Lord was utterly trustful. You need a trusting mind to sleep well, particularly in the middle of a storm when everybody else is awake. We have a picture of this terrific storm with the disciples nearly 'driven off their heads' with the danger of it, and there sleeping in the stern of the boat is Jesus. A stern of a boat is not terribly comfortable. He did have a pillow for his head but the rest was hard wood and there he is sleeping in the middle of the storm, a tired, trustful person.

The Sea of Galilee lies about seven hundred feet below sea level and there are deep ravines coming down towards the Sea through the Galilean hills. And from cold Mount Hermon, which is always snow-capped, in the north, the chilly wind rushes down into the Jordan valley as the hot air rises at about midday. This combination of the hot air rising and the cold air rushing in stirs up that little lake, which is only thirteen miles by eight, into a most terrible place. I have never seen this, but I have certainly heard of tourists in Israel who have been drowned because they ventured out on the Sea of Galilee in the afternoon in a small boat. If you go out on the Sea of Galilee, go out in the morning or go out on a big boat but don't run the risks. In fact a rule has been made that you are not allowed to go out in a small boat there as so many people have been drowned. This lovely lake looks peaceful, yet it can suddenly become dangerous. These were fishermen, and it takes a lot for fishermen to get upset. I began my ministry among fishermen in the Shetland Islands, and it had to be a really bad storm before they got concerned. This must have been pretty terrible.

For me, the interesting aspect of this story is the three rebukes. First of all Jesus is rebuked, then the storm is rebuked, and then the disciples are rebuked. Rebuke is necessary from time to time, but sometimes it is a wrong rebuke and sometimes it is the right one. Take the first. 'Don't you care?' What a thing to say to Jesus! Yet people are still saying it. They still say to God when troubles come, 'Don't you care?' It is the most terrible thing that you could ever say about the God who so loved the world that he gave his only Son. It is a terrible rebuke, and the disciples woke Jesus up. I do not know what they expected him to do — anything but what he did. I think it was just that they resented him sleeping while they were so worried. I have noticed again and again that people who are worried and going through the storm, and who are frightened of what is going to happen, resent those who are calm and peaceful. There is a kind of reaction to those who seem so free from cares and free from worries. They said, *"Teacher, don't you care if we drown?"* Well of course he cared, but there was no real danger. If they had really understood Jesus they would have known that he could not possibly have been drowned — his time had not yet come, it was not the Father's will that he should die by drowning. He had tried to talk to them about this and he was going to talk to them about it again. If they had really understood him they would have known that they were perfectly safe with Jesus in that boat, but of course they did not understand him so they rebuked him.

The second rebuke was to the storm. I am afraid I do not like the translation 'Peace. Be still.' It is a lovely, comforting calm word, but that is not how Jesus spoke. He spoke very sharply — 'Be quiet, get down', or literally, 'Be muzzled.' It is a word used to a puppy dog that jumps up at you. And he is saying: stop jumping up at my disciples, get down. Just as sometimes we have to say to our dogs when visitors come (maybe the visitor doesn't like dogs), 'Get down, be quiet!' That is how Jesus spoke to the winds. And that is the tone of voice that you get in the original language and in the modern translation, *"Quiet! Be still!"* It is a very strong term. Interestingly enough, it is exactly the same word that

Jesus used in Mark chapter one to a demon-possessed man who was 'spilling the beans' about who he was. I suppose 'Shut up!' would be about the nearest English equivalent, and Jesus could talk to the winds and waves like that!

The third rebuke in the story is to the disciples. You can imagine the scene now. Having been a sudden turmoil, now it is absolutely placid, and that lake is like a mirror nestling in the hills. You can imagine the feeling of the disciples. Now Jesus rebuked them saying, *"Why are you so afraid? Do you still have no faith?"* (Mark 4:40, *NIV*) They asked him whether he cared, and he asked them whether they trusted him. They wondered why he was not worried. This is the rebuke we often need from Jesus. We say, 'Don't you care? Aren't you worried about us?' And he would ask us why we are so afraid. Don't we believe that he cares? He presents this fundamental principle: you cannot have fear and faith in your heart at the same time — it is one or the other. If you are afraid, you do not have faith; if you have faith, you are not afraid. But the disciples did not finish with faith, they finished with fear; they were now more afraid of Jesus than they had been of the storm! Why? Because there was something supernatural going on, and they were saying, *"Who is this? Even the wind and the waves obey him!"* (Mark 4:41, *NIV*) He was a real man as they were, and yet what man can talk to the wind and the waves as you and I talk to a puppy dog and they do what he says? This made them afraid. I can imagine them all up in the bow of the boat, Jesus at the other end of the boat in the stern, and they are looking and wishing the boat were bigger and that they could get a bit further away from him. They were scared of Jesus now — a man who had such power was a man you had better not get too near, he could do extraordinary things.

The second story is of demon possession — from fear to faith. Their quest for privacy is frustrated immediately as they reach the other side. On the far side of the Sea of Galilee, in the south-east corner, there are very steep hills coming right down to the Sea – maybe 700 to 800 feet high. On top is a flat plain, and on that plain are ten cities called the Decapolis, and they are Greek cities, not Jewish cities, they are a little remnant of the conquest of Alexander the Great, and living in those cities are people who are not Jews but who follow a Greek way of life, and to this day you can go and see the theatres and the squares and the Greek architecture there. But between the cities on the plain and the Sea of Galilee is this terrible limestone hillside, pitted with caves, used only as a burial ground. It saves digging a grave, you just put the body in the cave and close it up. It is now dark and they land at the foot of the graveyard. It is an eerie time and it is an eerie place. I do not know what you would feel like if a man possessed with demons came screaming and running at you just after dark in a place where there is nobody near, but those disciples made for the boat I should think, and wanted to get back on the sea as quickly as they could. And Jesus just stood. This man came screaming and running up to him; he was stark naked, he was bleeding and scarred all over. There were marks round his ankles and wrists of iron fetters that had been smashed; he had long, uncut hair, long nails — you can see the picture.

Here is not a case of mental illness but of demon possession. All the symptoms are there. There is supernatural strength — a demon-possessed man has ten times the strength of anyone else. There is supernatural knowledge

— clairvoyance; spiritual knowledge about Jesus; an ability to talk with a language coming out of the mouth with the words that are said not coming from the man himself but from someone else. It was a real fight for Jesus to get this man healed. Jesus was saying *"Come out"*, and at first the demons resisted him. When Jesus started to talk to them they retorted very smartly. If you are going to have to deal with a demon, you must use the name of Jesus, but you will often also have to find out the name of the demon and address it by name in the name of Jesus, and confront one name with the more powerful name — 'Jesus, the name high over all in hell or earth or sky, angels and men before it fall, and devils fear and fly.' So Jesus asked this man for his name. The answer was a clever one: *"My name is Legion, for we are many."* Do you notice the plural, 'we'? There is more than one demon in this man. A legion was 6,000 Roman troops. Too many for you to know, the demons imply. Finally, Jesus comes to an arrangement with them. They ask him to send them into the pigs. That proves we are out of Jewish country because you would never see a herd of pigs in Jewish territory, you only see pigs in the far country. And it may well be that these ten cities, the Greek cities where all kinds of things went on, represent the far country in the parable of the prodigal son, because if a young Galilean Jew wanted to go away and have a good time he would make for the nearest Greek cities. In the far country there are pigs, and the prodigal finished among them. Here was a herd of two thousand pigs. I wrote earlier about a case where demons left a young boy and went into the farmer's pigs who started killing each other, and the farmer got his gun and shot the animals. Here, the large herd of pigs went rushing down a hill into the Sea. By the way, that tells me that Jesus values one man more than many animals. There is no false sentiment here. Jesus would rather the herd be destroyed and the one man saved, because the man is made in the image of God, the pigs are not. You have something of Jesus' scale of values here.

For me, the real point in this miracle lies in the reactions to it: the reactions of the people from the towns who came running to see, and the reaction of the man himself. Consider the people from the towns. They begged Jesus to leave. What on earth is wrong, that when people see a man cured of demon-possession and brought to his right mind, they should want Jesus to go? It is the most extraordinary thing. The answer may be that they thought too much about their pigs. I wonder how you would feel if you had a herd of two thousand pigs and were told, 'This religious leader who came here has made them all rush into the Sea.' I think you would be very anxious that he should catch the next bus out of town. It would affect business. But I think there is a deeper reason for it: they were afraid. There was something weird going on, something supernatural. I remember a lady saying to me once, and she was very sincere in saying it, 'I hope nothing supernatural will ever happen in our church.' Considering the reason why we met there — to meet God — it was quite a statement! (I do know what she meant, of course.) The supernatural disturbs; God breaking in disturbs; God doing things to people disturbs us, and we do not like being disturbed; we like things under our control, and we understand that.

I am not quite sure where the man who had just been healed got his clothes. I think the disciples would have had to share their clothes with him. But here he is sitting (that in itself is amazing), clothed in his right mind and clothed in clothes too. Here is this man who was once naked, tearing about screaming with supernatural energy; he had probably hardly slept and never sat down, and here he is calmly seated. He begged Jesus to let him follow him; he wanted to go everywhere that Jesus went. He would have been a missionary and gone to the ends of the earth for him. But Jesus said, *"Go home to your family and tell them how much the Lord has done for you, and how he has had mercy on you"* (Mark 5:19, *NIV*). Have you ever felt like this? It is sometimes much more difficult to go home than to go to China as a missionary. That is not belittling those who go as missionaries. But sometimes it would be easier to do some big thing for the Lord, go to the ends of the earth, make some huge sacrifice, than to have the Lord tell you to go home to those people you live with, your friends and neighbours, and tell them about him. But that man went home and told his friends. And the next time Jesus came to the Decapolis there were four thousand people who wanted to hear him. If you pray, 'Lord, I want to do anything for you, anything at all,' he may say to you, 'Go home, tell your family about me; tell the people you work with about me.' Tell others what the good Lord has done for you.

The third case is of sickness. Why did this woman come to Jesus? It was her last hope. The tragedy is that she had to try everybody else first. Isn't it amazing that we often consider prayer as the last resort? After we have tried everything and everyone else, we say, 'Well, there's nothing for it but prayer.' Why did we not pray first? Mind you, of course, he had not been healing in his ministry for all that period of twelve years. But here is a woman who regarded Jesus as her last hope. But more than that, she regarded him as her *best* hope. The faith of the woman shines out even before she met him. She was not saying, 'I'll try Jesus as a last resort and see if he can help me,' she was saying that she knew that he could. She must have heard something about him; she must have heard that he had helped others, and she was absolutely sure.

Of course, her condition rendered her unclean for both religion and society, so she was not allowed to mix freely with others. How could she get through to Jesus? Then she thought: I'll wait until he's in the middle of a crowd and I don't care if I am unclean, I am going to push my way through. *"If I just touch his clothes, I will be healed."* The word used, 'tassel', means Jesus wore the robe of the devout Jew — a large square shawl with tassels at the four corners, mentioned in the book of Numbers, and she believed that if she could just get through, near enough to Jesus to touch his tassel, that would be enough. What determination to get through! So she came to him.

The first two things we notice are these. She lost pain and he lost power. We note that they go together. Something was transferred from Jesus to her, and when Jesus heals we need to remember that something is being transferred: health, goodness and power. It was not that he gave her health in herself, he was giving her his. Here we come across a profound secret of the Christian life. If I need patience I need *his* patience in me, not more of mine. He is my wisdom, he is my righteousness, he is my sanctification, he is my life — if I get through to him, I can get his for me. So she came, and she realised that if she got close enough to him she could get from him what she needed, and we need to realise this too. The other side of it is that instinctively, immediately, she felt one thing in her body —health, which had come into her body — but Jesus realised that something had gone out of his body. In other words, she was living on Jesus. That is the relationship that ought to be. I ought not to be trying to be kind like Jesus, I ought to be living on the kindness of Jesus. That is the secret of Christ-likeness — not to try and imitate him but to feed on him. This is what is meant by the vine and the branches. He said, *"I am the vine; you are the branches"* (John 15:5, *NIV*). The branches draw everything from the vine. They do not produce fruit of themselves, they draw everything from the trunk, the stem, the stock, and so must we.

Jesus turned around and asked who had touched him, and the disciples' response showed that they thought this was a ridiculous question. He was in the middle of this crowd and said that! But Jesus repeated the question. Somebody had touched him. You can be in a crowd very near to Jesus and yet not touch him — I underline that. You can be sitting in church, part of a large congregation, and Jesus is there in the midst — he said he will be, and whether you are aware of it or not he is there. But you can be crowded near to him and yet go away without having touched him in faith. I put it this way: what is the need that you bring into a service? What is your particular burden? What is the particular resource that you are lacking and that you need? May I suggest that in the crowd, in the congregation, you stretch out the hand of faith, touch Jesus, and say, 'If I can get through to him I'll get what I need from him; he's got enough for me.' You can do that in a moment of quiet in the church, even as the minister speaks. In the crowd, reach through and say, 'By faith, Jesus, I take from you what I need.'

Why did Jesus want to know who had touched him? Because he was angry that he had lost something? Nothing of the sort. He wanted to get in touch with that person; he wanted to have a conversation; he wanted the truth to come out, and the truth wants to come out, so he turned around and she came. She told him all the truth. That is the best thing you can ever do with Jesus: tell him all the truth; tell him about your condition; tell him what is wrong with you; tell him how you feel; tell him the whole truth. Then when she told him the truth he told her the truth. There was nothing magic about his tassel, there was nothing in those garments, nothing different, it was her faith in him that was the factor. Now, that applies to the sacrament of the Lord's Supper. When we take bread and wine it is ordinary bread and ordinary wine, yet by faith we can have communion with Christ by taking it. There is nothing magical about the bread and the wine, it is our faith in Christ through the bread and the wine that makes this real to us and makes it a sacrament. Similarly with baptism. It is ordinary water which came from the tap and goes down the drain after baptism. But what is it that makes baptism a means of grace and a meaningful thing to us? It is that through the water we reach Christ, we are buried with Christ; by faith we are touching him. Jesus wanted this woman to know there was nothing magic about his clothes. *"Daughter, your faith has healed you. Go in peace and be freed from your suffering"* (Mark 5:34, *NIV*). Her faith, her belief in Jesus, is what matters. It was not touching the clothes that healed her, it was her faith that was determined to get through. So he told her the truth.

Now we come to the final story, one I used to love as a

boy. I think it was almost my favourite story in the Bible. I don't know why, but the drama of it! I have twisted the order of scripture a little because this woman's healing came in the middle of the last story. Here is a very prominent citizen losing all his dignity, all his pride, all his prejudice, to come and kneel before a travelling preacher. You have to be pretty desperate to do that, and he was desperate. He had a girl of twelve, and this girl was on the threshold of womanhood because a girl in the Middle East became a woman at twelve. She would be betrothed soon after, and married at fourteen or fifteen. And so twelve was equivalent to our eighteen or twenty-one. Here is a young girl on the threshold of womanhood and marriage, with all the possibilities of life before her, and she is desperately ill. That would make a father do anything. This man, who normally sat on the high seat on the platform, came and knelt before Jesus publicly. He did not care — he wanted Jesus to come and help his daughter. That man had tremendous faith. He did not start with fear, he just started with sheer faith, saying, *"My little daughter is dying. Please come and put your hands on her so that she will be healed and live"* (Mark 5:23, *NIV*). Then there was all this business about the woman who had been ill for twelve years. I can imagine his feelings: hurry, hurry, she's been ill for twelve years, can't she wait till tomorrow? Another twenty-four hours won't make any difference. But Jesus calmly stops to talk. How would you feel if a child of yours were desperately ill and the doctor talked to his patients on the way to your house —and in what might almost seem a leisurely way? You would be getting all worked up inside. Then they come across the mourners at the house, and it seems to be too late. At that point, the fear could have got in but the faith kept it out. We do not mourn in this country as they do in the Middle East. I remember looking out of my flat from the balcony down onto the street in the quarter of Aden known as Crater, seeing some of the funerals as they took place. The wailing, carrying the corpse within hours of death to the cemetery, and the people making themselves cry, telling the whole world death had happened, telling everybody this was the end — the noise they make when someone dies; everybody has to know! And Jesus told them the same as he told the storm. They were to be quiet; their behaviour was inappropriate.

Then he said, *"The child is not dead but asleep"* (Mark 5:39, *NIV*). Some have thought that he meant she was not physically dead, she was in a coma and they had mistaken the diagnosis. But it is interesting that Jesus preferred to talk of death as sleep. He said of Lazarus that he was 'asleep'. Why should Jesus say 'asleep'? The answer is that if someone is asleep they can be woken up. To Jesus, death was sleep because there was going to be a waking up. That is why many Christians have put this phrase on tombstones: 'Fallen asleep in Christ' — because if someone has fallen asleep you expect them to wake up again. This is the Christian approach to death: this little girl is asleep, we can wake her up again. Have you read the biography of Peter Marshall, the former chaplain to the United States Senate? He went to Washington as a Scots preacher and became quite a famous minister of the gospel. There is the part in the book where he has a heart attack and is being taken into the hospital that morning and he is not to live for more than a few hours. His last words to his wife Catherine were, 'I'll see you in the morning!' She wrote that very moving biography of her husband in which she says this is the message she clings to. That is why we say when someone has died they have fallen asleep in Christ: it means they are going to wake up again in resurrection 'morning'.

Putting the people outside, taking three disciples (and presumably we have got it from Peter, through Mark) Jesus took the parents and went into the bedroom. Then he said something so moving that we still have it in the original language and nobody has wanted to translate it: *"Talitha, cumi!"* Years later, the same Peter who was in that bedroom and heard those words, said it to a woman called Dorcas and she woke up too. These words were burned deep into the memories of those three men: *"Little girl, I say to you, get up!"* (Mark 5:41, *NIV*), and she got up. Then, with a divine touch of consideration, Jesus told them to get her something to eat. Why did he say that? Because she had been lying there without food for so long? I can think of another reason. Was it for the mother's sake? Out of sheer consideration giving the mother something to do; that was a profound touch of comfort and it is recorded in the Gospel. It shows again the sheer understanding of Jesus in such a situation. The mother now had to focus on getting something ready in the kitchen, getting something to eat, and she was gradually brought down to earth again. They were nearly out of their minds with amazement; putting the kettle on would just put it right.

Now we have looked at these four stories there are just two things I want to say to conclude this chapter. First, every one of these four situations is specifically said to be beyond man's control. The storm cannot be controlled by men, demon possession cannot be controlled by men, a woman had tried every doctor she could reach and she was beyond the help of men, and death is beyond the help of men. These four stories are saying when you come to the very end of human resources you are just at the beginning of our Lord's. These four stories tell us this hidden meaning: we are not dealing with a great man in Jesus, we are dealing with God. We are not dealing with a great human being; great as he was, we are dealing with something in another category. What manner of man is this? He is God himself. That is why those who read the Gospel and then say, 'Jesus was just the greatest man who ever lived' have not really read the story, they have not seen the hidden meaning of the miracles. The hidden meaning is this: here is a person who was in complete control of every situation that was beyond the control of men, and that means he must be more than man. This is why I can tell you that it does not matter what situation you find yourself in, however beyond the help of man you are, 'When other helpers fail and comforts flee, help of the helpless, O abide with me' — Jesus can help.

I underline this: faith and fear are incompatible, but faith has got to be faith in something or *someone*. And if Jesus is God, and still alive, and still able to help, then I have a ground for my faith and therefore I have a ground for conquering my fear.

7

ACTIONS AND REACTIONS
Mark 6:1–56

When we get to about chapter six in Mark's Gospel we need
an atlas in one hand and our Bible in the other, because our
Lord is constantly on the move now. He is travelling all
the time, moving from this side of the Sea of Galilee to the
other side and back again, moving out of Galilee altogether.
This is not aimless wandering. When we see the atlas we
realise why he kept on the move. In those days, that land was
divided up into little kingdoms or territories. The Romans
controlled one part, Herod controlled another part, the
Greeks controlled another area. On the Sea of Galilee there
were in fact three sections of shore belonging to different
rulers. Therefore, whenever Jesus crossed over to the other
side it was to get out of one territory into another. It was for
purposes of security; he was playing for time. He needed
more time with his disciples to teach them many things, so
he kept moving out of various territories, and so as soon as
he came to the attention of a ruler who would do him harm
before his time he simply got in a boat and crossed over to
the other side. Sometimes the purpose was to escape from
the crowd, but he never went anywhere without a reason.

I suppose if there were a competition for the most misunderstood man, Jesus would win it. As I read the central
chapters of Mark it strikes me that nobody really understood

him and therefore he must have been terribly lonely. Sometimes you feel lonely because you feel that nobody understands you, but bear in mind that Jesus was more misunderstood than anyone else.

There are six incidents here and in most of them we see misunderstanding. In most of them people take up an attitude towards him that is wrong, even when he is popular. We will study these attitudes as we go through the six incidents.

One of the things that you have to unlearn in life is the picture of Jesus you may have picked up in Sunday school. I certainly had it as a boy and I presume that is where I may have got it —because you cannot tell little children the whole truth about Jesus. I got a picture of Jesus as somebody tremendously popular, somebody liked by everybody, somebody terribly nice, and everybody as soon as they met him regarded him as nice, so wherever he went people would just come to him and they would make friends with him straight away. I am afraid this is far from the truth. There came a day only three years after he began his ministry when he said, 'The world hated me.' And we see something of these different attitudes coming out in this chapter six.

One day, Jesus came back to Nazareth. That required courage — he had been there once before and they had tried to kill him there. It says something for the compassion of Jesus that even though they tried to murder him on his first visit he wanted to come back and give them another chance, so he came. He came back to the people who had known him since he was a little boy with no shoes, running around the streets, climbing the hills around the town; to people who had taken him their furniture to be repaired. He came back now as the most famous man in the nation, and they took offence at him, they were resentful. In their case the old proverb 'familiarity breeds contempt' came true.

One of the most awful things that can happen to someone is to become so familiar with things of God that you are no longer aware of them. When you have gone to church twice every Sunday, Sunday in and Sunday out, you can become familiar with holy things and not see that God is near.

"Isn't this the carpenter?" They could not accept the words of his mouth, nor the works of his hands. They felt that those hands should have stuck to hammer and chisel. They almost resented him getting, in their eyes, 'too big for his boots'. And what they were saying would have been: 'He's only a working man, who does he think he is now? He only makes tables and chairs — who does he think he is, coming back like this with a great following and with this reputation?' And Jesus said, *"Only in his home town, among his relatives and in his own house is a prophet without honour"* (Mark 6:4, *NIV*). That must have hurt a bit.

The thing that strikes me most is their faithlessness, and the limit this imposed upon his power. It does not say he did no miracles there, it says, *He could not do any miracles there, except lay his hands on a few sick people and heal them. And he was amazed at their lack of faith* (Mark 6:5f, *NIV*). There was a blockage; he could not pour out his power in that place. So they may have said to each other after he had gone: 'Well, all this fuss about him, I didn't see anything. I don't know where the others have got these big ideas about the carpenter from because he did nothing in our synagogue.' Could it be written over our churches: there he could do no mighty work because they didn't expect it; they didn't believe it could happen? Let me challenge

115

my own heart and yours. We think of some difficult person. We would love to see them a Christian, we have prayed for them, and then we gave up because they did not seem to get any nearer. We just could not imagine them a Christian. He could do no mighty work because of their unbelief. Their faithlessness was the real blockage and their familiarity led to it. They had become so familiar with him that they did not expect it of him. And it is possible to become so familiar with church, with the Bible, that you do not expect things to happen any more, and they don't. The tragedy to me is what they missed, what they lost. Only a few sick people there could say, 'He healed me and he blessed me and he helped me,' and the rest said, 'Nothing much happened here when Jesus came.'

Now let us turn to the second incident in chapter six. It says that Jesus left Nazareth and began to move around the villages teaching, and he called to him the twelve and began to send them out two by two. Our Lord was wanting to multiply his ministry, to go to places he could not reach by himself, and he decided to send others to do the same work. This was the beginning of the ministry of the church.

An important point here is that the way you learn to do the things of Christ is to do them. The way I learned to swim was the hard way. I remember standing on the edge of the swimming pool at school and there we were trembling with the water before us and the PE instructor came along behind and pushed us in one by one. I understand it is not considered to be the best method now, and it is not used, but we somehow managed to reach the side. It was the hard way! But you learn things by doing them and Jesus knew that the disciples would only learn to preach by preaching;

they would only learn to deal with demons by dealing with demons — so he sent them out to do it. One of the difficulties we have as Christians is that we want to have a training course before we do anything, and if you announce a training course on evangelism, house to house visitation, people will come. But the best way to learn house to house visitation is to go down your road and knock on the doors. The school of experience is the best school! Jesus took the twelve and let them know that they must multiply his ministry. He wanted them to go out and do what he was doing. He wanted them to preach, to heal, to cast out demons.

He sent them out with two things. First of all, he sent them out in *austerity*. I remember Dr Billy Graham speaking of the most embarrassing and challenging thing ever said to him. When he was preparing to go to India he met a group of Indian Christians before he got there, and he asked their advice. He said to them all, 'Now, you tell me how I should behave when I come to India. Tell me these things so that I don't offend people and put my foot in it.' And one dear old Indian looked at him and said, 'Dr Graham, I hope you won't mind my saying this, but every Indian expects to see the signs of austerity in a holy man.' Dr Graham said that was the most challenging thing that had ever been said to him. Jesus sent these men out telling them not to take even a change of clothes, money, a bag, food. They were just to go out as they were. They would travel light, travel quickly and get out into those villages. They would have to depend on being received to live, they would have to depend on hospitality. He sent them out in *austerity*. That would mean a number of things of course, but above all it would mean that they would be utterly dependent on the success of their mission to go on with it. That was a very sharp challenge, and out they went.

The other thing he gave them was *authority*. Austerity and authority were the two marks of a missionary sent by Jesus. He gave them authority to cast out demons and to heal the sick. Imagine two of them going down the road, James and John. Maybe they were just hoping they would not meet anybody possessed or ill. They are creeping down the road into this strange village and thinking: how do we begin? They have never done it before. They have seen Jesus do it, but that was Jesus. So they come to a village, and there suddenly, shrieking at them, is a demon-possessed man. Can you imagine the hesitations? They must have been terribly frightened, terribly timid, then one of them would say, 'in the name of Jesus' — and it would be done. Can you imagine now the excitement with which they rush on to the next man? Can you imagine the eagerness with which they go on now? It worked! We learn elsewhere that they came back thrilled after that mission. (Even the demons are subject to us in your name!) I have known this again and again. People have gone out timid, frightened to speak in uncongenial circumstances, and they have come back and said, 'It works!'

I will never forget what happened when I was eighteen. A converted bookmaker took me out at about half past nine, put me in the middle of a pub parlour in Cannock Chase, Staffordshire, and said, 'Speak to them.' That was how I began speaking, and it is the only way to learn, but oh, are you timid and afraid when you start! Yet you come back rejoicing. I will never forget that night because in that pub I met a boy who had run away from a Borstal, a lad whose life was all mixed up. At midnight we finished up kneeling together in a little church in Staffordshire, and he came to Christ. He went home and he told his parents that night. He went in at about one thirty in the morning and they were asleep, but he burst into their bedroom and he woke them up to tell them. His parents got up and knelt by the bed and thanked God for it.

That is how it began — just thrown out, and that is the way to begin. But notice that the disciples went out two by two. The Lord, who you do not see, is with you, but to have another person you can see is a great help. There is something profound about the disciples having gone out in pairs. We are not meant to be individualists, we are meant to work together as a team in little groups and help one another.

Jesus sent out his disciples, his substitutes as it were, to be representatives for him. News of this mission began to spread out far and wide. Not only was one man preaching, healing and casting out demons, twelve were — thirteen including Jesus. Incidentally, we need to remember that Judas was one of those disciples.

They were all out on their mission, and the ripples spread south to a castle called Machaerus, which stood high on a rock overlooking the Dead Sea. It was in a most barren, dreadful place. Living there was an awful man, Herod, a puppet king of the Romans. He controlled the strip of land up the Jordan, and the whole of Galilee. Herod heard that a man and twelve others were beginning to turn his kingdom upside down and were beginning to have crowds go after them. So Herod was worried. This was not because of the military threat but because he had a guilty conscience. And well he might have done. If you read the history of his family you read a history of incest and murder the like of which you will never read again. It is almost impossible to draw up the family tree, because Herod, for example, married his niece and his sister-in-law, Herodias; Salome was married to her uncle and grand uncle, and through murder and incest this family became one of the most notorious of all time. They finished with the last Herod being eaten up by worms, a fact mentioned in the New Testament. Herod was frightened about what he was hearing, and he came to a most incredible and superstitious idea. He said, *"John, the man I beheaded, has been raised from the dead!"* (Mark 6:16, *NIV*) He must have been in a pretty bad state to think that this was the man whose head he had seen on a plate in his own dining room, yet he came to that superstitious conclusion.

I must now remind you of the terrible story of John's end. Those who think that to become a man of God is to make life easy and comfortable should read the story of John, the greatest man who had ever lived, according to Jesus. This man did not keep his mouth shut and lost his head for speaking out. I have been told sometimes by people who mean well, and who perhaps may be right in their criticism, 'Keep to the positive, don't ever attack anyone in the pulpit, just preach the positive side.' Well, that is a much safer way, but sometimes we are called upon to attack what is wrong as well as proclaim what is right, whatever it may cost. John was a preacher like that. He attacked. Repent and believe! He said publicly that there was a man governing that country in which he baptised who was illegally married, who was outraging public decency. He made an enemy the day he said that — not of the man himself but of his wife. Herodias did not like it one bit. Wherever she went, people now pointed at her and said, 'Living in sin.' People looked at her as at a dirty woman. She hated this preacher and resolved that he should die.

She had managed to persuade her husband to put him in the dungeon. Actually, it is still possible to see to this day the dungeons and the iron loops in the wall to which John the Baptist would have been tied. That terrible place is still there. Even though John, down in the dungeon, had been prevented from preaching publicly, every time they had a feast up above, Herodias would have thought of the man below. When you have a guilty conscience it can be hard to forget things.

There came a day when Herod had all his pals in for entertainment, and he had one of his own relatives do what only a 'woman of the streets' would normally do, and she danced in an erotic and obscene way. Herod must have been drunk because he said, 'I will give you anything, even my throne as queen.' That is what the phrase 'half the kingdom' means. If an eastern potentate said to a woman, 'I will offer you half my kingdom', he meant: I will make you my queen. And Herodias was sitting there! He was saying: I'll get rid of her and you can be the queen in her place. She went and she had a consultation with her mother. Can you imagine the hatred a woman could have to say: I'd rather have a man's head than anything else. What an evil woman! It shows her scale of values. And over the rest of the scene one just wants to draw a veil. The head is carried in of a man of God; a preacher who had fearlessly preached the Word of God for years; a man who had lived in the desert; a man who had experienced a hard life. That was how he ended — killed by a woman's malice.

Herod had this strange mixture: he liked to hear the

preacher and yet he did not like it. He was typical of so many men. They enjoy a good sermon and yet they do not like it if it gets near to the bone. This was Herod; he was a man of superstition. Why? Because he was a man of sensuality and the two invariably go together. Once you have given yourself to sensations you lose your sense. Once you have begun to live a life like this you cannot think straight. Here was a man who enjoyed John's preaching yet he did not enjoy it, but he kept him in the dungeon and had him up every now and again to preach, and then put him away again, as a man who listens to a preacher and has his conscience stirred on Sunday night but puts it away in the dungeon until the following Sunday night. Herod was so like many of us. Herod was the man who misunderstood, and John the Baptist was killed because Herod had to save his face. Do you know what Jesus thought of Herod? We know what Herod thought of Jesus. Herod thought Jesus was this man with his head back on — an incredible idea, but he thought it. But Jesus said of Herod, 'That fox.' This is not 'gentle Jesus meek and mild'.

Jesus moves out of Herod's territory; he crosses the sea. He is hoping to get some peace and quiet, but sometimes a boat has to tack across that sea against a contrary wind, and the crowd saw him going and they saw the direction of the boat and they ran round the lake. It would have been perhaps five or six miles for them but they got there before the boat. So here Jesus, seeking rest and quiet, is faced with a crowd. Any ordinary man would have said, 'It's my day off.' Any ordinary man would have said, 'I have been preaching, I have been working, I have been with you, I must have some rest.' But not Jesus. He saw them, and we read that he had compassion on them, because they were like sheep without a shepherd. What do sheep need from a shepherd? We know that in the Middle East the main need they had was for food. The chief need of a shepherd, or a pastor, was to get food to feed the flock. So he taught them. His compassion was for their minds that needed food.

Now there comes this great miracle, the multiplying of the loaves and fish. I am not going to focus on the miracle. It was a miracle, a creative act. But I want to look at the consideration Jesus showed. He said to his disciples, who wanted to send the people away to find food for themselves, *"You give them something to eat."* That shows tremendous consideration.

Now notice Jesus' carefulness. The first thing he did was to find out how much food they had. I have a little tin of sardines from Galilee at home. One of these days I will eat them! They had two sardines. From Capernaum in those days salted sardines were a really tasty export. They also had five loaves, although not loaves as we understand them, they were just little rolls, quite thin and flat, about the size of a pancake. Five rolls, two little fish, that was all they had. The disciples did not even consider this to be enough to be worth sharing, and they said that to feed the people it would take eight months of a man's wages! But Jesus told them to share what they had. We notice that he began to organise it properly. Our Lord was not foolish. Even though he had infinite resources he organised them into groups — of hundreds and fifties — all over the green grass. Then began something that can only be imagined. He took one of the fish in his hands. He broke it and there seemed to be twice as much. He gave some to the disciples to set before the people and, as he went on breaking, more came. Only God could do that; only God can create something out of nothing, man cannot do it. Then he took the little bread and broke some and went on breaking it. The disciples would have held out their hands, and then their arms, and filled them up. They walked to these clumps of hundreds and fifties. Then not only did Jesus assess the resources they had and use them, not only did he organise carefully so that it was well-managed, but thirdly they were able to gather up leftovers! We read that the disciples picked up twelve basketfuls of broken pieces of bread and fish! Here is a lovely little dig at the disciples. What could they gather it up in? Their own food baskets! There is a very subtle touch here. Each of the disciples carried a basket and carried food in it when they went on a journey or when they went on the boat. There was enough that they had to use their baskets. It was a subtle way of reminding them that their baskets were empty. They had been behind a bush somewhere eating while Jesus had been preaching earlier. That was what had been happening, and when he had told them to give the people something to eat they did not dare say directly that they had already had it so they just had twelve empty baskets!

Have you not discovered that to be utterly true, that even though you feel the little that you could do would not help anybody, when you did it and helped someone you found yourself with more blessing left over yourself? Of course you did. God's mathematics are not ours, they are not the mathematics my children learned in school. God's mathematics are: what you give away you gain; what you try to keep, you lose. Two fishes, five loaves: God's mathematics says give them away and you will have enough to eat yourself. What have you got that you could share with somebody else? Is it so little that you often say, 'Well, I'm not going to share it, it's too little'? Then share it and see what happens to it. So our Lord's consideration as well as his compassion comes through. There is no excuse for not being considerate, for assessing your resources properly, for organising distribution properly and for being careful so that none is wasted. And even though our God has cattle on a thousand hills, even though our God has infinite resources, the church must always be very businesslike and efficient in its use of God's resources. But the disciples still did not understand one thing about the loaves: that the only hands that could go on doing that must be God's hands. Although they thought it was something wonderful, they did not understand that this was something supernatural. Their hearts were hard. I suppose they would have been inclined to say: do that again. This is our instinctive reaction to something marvellous: 'Do it again, let's see if there's something up your sleeve' — instead of thinking about it and saying, 'How did he do that? Who did that?' So they missed the next opportunity which they had to see the truth.

The next attitude we come across is their hardness. Jesus now does insist on rest and quiet. He sends the disciples away on their own and he goes up into the hills to pray. Why does he pray? Because problems are piling in thick and fast. He is too popular with the crowds, they want to make him king. He has already made some serious religious enemies. He knows now that Herod is disturbed about him, and that probably spells his death, and so he goes up into the hills to pray. Imagine the scene. Here is a little boat that the disciples set off in at about five o'clock in the afternoon, and at three in the morning it was still stuck in the middle of the lake, so severe was the wind, and they were rowing hard. Jesus, up on the hills, saw them. He thought that they would be encouraged if they saw that he was still around and so he walked down the hill and he continued to walk straight out on the water. That should not surprise us. It should not have surprised them. Somebody who can take loaves and fishes and multiply them can surely walk on water. They should not have been surprised in the slightest at such supernatural power. We should not be surprised at anything that God does, but we are, and when we get an answer to prayer we talk to each other in shocked surprise! 'Do you know, that prayer we prayed last Saturday? It's been answered!' The very way we say it shows that we are surprised. Why should we be surprised when anything supernatural happens?

Jesus walked by them on the water. He just wanted to let them see him, and then he realised that they were frightened so he had to go to them. The same thing that we saw above happened again, and as soon as Jesus got in with them somehow it was alright, it was all calm. I know from my own experience that sometimes when you are very frightened, pulling very hard and getting nowhere, simply to be aware of Jesus being near — to know he is aboard — is to experience peace and calm. I could see a picture of the church in those disciples rowing vigorously and not making any progress because Jesus was not on board. It may be we could learn something from that.

So Jesus came to the other shore again, and we come to the last reaction. Why so many sick people? Because Tiberias was a health spa and people came to it from all over to take the waters. Now we find the opposite of the beginning. In Nazareth familiarity produced faithlessness, but here familiarity produces faith. Why? Because they had seen him not mending chairs but mending bodies, and they recognised him, so they rushed to bring the sick to him. Perhaps they brought the sick on the very beds that he had made, as he moved around the villages. But the Jesus who made beds makes bodies. One day he is going to make a whole new universe; without him the stars would not have been made; without him nothing was made that was made, and those hands that could multiply loaves and fishes could also heal and make new. I want you to notice that the people still just wanted health. The tragedy is that the demand was for what they could get from him. Nobody came and said, 'What can we give to him?' Nobody came and said, 'Let's follow him, let's help him with his mission,' they all came and they said, 'You can get health from him.' So they misunderstood him. They thought he just came to heal, but he came to forgive, he came to bring men to God.

Summing up this chapter, which provides a glimpse of many things that Jesus did, I am struck with this: the ministry of Jesus was a mixture of what he planned and decided to do and things that seem to have arisen quite spontaneously. I pray that my life and yours may have this same pattern about it, that there may be some things we plan to do for others in the name of Jesus, but that there may be many occasions when an opportunity arises that we did not plan — we meet somebody whom we did not expect to meet, we find ourselves in a situation that we did not expect to be in — and that we may know this same calm, helpful presence of Jesus. He can be in us meeting others' needs, and we can go out, maybe two by two, man and wife working together for the Lord, friend and friend working together.

We are now seeing the end of our Lord's Galilean ministry. Maybe just two years and a bit and it is over. Very soon he will leave Galilee; he will have gone because he did not come just to be a healer, he came to be a Saviour. Now the thunder clouds gather, the darkness thickens, the hostility grows, and Jesus becomes the most unpopular man in history, the man about whom they are going to say 'crucify him' — away, away with him, out of this world. How did it all happen? We shall see as we continue to study Mark's Gospel.

8

PLACES AND PEOPLE
Mark 7:1–8:26

One of the most surprising things about our Lord's ministry is that the people you would have expected to support and welcome him were those who were most antagonistic, and the most unlikely people became his most ardent followers. You might have expected the religious leaders of the Jews to welcome their Messiah and the Gentiles to turn him down, but it is just the opposite. Of the five incidents here, three are in the Gentile country and two in Jewish territory. In the Gentile territory Jesus got on famously, but in the Jewish territory he was in trouble. The first incident took place in a little area on the shores of Galilee called Gennesaret, and apparently the trouble was a question of Jewish ritual. But in this one incident, which is concerned with whether you should wash your hands before a meal, we see the whole clash between religion and Christianity.

I was asked to go and speak to a school as part of a series on the world religions. I was following Buddhism, and I was asked to speak on Christianity. So I gladly went, and I said, 'The first thing I want to say is that Christianity is not a religion, and until we see that we have misunderstood it. All the others are religions but Christianity is not.' And here in

129

this one little incident you have the contrast between religion and Christianity. What the Pharisees had was religion, and they had it bad, if I can put it that way, but what Jesus had was reality. They had ritual, they had all the outside of it, but he had the inside of it, and this is the difference.

Let us look at the incident that happened. A fact-finding theological commission was sent down from Jerusalem to report back on Jesus. They came and they watched him. They could not find anything in him to criticise but they managed to find something in his followers. Psychologically this is a very true account — you can see how minds work. They noticed that at one meal the disciples didn't wash their hands first. To you and me this would not be such a great matter as it was to them. Some Jews would rather die than break their food laws. There is a most terrible account of something that happened during the reign of Antiochus Ephiphanes, the Greek conqueror of Israel. There was an attempt to force seven brothers to eat pork, which was against their religion. Their aged mother was made to stand and watch. As they refused, one by one, they were tortured to death in front of their mother, who urged them to go on being firm and to die rather than eat the pork. This is what the eating laws of the Jews had come to mean. And to the basic laws which were to be found in the Old Testament, and which were part of God's Word, they had added a whole lot more that were not in God's Word but which they had come to regard as just as important. One of the disturbing features of religious tradition is that yet more tradition is added, which gradually becomes more and more fixed, more and more important, more and more a test of whether a person is truly religious, until you get to the point where the bit you have added is more important than what there was in the beginning, and the tradition becomes a substitute for that. Baptists suffer from it, so do Roman Catholics. Our traditions, the way we've always done things — if you don't do them this way, you are out.

This was what Jesus came up against, and the particular tradition here was this matter of washing of hands — not to get clean physically, but just in case they had touched the overcoat of a Gentile in the market place. It was a purely ritual act, to cover them from defilement. They would come in and wash their hands, then they would wash between each course, just in case they were unclean according to their religious tradition. It is said to Jesus that his disciples had not washed their hands, and Jesus replies with some pretty severe words. But he was right in what he said. That kind of religion and his teaching would not mix. The first thing he pointed out was this: they had turned religion into an external instead of an internal matter, so they had become terribly concerned with the outward appearance and outward actions. This is hypocrisy. He points out that Isaiah saw this in them five hundred years before. *"Isaiah was right when he prophesied about you hypocrites; as it is written: 'These people honour me with their lips, but their hearts are far from me. They worship me in vain; their teachings are but rules taught by men' "* (Mark 7:6f., *NIV*). This was to say: you honour God with the outside, you sing your hymns, you say your prayers, but your heart is a million miles away. To go through the ritual, to go through the acts and outside of religion, yet to have a heart that is far away from God, is sheer hypocrisy. Jesus indicated to them that they had become so concerned about getting their hands clean that they had forgotten that the heart needs cleaning. Let us accept this criticism from our Lord and apply it to ourselves. If we are more concerned about putting on our Sunday best clothes, getting our hair right and getting our face washed before we go to church than about getting our hearts clean and right before we get to worship, then we deserve exactly the same criticism. I apply it like that to my own heart because it is easy to blame those old Pharisees and say they were terrible people, but we all have a dose of this.

Secondly, they had substituted for the divine command a human idea. He told them that they were always doing this, and he mentioned a particularly bad example. The Pharisees gave very generously to God — the trouble was that they began to teach that if you were giving something to God that released you from other obligations, so you could say to your own aged parents, 'I'm sorry I can't keep you because I am giving this money to God' —and that was replacing a command of God with an idea of man. I have been asked about this more than once, and my answer is that supporting our family, whether it is our children or our parents, is a divine duty, and we should not be giving to God's work to the extent that those who are directly dependent on us are impoverished. To quote again that text from the New Testament, *If anyone does not provide for his relatives, and especially for his immediate family, he has denied the faith and is worse than an unbeliever* (1 Timothy 5:8, *NIV*). This is our first responsibility. And Jesus points out that Moses said in the law, which is God's Word, that we are to honour our father and mother. They were saying in effect, 'I can't, I'm giving all my money to God's work' —and that is putting an idea of man in place of the Word of God.

The third point was even more devastating: they thought of religion as a matter of physical action, when in fact it is a matter of spiritual attitude. In place of this kind of external tradition, the outside of religion, Jesus put the internal truth, and said something that has been described as the most revolutionary statement in the New Testament: *"Nothing outside a man can make him 'unclean' by going into him. Rather, it is what comes out of a man that makes him 'unclean'"* (Mark 7:15, *NIV*). Godliness is concerned with the heart. Being very direct, our Lord is teaching that if something dirty comes in at the mouth, the body has its own way of getting rid of dirt and it goes straight through the stomach and out. It is the things that start inside and come out that are really dirty.

Let us look at the things he said were inside. It is a horrid list and I do not want to spend much time on it for that reason. But I shall just run through them. Evil thoughts – that means a man who is planning what to do next that is wrong. Fornication — that means extra-marital relations before marriage. Theft means petty pilfering. The word used here does not refer to the big thefts, but could be applied to a little bit of shoplifting or taking something home from the office. That starts inside and it is dirty. Murder — that starts with anger. Adultery is the breaking of the marriage bond. Coveting is simply being greedy for things that other people have that you do not. Wickedness means the desire to hurt someone, to be a bully, to harm them. Deceit means to trick someone. Licentiousness means a person who does not want to be restrained or disciplined in any way. Envy means the evil eye that does not like other people having what you have not got. Slander means gossip and insulting people; pride includes contempt for others; foolishness means playing the fool. And Jesus highlights these as the dirty things that you need to get rid of, as the things that make a man a filthy man. It is not something that a person has taken in, it is something that he has given out. It starts inside and it works out; it does not start outside and work in. Fundamentally, Jesus has a completely different view of man to the view the Pharisees were holding. I have discovered that the Pharisees' view is the generally held view in England today.

The Pharisees believed that a man was basically good and clean, therefore he must be careful of outside influences on him. Jesus taught that a man was basically bad and dirty, and therefore it is the inside that he needs to be concerned about. Here are the two different viewpoints and it makes a total difference to your thinking, about yourself and other people in the world in general, as to whether you believe man is clean and is made dirty by things from outside, or whether man is dirty and needs to be made clean. Our Lord was saying of these things that he listed that you do not pick them up from other people, they are there inside to begin with. That is a very low view of human nature. Yet when I look into my heart, this is an accurate view. If you are concerned about the traditions of the external things, if you are concerned about your actions, the outside of it all, you have missed the real thing that needs dealing with and that is the inside of it all. It is a completely different viewpoint. Jesus was teaching: you are so bothered about washing your hands and you have forgotten about your hearts. They honoured God with their lips but their hearts were far away.

Therefore what we need is not religion but regeneration; that is why it is no use trying to reform a man and make him behave differently. On the farm we used to have Danish piggeries which are specially designed to keep pigs clean. In a Danish piggery the pig is the cleanest animal on the farm. You can change his behaviour and you can make him quite an attractive animal. But you let him loose out of the piggery and anywhere near the midden, and within five minutes his nature has reasserted itself. This is why sticking religion on the outside will never do the trick. You might manage respectable and decent behaviour, but inside there is the same old heart and the stuff is still there. That is the danger of drinking too much, because alcohol will release what is already inside and it comes out more easily. That is why when we get tired things come out that we are surprised at — irritability, loose speech. These come out when we are under strain. Why? Because they are there already, and that is why we need a new heart, and a clean heart, and the glorious gospel of Jesus Christ is that he does not come to reform you, he does not come to stick a new outside on you, he does not come to get you religious, he comes to clean your heart and to deal with these things at the source and to give you a new nature — that is what is meant by being born again.

It is very interesting that having discussed the matter of 'clean' and 'unclean' with these Pharisees, who regarded Jews as clean and the Gentiles as unclean, the very next scene shows Jesus in a Gentile country, an 'unclean' land — Tyre. Tyre should have been part of the promised land but the tribe of Asher never managed to conquer the people who lived there. It was part of the land that God gave to his people and Jesus was not stepping outside the promised land, but he was going into Gentile territory — unclean territory according to the Pharisees, but Jesus did not bother one wit.

He was escaping from the Pharisees to get a bit of quiet with his disciples, away from this opposition, and he went to a house. A woman heard he was there, even though he told his host not to tell anyone. We now get one of the most extraordinary sayings of Jesus. The woman came in and we read that she begged Jesus to drive the demon out of her daughter. Now come words that, if we did not have them in the Gospel, we would never credit Jesus with uttering. It is a proof of the truth of the Gospel record that nobody would have invented what he said. We read: *"First let the children eat all they want," he told her, "for it is not right to take the children's bread and toss it to their dogs"* (Mark 7:27, *NIV*). To us that does not come home with such horror because we like dogs, dogs are our pets, dogs live with us in our homes. But if you go out to the Middle East and call anyone a dog, they think of those mangy beasts that go from dustbin to dustbin scavenging things, animals that you run away from if they get anywhere near — horrible things. That is why dogs are so often used in contemptuous terms. *"Do not give dogs what is sacred"*, said Jesus. *Watch out for those dogs, those men who do evil, those mutilators of the flesh*, wrote Paul (Philippians 3:2, *NIV*). Why did Jesus speak in this way? I think the only way that I can understand it — and I can only give you my understanding and no more — is that he was saying to her that he had come to the Jews with his first duty to God's people. He had left them not because he was coming to start a mission to the Gentiles — not yet — he had been sent to the lost sheep of the house of Israel (he says this in another Gospel) and his first duty was to God's own people. He was saying this to stop this woman starting a mission for him among the Gentiles. He had not come to do this and it was a deliberate discouragement. But he left the door open by including the word 'first'. He said that the children were to be fed first. He was virtually saying the Jews are the children, you are the dogs — and everything was going to depend on how she took that. The most amazing thing is that she took it in just the right attitude. She could have had an inverted snobbery which is so common: 'Oh well, if they think we are dogs, alright — and if you are one of those Jews who thinks we are dogs, right, well I think you're dogs.' She could have resented this, she could have been proud. She could have been terribly upset. I would never dare to speak to a lady like this! She might never have spoken to him again. But instead she gave him this very witty reply: *"Yes, Lord," she replied, "but even the dogs under the table eat the children's crumbs"* (Mark 7:28, *NIV*). But there was more than wit that made Jesus say, *"For such a reply, you may go; the demon has left your daughter"* — there was humility. She accepted whatever he said about her — she was still asking. There was tremendous faith in this answer because she was saying that even a few scraps from him would cure her daughter. And Jesus told her that for saying this her daughter was well. She had accepted his challenge, she had not resented it, she had not been proud, but in humility and faith she had pressed for what little she needed and what little she may have been given. It is a tremendous story. Quite frankly, if we go up to take the bread and wine of communion we must come in exactly the same attitude as she came. 'We are not worthy so much as to gather up the crumbs under your table.'

Jesus travels from Tyre up in the north-west to the Decapolis, that group of ten Greek cities. He is still in the

Gentile territory; he is keeping well away from the Jews now. He needs time, and every time he goes into Jewish territory he is into difficulties. In the next chapter you will see what he was waiting for. Here he is simply able to relieve need. First of all, they bring a man who is deaf and therefore dumb; he had been that way since he was born. I love this story because Jesus did everything he could that would convey to a man who was deaf and dumb exactly what he was doing. He mimed in six ways. First of all, he put his fingers in the man's ears. The man could not hear, he could not speak, but he could feel fingers. And then Jesus spat, and that was something he would understand. Then Jesus touched his tongue with the spittle. You see how Jesus adapts himself to a man and meets him in a way that the man can understand — it is a lovely touch. Next he looks up to heaven; he is telling the man God is going to help us to do this. He has not said a word; he has been preaching to a man who is deaf and dumb. Then he sighs, a sigh of relief, a sigh that that man will be able to give when he has been healed, a sigh that says it is over. Then finally, he uses a word that is so much a word that can be lip read that it is no wonder we still have the word in our Lord's own language. He says *"Ephphatha!"* The man presumably could lip read. "Be opened!" It is a lovely little scene. How to preach to someone who is deaf and dumb; how to get through, how to begin where a man is, how to convey to him that God is wanting to do something for him right at the point of his need. When the cure came, as it certainly did, the people said something that is rather remarkable. They said, *"He has done everything well."* That is exactly what God said as he created the world. *"Let there be light,"* and there was light. God saw that the light was *good . . . . God saw all that he had made, and it was very good* (see Genesis 1:3ff; 31). What is translated into English as 'good' and 'well' is exactly the same in the Hebrew and the Greek here. They were saying about Jesus exactly what God said about his creation. They were acknowledging Jesus as the Creator. They may not have realised it but they are saying, in effect: you are making a good job when you do a job. You can take a person and make a good job with them, you can do it well. It is a lovely text.

Now we have the feeding of the four thousand. A huge crowd comes, partly because of the healing of the deaf and dumb man, but I think primarily because there has been another man speaking about Jesus for months, a man out of whom that legion of demons had been cast, and whom Jesus had told to go home and tell what he had done for him. The next time Jesus comes, four thousand people want to meet him, and they are prepared to listen to a sermon for three days. I won't underline that! But at any rate they are hungry when they are finished! Jesus says, *"I have compassion for these people; they have already been with me three days and have nothing to eat. If I send them home hungry, they will collapse on the way, because some of them have come a long distance"* (Mark 8:2–3, *NIV*). Would you listen for three days if Jesus were around? I would love to.

There are many similarities with the feeding of the five thousand and there are also some differences. There are seven loaves here; there were five last time. There are seven baskets full instead of twelve gathered up at the end. And a different word is used for 'baskets'. But the most extraordinary thing in this story, to me, is this. The disciples said, *"But where in this remote place can anyone get enough bread to feed them?"* That is a thing that I just cannot understand. They had seen five thousand men, to say nothing of the women and children — so presumably some ten thousand people — fed with five loaves and two fishes, and they dared to question how they could feed this lot, just a week or two later. Some have said they were being selfish again because they still had their own loaves this time and they did not want to give them up. That may well be true but I do not think it is the reason. The reason is this: you can see a miracle and still be so hard that you do not believe that it can be repeated. Let me challenge you as a Christian, as I challenge myself at this point. We have prayed about a certain matter, a desperate matter, and God has answered the prayer. We have usually been so surprised that we let it out in our surprised way of telling somebody that the prayer was answered. Then, maybe a few months or a year or two later, we come into an identical situation and we pray, and we wonder whether the prayer will be answered, don't we? I have been like that; it is hardness of heart. You can see God's wonderful hand, and then a few months later you can wonder whether he can do anything about this situation — 'how will he get me through this one?' This is so human and so realistic and so typical of us, and so the disciples wondered how they were supposed to feed this lot. It is proof that a miracle does not convince a man of the truth, which brings us to the fourth incident out of the five.

Jesus goes back into Jewish territory and he meets a group of the Pharisees straight away; they are waiting on the shore. And they ask him for proof, a sign from heaven, so that they might believe. Jesus is so frustrated, so exasperated, he sighs deeply, and he says, *"Why does this generation ask for a miraculous sign? I tell you the truth, no sign will be given to it"* (Mark 8:12, *NIV*). Why was he not willing to give them visible proof? Because he knew perfectly well they were sceptical — they were suspicious, and it did not matter how many miracles he showed them, they still would not have believed. From time to time someone says to me, 'Can you give me proof of the existence of God?' If they got proof they still would not believe if they did not want to. Such are the barriers we put up to the truth that if we get evidence of God in this way we find some other explanation for it, and we explain it away and want some more. So Jesus was not giving them the sign they wanted.

The hostile scepticism that came from Jesus' enemies was matched by a stupidity in his own disciples. They got into the boat again; they had to get away from Jewish territory as soon as they got back to it. On the way across the lake, the disciples heard a warning that Jesus gave, and thought he was referring to the fact that they only had one loaf of bread with them. It is very typical of a guilty conscience that you see references to yourself when none is intended. Perhaps you are feeling guilty about something and you think the preacher knows about it and he is constantly mentioning it all through the sermon. It happens quite frequently. People say to me afterwards, 'Who's been telling you about me?' And nobody has! It has happened to me, too, when I have been in the pew. Jesus said to the disciples on the way across, *"Watch out for the yeast of the Pharisees and that of Herod."* Hearing the word 'yeast' they thought he must be hinting that they had forgotten the bread, and Jesus meant nothing of the sort. What did he mean? What did the Pharisees and the Herodians have in common? They were two groups of

141

people you would have thought were miles apart in their thinking: the religious leaders, and the sensual political leaders. The one thing they had in common was that they both wanted visible proof. When Jesus was finally led before Herod — in chains — Herod was glad to see him because he hoped he would do a few tricks or signs for him. The Pharisees were asking the same thing. Both groups lived at the level of the senses. They could not rise by faith above their senses so they wanted the sensation and the sensual. Jesus told the disciples to beware of this attitude that can only look at material things, that cannot get beyond and see spiritual meaning.

In response to the disciples' interpretation of Jesus' words he said, *"Do you still not see or understand? Are your hearts hardened? Do you have eyes but fail to see, and ears but fail to hear? And don't you remember? When I broke the five loaves for the five thousand, how many basketfuls of pieces did you pick up?"* (Mark 8:17ff., *NIV*) They were not looking beyond the loaves of bread to what it all meant. They were so worried about bread, yet they had Jesus who had performed the miracles with the loaves. The Pharisees asked for visible signs and yet they seemed to think about nothing but bread. It is very interesting that after he said to them, *"Do you have eyes but fail to see. . . ?"* he healed a blind man. It is no accident that these two stories are together. I know people who are totally blind and who cannot see a thing, but who see spiritual things more than many sighted people do. So Jesus had this blind man brought to him.

They were now in Bethsaida — which was not Jewish territory — on the north-east coast of the Sea of Galilee. This blind man came, and again Jesus dealt with him as he was, quite differently from the deaf and dumb man. He got hold of his hand and took him for a walk to some quiet little place out in the country, then he spat, and then he touched and laid his hands on the eyes. The man began to look, and he could see some shadows walking. He had never seen people or trees, until this moment he had only felt them. It is hardly surprising that he now looked and said, *"I see people; they look like trees walking around"* (Mark 8:24, *NIV*). So Jesus took it further and he laid his hands on him again, and the man's sight was fully restored. Something remarkable about this miracle is that it is the only one that did not happen immediately, it happened in stages. Elsewhere, our Lord touched a blind man and he saw perfectly straight away. Does it matter if a blind man saw with one laying on of hands or two? Not at all. The wonderful thing was that Jesus did not finish with him until he did see clearly. It takes a bit longer with some folk than others before they see the light, but Jesus does not give up until you see.

9

TESTING AND TRANSFIGURATION
Mark 8:27–9:13

With this passage we have come to what I call the watershed of Mark's Gospel. Everything seems to build up to this point and then everything flows from it. It seems as if for two years Jesus had been waiting for something, and as soon as it happened he was off to the cross. So it all builds up to a peak. This is true not only of the meaning of the text itself, it is also true physically, because Mark's Gospel begins at the lowest point on the earth at the Jordan river, and now at this point we are at the highest mountain in the region, Mount Hermon. Then from the top of this mountain he comes down to the cross. In place of all the wandering around, crossing the Sea of Galilee, healing a person here, teaching there, we suddenly have a tremendous sense of purpose, and straight after this we shall find our Lord heading for Jerusalem.

We can say all this another way. You realise we are half way through the Gospel now, and in the second half we notice some very big differences. There are five differences that you will notice. (This is the advantage of taking great chunks of the Bible together; when you only read a few verses a day you miss all this, but when you read it through in large doses you see it all.)

Firstly, after this story, miracles and parables almost

145

disappear. You might never have noticed that before but you will notice it from now on.

Secondly, Jesus stops teaching the kingdom of God and speaks much more about the Son of Man.

Thirdly, he now deals primarily with the disciples and not the crowds, though the crowds appear from time to time.

Fourthly, whereas the first eight chapters are in the north, in Galilee, the second eight chapters are in the south, in Judea.

Fifthly, from now on it seems as if the sun goes out and the darkness comes. Have you ever been out walking on a lovely day with the sun shining from a blue sky, and then a little cloud has appeared and got larger and larger until it has blotted out the sun, and then the sky has gone darker and you think there is a storm coming? That is what happens from this chapter onwards. So far it has all been bright in the sunshine, people have been healed, and it has been so lovely. But now the clouds begin to gather, the storm clouds darken, and it is only a matter of time until tragedy strikes. It is most dramatic. So we have been building up to this and from now on there is a complete change.

What was Jesus waiting for? What was it that he was wanting in all his wanderings around Galilee? Why could he not get on with what he had come to do? He seems to have been frustrated to this point — what was this about? The answer is very simple: he was waiting for an answer to a question, and until he got the right answer to the right question he could not get on with his ministry. In this first passage we get the question asked and the right answer given.

I want to remind you of the place where the question was asked. Away at the furthest point in the promised land, far in the north, there was a little village in the Old Testament called Dan, nestling at the foot of a mountain 9,200 feet high and always snow-capped. This mountain comes down to the plain, not in a slope, but as a sheer cliff, and the village is at the foot of this high rock wall. From the bottom of the cliff, inexplicably, there comes a whole river. There is not a hole to see, it just bubbles out from the rocks. There must be some underground cracks. The river is called the Jordan. It seems to start nowhere and finish nowhere — a most dramatic river. Just above the place where the Jordan emerges is the village of Dan. Originally it was called after the god Baal, because this river seemed to them a symbol of life and fertility, Baal worship was fertility worship, and that was what had taken place there. But later, in the Old Testament period, God was worshipped there. Later still, when the Greeks came to this place, they found a little cave by the river and said that was the cave where their nature deity Pan was born — so they called the place after that god. Still later, the Romans came, and Philip, who governed this area for them, renamed it. Now it became Caesarea Philippi. Philip built a magnificent, gleaming, white marble temple on this spot, dedicated to Caesar, the emperor who was worshipped as a god. Here, then, was a place which has seen a cross-section of many religions. When I visited, it was the little Arab village of Banias, in Jewish hands since the Six-Day War. It was to this place that our Lord led those twelve men.

Now Jesus had a question to ask. It was a question in two parts. The first part was, *"Who do people say I am?"* He knew perfectly well, but he wanted them to say it. Some people, including some family members, thought that Jesus was mad; others accepted him as sane but thought of him as a great man of God, one of the prophets. But most people were saying this kind of thing: a young man of thirty cannot possibly be what this man is; a young man of thirty cannot be as clever as he is; a young man of thirty cannot be as powerful as he is — it is impossible. He must have had a previous existence; he must be a reincarnation of somebody else who lived a long time ago. So some of them thought that it might be Elijah back again. Others thought it was somebody greater than that, possibly John the Baptist. Such were some opinions of men.

Now comes the question which every person has to answer sooner or later: *"Who do you say I am?"* Second-hand opinion is no good for Jesus to build on. Your mother and father and grandmother and grandfather may have had the right ideas, but it is no use telling Jesus what other people think or what you have been told to say. What do *you* think? And the disciples stood there stunned and shattered: What do we think? We have lived with him, we have talked with him, we have eaten with him, for two and a half years. What do we think? Who is he?

They had some extraordinary facts to go on — some of their own observations. He was a man who never lost an argument. That is a remarkable fact. He was a man who was never beaten by anything or anyone; he never lost control of a situation. He was a man with no faults in his character. He was a man who had remarkable insight into other people. He was a man with complete self-confidence and authority. He was a man who knew God better than anyone else. *"Who do you say I am?"* In the silence, Peter spoke out. He sometimes opened his mouth and put his foot in it, but this time he did not. He opened his mouth and did not declare that Jesus was a prophet but: *"You are the Christ."* Note the word 'the'. Jesus is unique. You have to be a Jew to get the flavour of this word 'Christ'. They had been waiting for hundreds of years for the Christ, the Saviour, the Messiah, the one who would solve all their problems, to be sent from heaven to earth. Peter said, *"You are the Christ"*, and with this key the door was unlocked and they saw the truth. The question was answered rightly. Now they were in a position to learn far more about him, and for the first time Jesus began to speak about the cross.

There are a number of things that I would like to say before we move on. First, you will never understand what Jesus did for you until you know *who he is*. There is no point in talking to you about the cross until you believe that the Jesus who died on it was more than a man. If he was just a man dying for you then there is no sense to it, there is no meaning in it, the cross cannot do anything for you. That is why Jesus never mentioned the cross until they had answered this question rightly. Because if Jesus was only a man, however great a man, if he died on a cross then he is dead and gone, but if he was the Son of God then he is still alive.

The second thing is that it is no use having a second-hand opinion about Jesus Christ. I was brought up with the right opinions about him because my parents held the right opinions and they taught them to me, and I went to Sunday school and church. But I went away from home at the age of sixteen and I got away from second-hand opinions and found out very quickly that I had no first-hand opinion about Jesus. I had never thought it through for myself. If somebody had asked me, 'Who is Jesus?' I would have said the right words: 'The Son of God, the Saviour of the world' — but it would have been a second-hand opinion, not mine; it would have been what others had said he was in my presence; it would have been something I had picked up from my environment. The important question is: Who do *you* say . . . ?

Have you ever thought it through? Have you ever read the Gospel of Mark right through and then said, Who is he? Who is he in that storm? Who is he in great distress? Who is he that rose from the tomb? Who *is* he? Nobody else can answer that question for you.

At this point, Jesus qualified what had been said with two shattering additions. Firstly, he told them not to tell a soul. They were bursting! People had been waiting for hundreds of years to meet the Christ, the Son of God. And now that he was here they wanted to tell the whole wide world, yet he told them to keep it to themselves. Why should he say that? The answer is very simple: because people had the wrong ideas about the Christ. They wanted a political saviour. They wanted someone who would come and put all their troubles right, except one — their own sin. They wanted someone who would release them from the Romans, someone who would release them from fear, but not from self.

Jesus now adds the second qualification. The Christ must suffer and be killed. They had not thought about this. What kind of a leader, what kind of a liberator, what kind of a hero is it who says that he has to suffer, and be put to death? They had been like most other people in reading the scriptures: they had remembered all the nice bits and none of the 'horrid' bits. They had remembered all the wonderful bits said about the Christ, but not the passages that said he will have to go through it, he will have to suffer. Peter, having said the most wonderful thing, now opened his mouth and put his foot in it badly. We are told that Peter took Jesus aside and began to rebuke him. Jesus now had to correct Peter, his friend. It is a tragic scene. If the devil came to me as a little black imp with horns and a spiked tail and tried to tempt me I should recognise him straight away and I would say, 'Get out of here.' I should do what Martin Luther did and throw my ink pot at him. But I have never met a devil who came like that. You meet a devil who can dress up as a messenger of light, a devil who can speak to you through your family, through your nearest and dearest, through your friends. And when Jesus turned around and looked at that fisherman he saw the devil speaking through him, and he said, *"Get behind me, Satan!"* Can you imagine what Peter felt like then? Peter was so human, so full of impetuosity. Are we not all a bit like this sometimes? Having said something good, true and helpful, we cannot shut up, we have to go on talking, and the next thing we say is just the opposite. Having said the right thing just moments before, Peter thought he could open his mouth again and that the right thing would come out again — but it does not. You can be inspired by God one minute and speaking words that are of the devil the next. There is a time to speak and a time to be silent. Peter is in the grip of human logic. He is thinking like men; he is not on the side of God now, he is on the side of men. Men want the easy way, men do not want to suffer; men want the easy and comfortable road to glory; men want the glory first. Men are not content to have the struggle in this life and the joy in the next, they want the joy in this life. This is the human way of thinking, not suffering, not difficulty, not discomfort, not being killed, but life, enjoyment and happiness *now*.

So Jesus calls together the people who know him, in order

to tell them something they need to understand.

"If anyone would come after me, he must deny himself and take up his cross and follow me. For whoever wants to save his life will lose it, but whoever loses his life for me and for the gospel will save it" (Mark 8:34f., *NIV*).

To follow him would mean sharing the suffering. It is not easy or comfortable to follow him. If the Christ must go through suffering to glory, so must they. Be thankful that Jesus was honest, because I find so many Christians today — I would call them 'mini Christians' — have either never been told or never realised that it is the toughest life to be a Christian, that it is going to be tough, and there is going to be suffering from now until you die. Whoever would live a godly life in Christ Jesus will suffer, says the New Testament. Before any youngster says 'I want to be a Christian' I want to say, 'Have you counted the cost? Do you realise that you are going to follow Jesus, the Christ, and that he says that the glory is on ahead but the suffering is here? In the world you will have tribulation, and if we want to follow him it is not a bed of roses, it is a crown of thorns?' Jesus communicates to the crowd (as has done to the disciples) that the pathway to glory is through suffering in this world. He is now letting anybody who is thinking of following him know there are four things that you have to rethink. First, if you are going to follow him you will just have to deny self. You have got to take that self and crucify it — it is a life of a cross and you will be crucified.

I remember talking to a missionary out in Africa. She was killed by bandits just a short while after I talked to her. I remember asking her about the danger that she faced as she walked those hazardous roads alone. I asked her if she was ever afraid to die, and I will never forget her answer. She said, 'I died ten years ago.' A few weeks later, when she was killed just for the contents of her handbag, I remembered that phrase. To be a Christian is death to self. It is to take the capital 'I' and cross it out. Jesus taught that to follow him one would suffer the loss of self — because it has to be crucified.

Secondly, if you are concerned with security and safety then do not follow him. I had a very interesting letter many years ago, telling me that I was quite wrong to go into the Baptist ministry because it had no security. It was from a minister of another denomination. Is that really what we are after in life? Do we want security? Do we want safety? Is it all self-preservation? Must we look after number one? Let us be fools for Christ's sake. He who lives for his own self-preservation will lose his life, but once you have lost it for Jesus' sake, and security and safety are no longer your concern, you find your life. History is full of examples of Christians who in the eyes of the world have lost their lives, but in Christ have found life.

Thirdly, success must be devalued. A man may gain the whole world, he may build a business, he may extend his branches and 'get on' as we say, and Jesus said, *"What good is it for a man to gain the whole world, yet forfeit his soul?"* (Mark 8:36, *NIV*) You may be so busy making a living that you never live. Success has to be rethought by the Christian if you are going to follow Christ. In the eyes of the world you may be a miserable failure as a Christian, but in the eyes of Christ you may have found the only success that really matters — to live for him.

Fourthly, you will have to defeat shame. Jesus spoke

of an adulterous and sinful generation, which means that as soon as you follow him you will be a misfit; as soon as you follow him, people will laugh at you; you will be in a minority, and you will be tempted to be ashamed of him, and you will be tempted to keep it under your hat that you belong to Christ — because people do not like God in this world. The world has gone after other gods. And Jesus said, *"If anyone is ashamed of me and my words in this adulterous and sinful generation, the Son of Man will be ashamed of him when he comes in his Father's glory with the holy angels"* (Mark 8:39, *NIV*). Some time ago a man came to me and said, 'Do you know what, I've found another Christian in our office.' I replied, 'That's fine.' He continued, 'I'm a lay preacher and he's a lay preacher, too —isn't that great?' I said, 'That's wonderful.' Then he added, 'Isn't it amazing, we've worked in that office for twelve years, and we never guessed.' That somehow took all the edge off that discovery!

How can it be that if we are ashamed of Jesus now he will be ashamed of us? Well, can you imagine this scene: Jesus is coming again and every eye sees him, and all those other people in your workplace see him. Suddenly they would see you alongside him. And they would say, 'Well, I never knew you had anything to do with him.' How would you feel then? When Jesus comes again in glory we shall be so proud of him, so thrilled for people to see his glory and to know that he really is the Lord of lords and King of kings, but how will we feel about ourselves when people see us alongside him and say, 'I didn't know you had anything to do with him'? Jesus was letting those who followed him know it was going to be really tough.

But here are two incentives. The first lies in the future.

You will see Jesus coming in glory one day. Won't that be worth it? Won't it be worth all the suffering, all the struggle, all the ridicule, all the tribulation that you go through, to see him come in glory with all his angels in the clouds and to know that he is coming for you?

The second incentive is they would not even have to wait to see him coming in glory to have some encouragement. He said, *"I tell you the truth, some who are standing here will not taste death before they see the kingdom of God come with power"* (Mark 9:1, *NIV*). What did he mean? The key word is *power*. When did power come? The answer is on the day of Pentecost when the Holy Spirit came. And one of the encouragements and incentives to the Christian to help him through this struggle and this hard road is the presence and power of the Holy Spirit. The kingdom of God is righteousness and peace and joy and the presence of the Holy Spirit now — that is what makes it worthwhile. So with the power now, and the glory hereafter, can't we face the struggle? Can't we follow him?

Now we come to the third and final part of this section. Peter had already said, *"You are the Christ"*, now he was going to see it. The great confirmation, the beginning of phase two begins very like phase one — a voice from God. At the baptism in the Jordan, God had said, *"You are my Son, whom I love; with you I am well pleased"* (Mark 1:11, *NIV*). Now phase two begins with another voice from heaven, at the top of the mountain: *"This is my Son, whom I love. Listen to him!"* (Mark 9:7, *NIV*)

It is a week later, right at the top of this mountain. Just the four of them — Jesus, Peter, James and John — have climbed up. It is towards evening and the snow is glistening in the dying embers of the sunset. They are desperately tired so the three disciples settle down for the night and pull their robes around them to keep warm. They are ready to go to sleep and Jesus is a little way off, praying. They never did get to sleep, according to my Bible. Something happened that kept them awake. Suddenly, instead of the darkening sky it seemed as if the whole place was getting brighter and brighter. When they looked around they had a most extraordinary vision. They saw Jesus so bright they could hardly look at him. The description tells us that the light was coming through his clothes from inside them. It was not that a light was shining on him, it was a light shining out of him, and his clothes were almost transparent. Have you ever put a torch behind a piece of cloth? That is the kind of thing they were describing. Peter, with down to earth language, described it to Mark years later. We read: *His clothes became dazzling white, whiter than anyone in the world could bleach them.* No detergent on earth could have bleached his clothes that white — they were just shining, glistening white. If you get your clothes the whitest they can be in the next wash, then go and hang them up in a snowstorm against the snow; see what they look like against the snow and you will see the difference! Yet he was glistening whiter than snow on the top of Mount Hermon; it was a most amazing, mysterious, almost weird experience and they were terror-stricken at first.

Then they looked closely and saw two people, Moses and Elijah, talking to Jesus. Have you ever wondered how they knew which was Moses and which was Elijah, or which was anybody? It is one of the proofs to me that when we get to glory we shall recognise everybody straight away. People have asked me, 'How will I recognise my loved one? I have got older since they went, how will they recognise me?' The answer is in exactly the same way as Peter, James and John knew it was Moses and knew it was Elijah. Don't you look forward to getting to heaven and saying, 'Why there's Simon Peter! I always wondered what he looked like, and there he is! And there's Paul. Well, he's not a bit like what I expected, but there he is!' Above all, have you ever wondered how you will know Jesus? You will know instinctively straight away, because then we shall know as we are known now. So they knew it was Moses and Elijah talking. They were on the edge of the universe, they were on the edge of eternity, they were having a glimpse into another world. What was the significance? Let me just mention a few things.

First, it means that Moses and Elijah were not dead but still alive; God is the God of Abraham and Isaac and Jacob. When I stood in Hebron and looked at the tombs of those three patriarchs, I thought: they are not there; their mouldering bones are there but they are alive. God is still the God of Abraham; Abraham is still loving God, and so is Moses and so is Elijah. Some people I meet try to drive a wedge between the Old and the New Testament, as if the Old is not true and the New is. Moses and Elijah and Christ belong together — you cannot drive a wedge. They talk together. It links the past with the future, the total plan of God through the ages is revealed in this event.

It also leads to something about the future. They were seeing something that one day every Christian (and indeed everybody) will see: the glory of Jesus. They were catching a glimpse of what Jesus looks like when he is in heaven; they were catching a glimpse of his glory that he left behind when he was born in Bethlehem. Many years later they still talked of it as if it happened yesterday. Listen to John writing at least sixty years after the event: *We have seen his glory, the glory of the One and Only, who came from the Father, full of grace and truth* (John 1:14, *NIV*). Listen to Peter writing years later: *We ourselves heard this voice that came from heaven when we were with him on the sacred mountain* (2 Peter 1:18, *NIV*). They were seeing the glory of Jesus. In other words, Peter said, "You are the Christ", and now God confirms the truth of this statement. Peter was indicating he believed that Jesus lived before, not on earth as a man, but in heaven as the Son of God. It was confirmation of the great confession of Peter — it was proof to him.

Peter opened his big mouth again. Poor Peter! Did he want to join in the conversation, or what was it? Did he feel a speech was necessary? There is always someone around who feels he should make a speech, and perhaps Peter felt this way. He said, *"Let us put up three shelters – one for you, one for Moses and one for Elijah."* People would then be able to come to the mountain top and remember. Peter had made two terrible mistakes. He was not rebuked by Jesus who did not speak to him, he was not rebuked by Moses, he was not rebuked by Elijah, he was rebuked by God himself. It was the first time that Peter ever heard the voice of God direct — it must have been like thunder. God thundered from the sky, *"This is my Son, whom I love. Listen to him!"* That voice of God tells us the two mistakes that Peter made. At the foot of the mountain, Peter's confession signified that Jesus was not one of a group, not one of a category; he had acknowledged that Jesus was unique — the Christ. But now what is he saying? He is implying that Jesus is one of the three he sees. Do you see the mistake? He is putting Jesus back among the great men of the world, back among the great prophets; he has reduced Jesus to one of a crowd. And God says, *"This is my Son, whom I love"*, and the cloud blots out the other two so that they only see Jesus. Peter is shown that he is to stop talking about these three. Peter has gone back on his earlier declaration by putting him among the others.

The other mistake that God rebuked was the fact that Peter was not listening. He should not have been talking at this point, but rather listening to what the Lord had to say. If Peter had listened, what would he have heard? What was Jesus talking about to Moses and Elijah? He was talking about the cross, about his death. Jesus needed to talk it over with someone, and his disciples would not understand, so Jesus had to go into heaven to understand; he had to reach for two saints of God from centuries past to talk about the cross. Moses understood, Elijah understood. So God tells Peter to listen to Jesus. If you are going to understand anything you must listen to Jesus. Sometimes in church we do too much talking and not enough listening. Sometimes in our personal prayers, we may need to be reminded: listen to him, stop talking and he will tell you things that you need to know.

Now Jesus turns to them and tells them again that they must not tell anyone what they have seen — not until he has risen from the dead, and then they can tell the whole world. The world would not have understood it until he had died. But after he has died and risen again they will be able to tell of how they saw his glory. Then they asked him a little question about a Jewish belief based on the Old Testament, that before the Christ, the Messiah, came, a messenger had to come to prepare the way for him. Many Jews thought it must be Elijah who had to come first, so they asked about this belief that if Jesus really is the Christ, then why has the messenger not come first? Jesus points out that he did come. When it says of John the Baptist that he wore clothing made of camel's hair, with a leather belt, do you know that there is only one other man in the Bible mentioned as wearing that type of clothing? Do you know that when it says that John ate locusts and wild honey there is only one man in the Bible otherwise mentioned who ate that — and that is Elijah? Read 1 Kings 19, it is mentioned there. 'Elijah' has come — not the Elijah who lived long ago, but the messenger. It is all taking place according to plan. But Jesus goes on to point out that the scriptures — that tell that the messenger would come — tell also that the Messiah will suffer. If they killed the messenger they will kill the Messiah too. Do you see what he is explaining to them? We will find it at the end of chapter nine, we will find it in chapter ten, we will find it in chapters eleven, twelve, thirteen and fourteen. Jesus is trying to get it into those disciples' minds that suffering is the way to glory, trouble is the way to triumph, apparent defeat is the path to victory — it is there in the scripture. Consider what was done to John. Could they not see that when a really good person lives in this evil world they are bound to suffer? But the tragedy is that they could not see this.

There are two more lovely thoughts to add before we leave this chapter. The first is simply that Jesus came down from the mountain. Do you realise that Jesus could have stepped back into heaven with Moses and Elijah as easily as he liked? He could have avoided the cross and all that suffering; he could have gone back into glory. But he came down from Mount Hermon, voluntarily, and would go all the way to Calvary.

Secondly, there is something which I find more thrilling still. Jesus is coming down from heaven again one day and he will come with that glory, that shining, burning light. He says it will be like lightning from east to west when the Son of Man comes — blazing light in the sky. I can scarcely imagine what it will be like. But two things I know. First, we shall see him as he really is. The experience that only Peter, James and John had that evening is an experience you can have. Do you realise that one day your clothes could shine like that? Do you realise the Bible teaches that if he calls anyone he will justify them, and if he justifies them he will glorify them. It is quite legitimate for the Christian to look forward to the day when we shall be changed; day by day we are being transformed, so that one day his glory will shine from us.

10

LESSONS AND LIFE
9:14–50

Last chapter we were on the mountain top, and in this chapter we are in the valley bottom. One of the lessons that every Christian has to learn, and which can be one of the most difficult of all, is how to get down into the valley again properly. We have our mountain-top experiences but we cannot live up there, not until we get to heaven. There are moments when we do not know whether we are coming or going — we have one foot in glory — and then there are other times when we are way down in all the mess of human life.

This passage is set in the valley bottom. They have been on the mountain, they have seen tremendous things, but now they have to come down, and Jesus brought them down. It may be that some Sundays you have one of those days when you feel in church that you were very near things that cannot be spoken of. Then it is Monday morning and you are at the kitchen sink or the office desk or the factory bench, and you are down to earth with a bump. We have to live in both. These disciples had to learn how to come down again to ordinary life and how to cope with the problems it presented. I am afraid they did not cope with them terribly well.

Here are five things that they lacked. I find this a great comfort, because if the Lord could manage anything with those twelve men he can do something with David Pawson!

The first thing is they were *impotent*. They were trying their best, they were trying so hard, and they could not do anything. They had let someone down badly. In the scene which Jesus found at the bottom of the valley when he got down from the mountain, we can see in miniature a picture of the situation in which we have to live. Here is a young man in the grip of evil, and nobody can help him. There is something terribly real about that. Here are some anguished parents who would do anything to help him, and they can't. Here are some followers of Christ. They have tried to help and they have just messed up the situation. And here are some scribes —there are always people like this: critical, arguing, discussing their failure, taking advantage of their embarrassment. We are reminded of the mess that we find in the world today: people in the grip of evil, parents anxious about youngsters, Christians desperately trying to help, and often getting discouraged because they seem to make the situation worse, and there are always the critics around. Here, Jesus puts his finger right on the spot of what is wrong, in words which reflect something his own Father had said about Israel centuries ago. He referred to them as an 'unbelieving generation', and he said, *"How long shall I put up with you?"* It sounds almost an expression of frustration. He put his finger on it: the real trouble with them is that they are faithless. They do not believe in God's power to do something. They are all trying to put the problem right themselves. And he tells them to bring the boy to him.

At this point I would like to focus your attention on someone who doubted too much and someone who was too confident. First of all, someone who doubted too much. The boy's father does not believe enough. He comes to Jesus and says something he should never had said to him, and if he had known him better he would not have said it. But when you do not know Jesus you say things that you should not say. When you do not know enough about Christianity you say things about it you should never say. He said to Jesus, *"If you can do anything, take pity on us and help us."* Jesus took him up on this and he said, *"'If you can'?"* There is not only disillusion in this man's remark, there is despair. I have met people who despaired of Christ ever helping them because they had asked Christians for help and not had it.

The man is saying something like this: your followers couldn't help me, I wonder if you can; if your followers who have your authority can't help, I doubt even if you can. May I appeal to you, if you are in this position, if you have been disillusioned with Christians, if you have sought help from the church and not found it, may I beg you not to assume that Christ cannot help you because of this. It would be a tragedy if you judged him by them. Alas, and I confess it freely, those of us who follow Christ are far from being the best advertisements for him. That is why we say do not put your faith in us, we say put it in Christ. If you put it in us you would be disappointed; you would be like this father; you would begin to say, 'if there is anything in it'. But when you come to Jesus you do not say 'if', you say something else. Do you remember the leper who came to Jesus? He said: if you will, you can make me clean — and that is the right thing to say. This man did not say if you *will*, he said if you *can*. Of course Jesus can. Jesus says to that man, *"Everything is possible for him who believes"* (Mark 9:23, *NIV*). Later we read of Jesus speaking to a tree, and it was dead the next morning. Peter exclaimed, *"Rabbi, look! The fig-tree you cursed has withered!"* (Mark 11:21, *NIV*) And Jesus told him to have faith in God, adding, *"If anyone says to this mountain, 'Go, throw yourself into the sea,' and does not doubt in his heart but believes that what he says will happen, it will be done for him"* (Mark 11:23, *NIV*). You do not need very big faith, you do need faith in a very great God, and Jesus let that father know that if he had faith there would be no limit to what was possible.

Now comes one of the most honest prayers that has ever been prayed: *"I do believe; help me overcome my unbelief!"* One of the greatest virtues in prayer is sheer honesty. A minister was telling of a young man who said, 'I don't believe in God, I'm an agnostic.' He then asked him, 'Have you ever told God that?' He had not, so he asked him to tell God that, to get on his knees and say: 'O God, if there is a God, I don't believe in you.' Prayer begins when you are really honest with God. And this father had doubts; he knew that he did not believe enough. He had a bit of faith and asked the Lord for help to overcome his unbelief. He wanted Jesus to start with him as he was. The glory of it is that Jesus can start with a man wherever he is, provided he is honest and provided he tells Jesus the truth about himself. Jesus healed that boy.

When they got into the house the disciples came and asked him why they could not do anything. They now learned the lesson of their impotence, and it is a lesson that most of us who are Christians learn the hard way. It is a very important lesson, a deep one. Why could they not do it? After all, just a few weeks before, Jesus had sent them out to cast out demons, they had gone out and they had succeeded in doing it. Now here was just one boy and nine of them could not do a thing. What had gone wrong? The answer is they were now too confident. They thought they could do it themselves. Jesus was teaching them that what had gone wrong was that they were not plugged in anymore. He said, *"This kind can come out only by prayer."* Here is the lesson, and people ask me again and again this kind of question. They say, 'I remember when I had a tremendous sense of God's presence. I had power, I had joy, I had peace, I had wonderful things, but where are they now?' The answer is you are not plugged in. We must understand that we can never have anything ourselves. We can only have power in Jesus, we cannot have power ourselves. We can have peace in him, we cannot have it in ourselves. We can have joy in him, not ourselves. The tragedy is that when we get through to Jesus we experience these things and then we think that we can have them. So we go out, as at other times, and think that we can have them, and we are no longer plugged in. If somebody says, 'Where is what I once had?' My first question would be, 'What has happened to your prayer life?' Prayer means being plugged in and switched on, and if we do not keep up our prayer life we cannot expect to have what we once had; we cannot expect to have the power that we once had; we can only have it in him. I would guess that the greatest need of every church is more prayer on the part of members who are plugged in. We cannot because we once did things in the past do them again if we have lost that contact.

The strongest man in the Bible was also the weakest — Samson. There he was with a great big physique, rippling muscles, a big, tough chap. Time and again, he took others on and he beat them hollow. Then came a day when he just fell flat on his face. Why? He thought he had the power and in fact, the Lord had the power, and he had got unplugged. The Lord had departed from him. So of course the disciples could not do it. Did they not realise that Jesus drew his power by constant prayer with the Father? Did they think that having done a thing once you can just go on doing it without prayer?

The second trouble was they were ignorant. You will never make a good follower of Christ unless you *learn*. Knowledge is important to the follower of Christ. There is so much we need to learn. They were now passing through Galilee; the great journey south had begun. Jesus was heading for the cross and time was short. He wanted an intensive mission now, not an extensive one. He did not want the crowds so he was travelling incognito. He had just a few weeks to teach his disciples. We are told that he kept on teaching them two things: he was going to die; he was going to rise again. They needed to learn that Christianity is primarily concerned with death and resurrection. There are people who think Jesus was a great man, a great teacher, a great leader, and that if we all tried to live the Sermon on the Mount and to do what he did we would have a wonderful world, but that is not what Christianity is. These twelve disciples were not getting the message. They thought it was a matter of going around helping people and healing and so on, and it included that, but the heart of it was, and is, death and resurrection. Still to this day I meet people who think that Christianity is a matter of trying to do good. It is not; it is a matter of learning that Jesus died and rose again, and the meaning of those two events.

Jesus knew there was a traitor in the camp because he said,

"The Son of Man is going to be delivered into the hands of men. They will kill him, and after three days he will rise" (Mark 9:31, *NIV*). Already he is beginning to hint, and I wonder what Judas felt when he said that. He is saying that men are going to kill him, God is going to raise him. Men are going to put him out of the world, God is going to put him back in. This is what it is all about and this is the heart of our faith. If we are ever going to follow Christ we must so understand the death and resurrection that we can explain to someone else why Jesus died and why he rose again. But the disciples did not get it. In chapter ten Jesus is telling them again; in chapter eleven he is telling them again; in chapter twelve he is telling them again. They did not get it. And still to this day we preach Christ crucified and risen, and people still think we are trying to tell people to live right. Christianity is to come and say: Christ died for my sin and rose again to be my Lord. This is what we need to grasp, and these twelve men had not grasped it; they were still ignorant of the fundamental gospel.

The third thing that was wrong about these twelve men was they were too self-important. As they walked south to Jerusalem they would walk in a kind of file, with Jesus ahead. He always seems to walk ahead of them; they are always strung out behind in twos and threes. As he walks down the road he overhears bickering behind him, and raised voices. So when they got into the house for the evening meal he asked, *"What were you arguing about on the road?"* They did not dare tell him, because they were ashamed. It is as though Peter was saying: 'I'll be most reverend and you'll be right reverend, and you'll be not so reverend'! Who will be the greatest? They had been discussing the grades of status;

169

they were still thinking of the kingdom of God in terms of power politics. And I have no doubt that Peter, James and John, having been up the mountain and seen that, were saying to the other nine: well now, that makes us a kind of trio up at the top. We three are going to be more important than you nine, and we have got this kind of graded hierarchy. This is what they were discussing: who was to be the most important. Christ cannot do anything with people until they have stopped discussing their own importance; pride is one of the most difficult things to deal with.

What did Jesus say? He gave them a verbal rebuke and a visual one. The verbal rebuke was very simple. He wanted to take their social values and turn them upside down. He told them, *"If anyone wants to be the first, he must be the very last, and the servant of all."* They were to go to the bottom. If they pushed out to the front they would find themselves at the back; if they tried to get to the top they would find themselves at the bottom. If they wanted to be the greatest they should chose the humblest, most menial position and become the slave to the others. This was something they did not get hold of; it is something we have not yet. We still talk about who is important, in the wrong way. To jump ahead slightly, when it came to the Last Supper they went into the upper room. Nobody was there because it was a secret rendezvous; there was no servant there to wash their dirty feet as they came in, which was normal hospitality. And I have no doubt that all the disciples looked at the bowl of water and the towel, each saying, 'Well, I'm not going to do it for the others,' so they all sat down with dirty feet. And Jesus got up and took his coat off. He picked up the bowl of water and told them that he was going to wash their feet. It must have been shattering. Jesus teaches us that we have got to think upside down to the world; we have got to turn the world right way up. If you want to be great in the kingdom, then serve — chose the bottom position.

Then he gave them a visual rebuke. He took a little child — possibly Simon Peter's son, for they were in Capernaum — and it says, *Taking him in his arms* [a lovely touch] *he said to them, "Whoever welcomes one of these little children in my name welcomes me; and whoever welcomes me does not welcome me but the one who sent me."* (See 9:36f.) If we think we are important, not only must we reverse our idea this way, we must also minister to 'unimportant' people. A person who thinks he is important will probably spend all his time with important people, name dropping, getting introductions. But Jesus was teaching them that if you give your time to a little unimportant child who cannot give you anything in return — and you won't go up the ladder of anyone's estimation by spending time with a child — if you do it in his name you will receive Jesus and the Father. That should be a tremendous encouragement to a Sunday school teacher, to someone who spends a bit of time among young people, to someone who is going to give themselves to those who are not high in rank or important in society. The disciples are challenged: why are they discussing importance? —everybody is important.

Fourthly, they were intolerant and they should not be. Mention of the name of Jesus at this point raises something that they have just done. John, who was a choleric, a son of thunder, came and he said: *"We saw a man driving out demons in your name and we told him to stop, because he was not one of us"* (Mark 9:38, *NIV*). This was rather like

171

saying they stopped it because the man was not in their trade union, not one of us. Notice the word 'us'. They did not say, 'he didn't follow *you*', they said, 'not one of *us*'. They were thinking that, after all, they were the only true disciples. So they told the man to stop it because he was not joining the right group. John was proud of this and thought Jesus would be pleased, but this was just rank intolerance, so we read, *"Do not stop him," Jesus said. "No-one who does a miracle in my name can in the next moment say anything bad about me, for whoever is not against us is for us"* (Mark 9:39f., *NIV*). A man who can use the name of Jesus to release someone from the powers of supernatural evil will not be against Jesus, he is for him. Do not stop him just because he does not follow you, just because he does not join your church, just because he is not in your band of disciples. This man was doing something for Jesus, and no-one is to stop that.

Casting out a demon is a very difficult thing to do, but Jesus says something else here that is very easy: *"I tell you the truth, anyone who gives you a cup of water in my name because you belong to Christ will certainly not lose his reward"* (Mark 9:41, *NIV*). If a person just gives you a cup of water because you belong Jesus, because you are a Christian, then that counts too. You must not even stop that. So whether a man is doing a difficult thing or an easier thing, if he is doing it in the name of Christ and in the power of Christ, you must not stop that. I remember when I had to learn this lesson. I was a chaplain in the Royal Air Force in Aden. I got a message from the Chaplain-in-Chief in Cyprus saying that some strange things were happening on the RAF station up at Bahrain in the Persian Gulf, and would I get up there and stop it quickly, because there was no chaplain there to keep control of it all. I went up, and I found there a young man anointed by the Holy Spirit leading his fellow RAF men to Christ, and he had led about twenty of them to the Lord. He had baptised them in the swimming pool and they were meeting together. There was no chaplain there, but there was something real happening. It was of Christ — how could I stop that? How could I say, 'That's wrong'? I preached to them for three and a half hours. It is the longest time I have ever preached but they said, 'We won't see you for three months; will you teach us enough for us to have for those three months?' So we just went on and on and on talking about the things of God. I will never forget that night. I did not know what to say to the Chaplain-in-Chief! Something may not be within our church programme; it may not be within our organisation; it may not be as we planned it; it may be most extraordinary. I wonder whether you know how the Salvation Army started. It was because William Booth, a Methodist minister, would not toe the line, because they wanted to fit him into the straitjacket of the Methodist system as it had developed. And in the meeting where they told him this there was a woman's cry from the gallery, 'Never William, never!' The Salvation Army was born that way. Church history is strewn with people doing things in the power of Christ that did not fit into the pattern of ecclesiastical organisation — 'not one of us'. But Jesus was telling his disciples that they had to have a big enough heart to recognise Christ's work wherever it happens. Rejoice in it.

Now the final thing that was wrong with the twelve men: the real problem is that they were intolerant with others and tolerant with themselves. This often happens. You can be terribly strict with other people and slack towards yourself. Jesus' teaching is that it is **you yourself** that you should be strict with, it is yourself that you should be intolerant toward.

Now Jesus says a certain thing negatively then positively. It is very clear that it is not meant to be taken literally, but it is meant to be taken seriously. He says, *"If your hand causes you to sin, cut it off."* He goes on to say, *"And if your foot causes you to sin, cut it off."* He also says, *"And if your eye causes you to sin, pluck it out."* What does he mean? It is picture language and it is clear that Jesus does not mean it literally because if my eye offends me and I pluck it out, I have still got the other eye to look at the same thing. Let me put it into simple English, because we do not think so much in pictures as they did then. Here is what he means: if there is anything you are doing, if there is anything you are watching, if there is anywhere you are going that is hindering you from being a good Christian, cut it right out. It is as simple as that. You will realise that this will vary from person to person, and the tragedy is that we often become so strict with each other that we make rules for one another that Jesus never made. It may be perfectly alright for one Christian to go and watch a good film in a cinema, and it may be thoroughly wrong for another to go near that place. It may be alright for this Christian to have a television in the home, it may be all wrong for that one to have one. We must not judge each other in these secondary things. What Jesus is teaching here, he teaches each disciple individually: if this is offending you, cut it right out. It may well be necessary for some Christians to be total abstainers, but you cannot establish from the Bible that all should be. It may well be necessary for some Christians to cut out this, and to cut out that, and not others. The point is: is this something that I am doing or watching or going to that hinders me from doing the work of Christ? If so, cut it right out because any of these three things could lead a person to disaster.

Here we come to some very serious teaching about hell. Jesus is the one who taught us about hell — nobody else really did. He always pictured it as the valley outside Jerusalem. Just imagine the city of Zion, up on the hill with the wall around it. On the south side is a deep, dark valley, the bottom of which never sees the sun but is in permanent shadow. Down in that valley was the rubbish of Jerusalem. If you had any rubbish you tipped it over the wall and it tumbled down into the valley. There were maggots eating up the food that remained, and bonfires were kept burning to keep the rubbish down — it was just one heap of useless garbage. And Jesus is teaching this: beware; the things a man looks at are enough to ruin him to the point where he is just rubbish and no use for anybody or anything. The things a man does can bring him down to that, and make him utterly useless to man and God. The places he goes to can ruin him. Better to cut these things out and be called narrow and live a narrow life in other people's eyes than ruin yourself and bring yourself to the rubbish heap. Jesus was being so true to life. It was our Lord who described hell in terms of a rubbish heap where the worm dies not and the fire is not quenched, where men and women go who are no use to God and men any more. It is what the word 'perished' means in John 3:16: *"For God so loved the world that he gave his one and only Son, that whoever believes in him shall not perish but have eternal life . . . "* (John 3:16, *NIV*). Rather than perish, rather than become useless, rather than be thrown out as rubbish

and ruined, it is better to cut it out, right out, for yourself
—and enter into life.

Now he puts the positive side. Jesus told the disciples that
they needed this discipline of cutting these things out for
this reason: if they did not, they could not be the salt of the
earth, they would not have the right flavour, they would not
have that distinctive quality which makes salt useful. They
used salt for two things in those days. They did not use it
for flavouring food as we do. They used salt first of all for
fertilising the gardens because it came with quite a lot of
potash. They used it also to disinfect their equivalent of the
closet at the bottom of the yard, which was just a heap of
earth called the dung hill. They used salt to promote good
growth in the garden, and to disinfect and inhibit the evil
and the disease of the dunghill. Jesus said, *"Salt is good,
but if it loses its saltiness, how can you make it salty again?"*
(See Mark 9:50.) How could it be used for the field or the
dung hill? How does salt lose its savour? Sodium chloride
does not lose its quality, it is always salt. The answer is very
simple. Some sharp-practiced grocers used to mix other stuff
such as sand with the salt. It weighed more heavily then, and
they could sell it for more money. And sometimes a poor
housewife would buy a packet of salt and she would taste it
and discover that there was no salt in it, just sand. It would
then be thrown out into the street and trodden under foot by
men. It was of no use for any purpose; it could not disinfect
evil, and it could not fertilise good. Jesus was teaching his
disciples that unless you are prepared to cut out anything
you do, anything you watch, or anywhere you go that causes
you to stumble, the salt will lose its savour and you will
neither cause good things to appear nor will you hold back

the bad things. And this is what a Christian disciple is to do. A Christian working in an office or in a factory should promote the good and disinfect the evil. His very presence should inhibit smutty jokes; his very presence should help people to feel more kindly towards each other; he is to be the salt of the earth. This is the intolerance a Christian needs: that he will cut out everything in his life that stops him being the salt of the earth.

So the disciples were impotent, they lacked faith; they were ignorant, they lacked knowledge; they were too self-important, they lacked humility; they were intolerant, they lacked love; and they were indulgent, they lacked holiness. Yet the whole future of the church depended on men like that, and Jesus had only a few weeks to knock them into shape before he had to leave them. I repeat: if he could do something with men like that, he can do something with you. Some people have the idea you have to be terribly religious or terribly good or terribly mystical to be a Christian, but those disciples were people just like us. If he could change them, he could do it for any one of us. If we are a bit self-important, and if we are a bit helpless to help people, and if we are a bit intolerant of each other, and if we are a bit indulgent with ourselves and do things we ought not to do, Jesus can still change us, provided we let him, and provided we follow him all the way.

11

TOUGH AND TENDER
10:1−52

Imagine a very deep valley, the lowest point on the earth's surface, a great big crack that extends from the Jordan valley down; it fills up with sea and becomes the Red Sea, then the crack extends right down as far as Uganda. The lowest part of that deep valley is the Jordan valley. There is the Sea of Galilee and there is the Dead Sea, and there is the river Jordan that comes from nowhere and goes to nowhere. Christ is walking down the east side of this river. It is a strip of land called Perea (in the British occupation Transjordan; today it is the kingdom of Jordan with Israel on the other side). Between the Sea of Galilee and the Dead Sea five things happen, and chapter ten covers this part of the journey. Jesus comes lower and lower down that valley, so the storm clouds seem to gather, and the picture looks pretty grim. There is no relation between these events but I am struck again and again by how much Jesus taught people quite spontaneously as a situation arose. He seems to have been able to use everything that happened to teach them something. Wherever he went, down this valley, the crowds came, and when they came he taught them. Jesus was a great open-air preacher; they did not come to be preached to, but that was what they got when they came to him. He would tell them something new. The only thing in common between these five events is this: in every one of them, people's ideas were changed. Occasionally people say to me after a service, sometimes even with a tone of resentment, 'Well, you made us think tonight,' as if that is the last thing they came to church to do and the last thing I should make them do! Nevertheless, we find again and again, at a much deeper and more wonderful level, that Jesus was always making people think, and he was always turning their ideas upside down and making them think again about something that they had already made their minds up about wrongly.

The first question that came up was the question of divorce. Let us see how it arose. There were enemies of Jesus who were always trying to trap him with questions. It is very interesting, whenever you have a question session, you can soon sort out those who are asking a question because they genuinely do not know the answer and want to, and those who are asking questions to try and trap you and make you contradict yourself, or make you unpopular with certain groups. If you went to Speakers' Corner in Hyde Park, London, you would find there some regular hecklers whose amusement lay in tying the speakers in knots — not asking questions because they want to know, but to embarrass and if possible confuse the speaker. And the Pharisees were professional hecklers to Jesus. Of course, a lot was at stake. If he was right they were wrong; if his way was the truth, their religion was false, so they tried to trap him. And one of the debated issues of the day was this matter of divorce, because in those days divorce was becoming more and more common, as it is today. Indeed, in the Roman empire and in the Greek countries, and even in the Jewish country, people were divorcing their wives for something as trivial as burning the breakfast, and provided they wrote out a proper certificate at the time they could get away with it.

Among the Jews there were two groups of people, one headed up by a rabbi called Hillel and the other headed up by a rabbi called Shamai. Hillel's was the broad party and they said you could divorce your wife for this, that and the other: if she had a voice that was too loud you could divorce her for that. On the other side, Shamai said no, there are only a limited number of things for which you can divorce her. So there was a big debate going on among the Jews as to how many causes there were. They came to Jesus thinking that whatever he replied he was going to get into trouble with at least half of them. They asked one of those trick questions like, 'Should we pay tax to Caesar?' Now they came to him and asked him straight out for his views on divorce. He did not quote the scribes and the rabbis and the clever scholars. He went straight back to the scriptures and he asked them what Moses had commanded. The first place to start is with the law of God. *They said, "Moses permitted a man to write a certificate of divorce and send her away"* (Mark 10:4, *NIV*). So the husband gave the wife a certificate and sent her packing. The first thing to notice is that this law of Moses was a permission, not a command. Furthermore, it was a very limited permission. And it was for nothing that happened after marriage, it was solely in the case — if you read the book of Deuteronomy you will find it — where a man married a woman and found out something about her afterwards that he did not know, which made the marriage less than that which he expected it to be, and in that case Moses allowed it. Moreover, Jesus taught that it was a concession to the hardness of hearts (see 10:5). We have to realise that when you are forming laws for society you will have to make concessions to human nature. There is no way of governing society if you do not recognise the hardness of men's hearts, and Moses was being given laws for society. But Jesus takes them to another part of the law of Moses. He takes them right back to the very beginning — who made sex and why? God made sex, and that means that sex is not a dirty thing in itself; it is we who make it dirty. God made it and called it good. God made male and female.

Secondly, Jesus pointed out that what is involved in a marriage is this: you are breaking up one family in order to form another. There is always a breaking before there is a making. This is one of the points of getting engaged. Sometimes young people say to me, 'What's the point of getting engaged? It's just between the two of us.' The point is that in the engagement you are telling others that you are going to get married, and you are recognising that marriage is not just a private arrangement, it is something public. In marriage, a man leaves his parents and, with his wife, forms a new unit. Something has happened that is quite decisive in God's sight.

Thirdly, God has joined them together. He does not say that if you get married in church God has joined you together, he says that the two will become one. God has joined the couple together, and what God puts together no man should put asunder. In a Christian wedding service this is said most clearly. There is only one thing that can break such a unit in God's sight, and that is death. This is the standard that Jesus took. In other words, he was saying that he was not going to give an opinion on divorce, he was going to take them back to the beginning: who made sex? Why? And how was it meant to be used? That is where you start. If you start from the divorce side rather than the marriage side you get a distorted view. Start with what was intended.

The disciples were a bit worried about all this, they thought Jesus was taking much too strict a line. So when they got into the house they asked him again. And Matthew tells us they asked him because they thought that nobody would ever get married if he was so strict about divorce. This may throw some light on the apostles' married lives, but it is amazing that they thought that marriage would be impossible under such circumstances, and that they brought it up. It was then that Jesus taught quite simply that once you allow remarriage you are then breaking one of the ten commandments — it is as simple as that. Jesus had the highest possible standard. It even upset the disciples, never mind the Pharisees. But we notice that Jesus loved people so much that he could not reduce the standard. And in a world in which women were being treated like objects and were being passed on from one to another, what Jesus was fighting for was the dignity of womanhood. Until you realise that that is why he fought this, and that is why he raised the standard, you will misunderstand him. He was lifting womanhood until women could be of equal honour and status with men in God's sight. This was a thing that they did not have in the Greek world, they did not have in the Roman world, and they did not even have it in the Jewish world of his day. He was being fairer to the women. And you notice that the Pharisees were only concerned with the man's privilege to divorce. So he was lifting womanhood to where womanhood was meant to be. It is a remarkable statement and this is our Lord's standard.

Having said that, may I add straight away to be divorced or to have committed adultery is not the unforgivable sin — we must never treat it as if it were. It can be forgiven, and as soon as we come to Christ he does forgive. The woman taken in adultery and the story of how Jesus dealt with her should be enough to tell anybody that it is not the worst sin in the book. You notice Jesus did not say it was not wrong, but he said, *"Neither do I condemn you, go and sin no more."* He called it sin, but not the unforgivable sin. Off you go, don't do it again. That was his approach, and it was straightforward and it was clear.

Again you see Jesus changing people's ideas. The common idea was: woman is low, divorce is easy, change partners as soon as you are sick of one. And Jesus lifted womanhood up, so that they had to revise their ideas and see a woman as someone to love 'till death us do part'.

The next group of people brought to Jesus' attention were the children. The disciples implied that children are not important. Once again, he reversed their ideas. May I remind you that it was not the mothers who brought the children but the fathers — the adjective is masculine. It is a reflection of our day and age that every hymn written about this event in the nineteenth and twentieth centuries refers to mothers of Salem bringing their children to Jesus. I want to lay stress on this: in God's sight the father of the house is responsible for the religion of the children, and in 99% of homes outside the church today I find that the father takes not the slightest interest — that it is left to the mother to do anything religious for the children. This is a complete reversal of God's plan. Every father will be held responsible by God for his children in their religious life. The fathers were bringing children to Jesus, but the disciples' attitude was: no, we are having an important theological discussion; we are discussing divorce; it's not for children, it's an adult matter; we are really much too serious for them, keep them out. You can see why. At this point they were having a very adult discussion. Jesus heard them, and he told the disciples to let them in, implying: children are very important; you have got your ideas all wrong; your idea is that these children cannot have anything of this until they are like us adults. *"I tell you the truth, anyone who will not receive the kingdom of God like a little child will never enter it"* (Mark 10:15, *NIV*). It is a reversal of ideas. We live in a sophisticated adult world but in all our sophistication the words of Jesus still apply: unless you become like little children . . . .

I remember a prayer meeting in the Shetland Islands. There was a great big fisherman called Dordie Pottinger, who was a large man, and the captain of the local fishing boat. I shall never forget him getting up in a prayer meeting and calling God 'Dad'. This big, tough man was just looking up to heaven and saying, 'Dad', just pouring out his heart like a little child. It was lovely. Our ideas are so sophisticated, we all have to be terribly grown up and so intellectual, and Jesus teaches that our ideas are all wrong, we will have to become like little children.

What is it about little children that was so important? I do not think Jesus meant that they are innocent because our three were not, and I do not think others are. I think there are three things that you will find in every little child that you will need before you can ever get into the kingdom of God. You first of all need a mind open to Jesus. Have you noticed how a child is ready to believe? The older we grow, the more we close our minds, the more we want to argue, the more we say 'I don't believe it', but if you tell a little child something they accept it with an open mind willing to receive the truth. The second thing about a child is an open hand — they are willing to receive. And the further we go in life the less we are willing to hold out our hand to someone else, until we get to the point when we are old-age pensioners and we could get assistance, but we are too proud to have it, and we call it 'charity'. A child is not like that. A child does not say, 'I won't have that chocolate, that's charity'! A child does not talk or think like that. A child is willing to open a hand and take it. Jesus said, *". . . anyone who will not receive the kingdom of God like a little child will never enter it."* So we must be willing to come as a little child and say, 'I will have that from you. I cannot save myself, but I will take it from you.' The third thing about a little child is an open heart. If you try to love a child properly, the child will respond to you in love. If you try to love an adult they may well say, 'I wonder what he's after now.' We get suspicious, we are let down by people, we stop trusting them, we become cynical and resentful and we think that everybody is trying to bring us down. A little child does not think like that. I am afraid a child is spoiled by experience of life and the heart closes up. Jesus taught the disciples that they had got it all wrong. They thought that faith in Jesus was for sophisticated adults and they were pushing those kids out. They were fond of those grown-up discussions about divorce and all the rest, but — until you can become like these little children . . . Jesus took the children in his arms. Can you imagine the scene? Jesus is saying that these are the sort of people he likes; this is the kind of people he wants in the kingdom.

A young man comes running up. I would call it the story of the poor rich man. He was a lovely young man. Jesus loved him for these things:

Firstly, this young man wanted life, and he wanted real life, eternal life. He knew what he was after; he was just existing, and he came running to Jesus.

Secondly, he admitted that he had not got life. It is tremendous when you meet a young man who is prepared to admit he has not got it. Although he was very rich and powerful — a rich young ruler — he did not have real life.

Thirdly, he recognised that if you are going to get life someone has got to give it to you, and he used the word 'inherit'. That was probably how he got his money — somebody had left it to him. So he asked Jesus, *". . . what must I do to inherit eternal life?"*

Fourthly, he was prepared to do anything to get it, which is why he asked what he had to do.

Fifthly, he believed the answer lay with Jesus. It is tremendous when somebody realises that if you want real life and you have not got it and you are prepared to do anything to get it, the man you need to go to is Jesus.

And he said, *"Good teacher"*. Our Lord's comments are very interesting. Jesus says, *"Why do you call me good? No-one is good — except God alone."* Is Jesus saying that he is not God? No, nothing of the sort. In effect, the young man is being asked whether he thinks Jesus is God. Jesus is asking him why he is calling him good, since that is only a word that should be used about God — and Jesus is God, and so can give him life. I do not know if he saw the point of our Lord's question, but Jesus then went on to ask a question about the Commandments which would show how good the young man thought he himself was. He answered Jesus, *". . . all these I have kept since I was a boy."* He was not claiming to be perfect. When he says he has observed all that from his youth he is saying that he has tried to be good, he has tried to keep the commandments, he has tried to live decently — it does not bring life. Jesus loved him for his honesty and sincerity. Here is a young man who has tried being good and found that it did not lead him anywhere. He has tried to find life but he has not found it. He is prepared to do anything to get it, and he asks what he needs to do. Then Jesus told him of the one thing he needed to do.

What was that one thing? Every commentary I have read suggests that the one thing this young man lacked was poverty. But that was not what Jesus said. He said *"One thing you lack"*, not: there is one thing you have got that is causing the trouble. What was the one thing this young man did not have? It was not anything to do with his money. Jesus told him that the one thing he lacked was Jesus: *". . . follow me."* But the trouble was that there was something that was going to get in the way. He is not saying the one thing you lack is poverty, get rid of your money, he is saying the one thing you need is me, Jesus Christ — that brings life — but there is something that is going to get in the way. Let me say utterly sincerely to you that you cannot have Christ and everything else. I do not care who comes to Christ, there will be one thing in that person's life of which Jesus says: get rid of it, and then you can have me. Go and deal with that and then you can follow me. It may be something you possess; it may be some person with whom you have a relationship. Jesus says you cannot have that and me, cut it right out. It may not be money, as it was in this man's case, but he is teaching this: follow me, that will bring you life. Forsake that or you will not be able to follow me.

There are rich people who have found Christ, but it was Jesus that the young man lacked, and at that point the young man turned around and went. Nobody is quite so unhappy as someone who has come as near to Jesus as that and turned away because they were not prepared to pay the price. The young man's face dropped and he looked so unhappy. He would have brought that money to Jesus if Jesus had let him. But Jesus told him, *"Go, sell everything you have and give it to the poor, and you will have treasure in heaven. Then come, follow me"* (Mark 10:21, *NIV*). Jesus loved him so much that he would not reduce the standard. Jesus, who said to the disciples, *"I will make you fishers of men"*, seems to have lost a fish that day. The fish got off the hook and went away, and it was a big one. But Jesus preferred that the young man went away than follow him under false pretences. Christ lost that young man who did not want eternal life more than anything else, and when the choice came he let it go.

When he went away, Jesus sighed and said, *"How hard it is for the rich to enter the kingdom of God!"* (Mark 10:23, *NIV*). The disciples were astonished. They thought everything came more easily for the rich. I have met many people today who think that if you have a big bank balance everything is easy. The problem with this is that because things come easily to you on earth when you have money, you may think that things come easily to you in heaven when you have money. But Jesus was showing the young man that all his money was invested on earth. Give to the poor and get it invested in heaven; there is nothing in heaven to your account, we must get this sorted out.

So the disciples said, *"Who then can be saved?"* If the rich man could not get into heaven, who could? Is that not an amazing revelation of their outlook? Imagine thinking you can sign a cheque to get salvation! Jesus had taught that little children can walk in, but now he explains that, *"It is easier for a camel to go through the eye of a needle than for a rich man to enter the kingdom of God"* (Mark 10:25, *NIV*). We have all sorts of literal explanations of this, but Jesus was being jolly funny at that point. He has a lovely sense of humour, and if you read the teaching of Jesus in the Middle East, people will see the funny side of the picture. But we are so literal that you will find preachers telling you about little gates called the needle's eye, and you can squeeze a camel through without the baggage on its back, and so on. Jesus was talking about a needle's eye. If you have ever seen a camel's expression you will know that if you ever mention one you are being funny. A camel is a horse designed by a committee! Here Jesus is teaching that you might as well try and shove a camel through a needle's eye as try get a rich man converted. For man it is quite impossible, but God can do it. God could get a camel through a needle's eye. God can get a rich man through the gate of repentance into the kingdom — it is amazing. And once he is through, what a power that man can be for good. So with God it is not impossible.

Peter's typically human reaction is, *"We have left everything to follow you!"* Well, these rich men can't but we can; we dropped everything, we came! Jesus said two things to Peter. First, *". . . no-one who has left home or brothers or sisters or mother or father or children or fields for me and the gospel will fail to receive a hundred times as much in this present age (homes, brothers, sisters, mothers, children and fields — and with them, persecutions) and in the age to come, eternal life. But many who are first will be last, and the last first"* (Mark 10:29ff., *NIV*). They did not lose by it, no-one loses by it. Whatever they dropped, they were repaid a hundredfold. I personally think of how few friends I would have if I were not a Christian, locked up in my own set, locked up with people of my own interests. I found that through Christ I have thousands of friends, thousands of homes of all descriptions I could go to and be at home. How rich you become when you drop everything to become Christ's! Jesus teaches us that if we give up relationships here he will give us a hundred more relationships even in this life. If you leave behind a family he will give you a great big family a hundred times the size. Nobody who ever gives up anything for Jesus loses by it. Peter was talking as if he had made a big sacrifice, but he needed to remember that he gained a whole lot by it. In this world far more people related to him than he ever had before; and in the next world, eternal life. But such was the honesty of Jesus that he told Peter that he had all this *with persecutions*. Our Lord was never dishonest.

He also made clear to Peter the need to remember that you can lose what you have gained. He may have been the first to drop everything, but the first can become last. It is not how you set out in the race, it is how you continue; it is not what you gave up when you first became a Christian, it is whether you are prepared to go on in the sacrifice. The last person to join can become first. I have noticed in church life that sometimes there is a person who has been a member for say twenty years, that they had a great beginning and then somehow it never developed. But there can be a person who is just two years old spiritually, and they seem to be streaking past. The last can become first and the first can become last. Jesus knew that Peter had left everything, but he was explaining the need for him to go on this way.

Then (from 10:32), we see a most dramatic picture: Jesus is striding out ahead down the road to Jerusalem — and they know what danger lies there — the disciples following behind. I remember as a boy going to a circus and watching a man put his head in a lion's mouth. My feelings and my face at that moment were exactly the same as I think the disciples' here must have been. They were amazed. Jesus turned round with two things to tell them. First, he explained that he knew what was going to happen to him. Men were going to spit on him, they were going to kill him. Despite this, he would go — and they were even more afraid. He knew it all. This tells me that the cross did not catch Jesus unaware. He knew what was going to happen; he walked straight into it. The cross was no accident, it was utterly deliberate. Then he said something else: *"Three days later he will rise"* — but they did not understand that then.

There was a tremendous sense that things were building up to a climax. Something was going to happen soon. They were coming to the capital city, and James and John instead of thinking of a cross thought of a crown, because they were expecting Jesus soon to be on the throne, soon to be the king. They said to Jesus, *"Let one of us sit at your right and the other at your left in glory"* They had seen Jesus' glory on the mount of transfiguration, and Moses and Elijah on his right and his left. They had thought about how marvellous it must be to be in glory and have Jesus in the middle and themselves right and left. James and John had a very ambitious mother and she wanted this for them as well. Jesus told them that they did not know what they were asking. *"Can you drink the cup I drink and be baptised with the baptism I am baptised with?"* They did not know, but they could. So he told them that they would. And they both suffered very dearly for the Christian faith in later years; they did drink that cup, they were plunged into the suffering in which he was plunged. But he told them that even if they were able to, he could not tell them who will be at his right and left. Is it not ironic that on his right and left when he won the world's redemption were two criminals, not James and John? James was running for his life and John was busy looking after our Lord's mother. James and John were not on his right and left, a couple of thieves were.

He told the twelve to come so that he could tell them something. He told them that they should not be like others, who like to lord it over people and tell them what to do. *"Not so with you. Instead, whoever wants to become great among you must be your servant, and whoever wants to be the first must be the slave of all. For even the Son of Man did not come to be served, but to serve, and to give his life as a ransom for many"* (Mark 10:43–45, *NIV*). He was also telling them for the first time the meaning of his cross, that it was going to be a ransom. When he died he was going to be serving people more than he had ever served them before. He was going to be the means of setting them free. That is what a ransom is.

Now we come to the last little incident in this section, and my favourite. Jericho was the oldest city in the world and the most immoral: the city of Rahab the harlot. Rahab was one of the people in Jesus' family tree, and I am sure that as he came to Jericho he remembered that a prostitute in the streets of that town was one of his ancestors. It is an amazing moment. There was a big crowd around him when a blind man heard a commotion down the street, and he heard — note the word 'heard', it is a lovely little touch — that it was Jesus of Nazareth. The blind man realised this was his only chance. He started yelling at the top of his voice, *"Jesus, Son of David, have mercy on me!"* Again, people had the wrong idea about who was important. They thought Jesus would not be interested in blind beggars. Little did they know Jesus. Jesus told them to fetch him. Then came the great moment. The blind man was told that his faith (and remember he was going on asking and yelling until he got through) was going to make him well.

There are two especially wonderful things about this man. Here is the first: the end of the story is that the blind man rose up and followed Jesus. To the rich man Jesus said "Follow me", but he had too much money and could not follow. The beggar had nothing to lose so he jumped up and followed Jesus. The richer you are when you come to God, the harder it is to follow him; the poorer you are, the easier it is. When you have nothing to lose you can just get up and come. That is why Jesus said in his lifetime that publicans, harlots and sinners got into the kingdom of heaven before respectable religious people. It is still true that when a man is at the bottom and has nothing to lose he finds it easier to follow Jesus than those of us who have so much. That is the first wonderful thing about him.

The other wonderful thing is what he said. He called Jesus 'Son of David'. There was only one man who had called

Jesus that before, another blind man. These were blind men who could see, and they saw the truth about Jesus. Just a few days later, a crowd was going to shout, 'Hosanna, Son of David' — but it took two blind men to see it first. You cannot physically see Jesus passing through your church, but when he does pass through and you realise that he is present, that is the moment to seize because you may never have that opportunity again. This blind man did not see Jesus but he heard that he was near, and he started calling on him and saying he needed something from him. And he heard Jesus say, *"What do you want me to do for you?"* Even though you cannot see Jesus, I tell you that you can call on him and say: 'Son of David, have mercy on me.' You will hear him say, 'What do you want me to do for you?' And you can rise up and follow him, but it is easier to do that if you come as a spiritual beggar. It is one of the hardest things in the world not to come with your hands full of all your good deeds, all your spiritual possessions, saying, 'Lord I have done this, I have done that, I have not done anybody any harm; and I haven't done this and I haven't done that; Lord, will you accept me?' It is much better to come with empty hands and say, 'Lord, I am a beggar; have mercy on me.'

12

COLT AND CROWD
11:1 – 11

In the month of March or April (it varied a little because of
the Jewish calendar) about 2 – 2.5 million Jews left home and
set off on a pilgrimage that would take them away from home
for a few days. In the year AD 29, which I take to be the year
in which Jesus died (that is as near as I can get), they set off
with one question being discussed by everybody travelling
up to Jerusalem: will Jesus come to the Feast? They realised
that if he did come it would mean the big showdown, it
would mean a crisis in their national life. Everybody must
have been asking everybody else: have you seen him on the
road? Some had, but not many. He had been making his
way up, healing people, teaching them on the way. Imagine
the scene with this vast crowd. Jerusalem could not have
coped with that many visitors and they would have to camp
out around the hills. If you can imagine a night light in the
middle of a soup plate you have got the geography of the
city of Jerusalem. There it is nestling in a hollow with a
rim of hills all around about a mile away. And those hills
are higher than the city itself, so that you do not see the city
until you come up over the rim of the soup plate, and there it
is nestling like a jewel. It is a wonderful situation. On these
hills all around, millions camped for the Passover, and this
is the setting for Palm Sunday. On that morning Jesus left

the home in which he was staying, in Bethany, just over the Mount of Olives, just over the top of the rim on the Jericho side. The last time we saw Jesus he was down in Jericho, now he has climbed nearly 3,500 feet. That morning he set out and he sent the disciples for that colt. If I were to preach on the use of our possessions I would use the story of this colt as an illustration of a man who said that when the Lord needs it he can have it — as he may say to you on a Sunday morning: I need your car. The man immediately let him have the colt. To get on a colt on which no man has ever sat, and then to ride it through a shouting mob numbering thousands, was remarkable. It takes a police horse years to learn to move through heavy crowds. We get a unique impression of our Lord's control of men, of animals, indeed of every situation, but that is not the main theme in this chapter.

I want to ask the question: what was really happening? I know we have heard the story since we were children. I know we think it is all exciting and tremendous, and Jesus was riding in with the crowd's adulation. Nevertheless, when we ask this question we are a bit shaken when we discover the truth. To the crowds it was a day of tremendous triumph; to Jesus it was a day of terrible tragedy.

Let us look at it first from the point of view of the crowds and the disciples. The people had waited a thousand years for this day. Fathers had passed on the dream to sons, and sons had passed on the dream to grandsons. They were all waiting for one thing to happen. They were waiting for David's throne to be occupied again. A thousand years before this day they had known a time of peace, prosperity and a king after God's own heart. Back then, it was the golden age of their history, and it had never been the same since. It is a sorry tale but I want to give you just a little bit of the sorry tale of this thousand years.

Very soon after King David died, because of his son Solomon's policies there was civil war and the nation divided, never to unite again. From then on they had a succession of kings, some of them good, most of them bad. After that, they began to be invaded by other powers. Assyria came, Babylon came, and they lost the land altogether for about seventy years. Some of them managed to crawl back and build a small temple on the site of the big one that Solomon had built, and they tried to maintain their life there. But other invaders came from another direction. The Syrians came, the Egyptians overran them, then Alexander the Great marched and the Greeks took over, and finally the Romans marched. By the time Jesus began his ministry the land was cut up into little bits. It was not even one land, it was divided far worse than Germany was after World War Two. A little section in the north was ruled by a man called Philip, whose capital was Caesarea Philippi. Galilee was governed by Herod, the grandson of the man who had killed those babies in Bethlehem. A chunk in the middle was home to the Samaritans. Jerusalem and the area around that was governed by a Roman governor, Pontius Pilate, who had taken over direct control. The people lived for the day when they would have their own land to themselves again. It is quite natural that all these hopes should be expressed in one word, 'David'. When any Jewish boy was born, the parents would rush out into the street and shout 'David!' meaning a boy has been born and it might be another 'David' who could help get back the land for them. Every mother who had a male child hoped that their baby would be that king and sit on the throne. It is a wonderful story of how for a thousand years they kept alive the hope that one day there would be another king like David.

Being an enemy-occupied territory this had bred collaborators, tax collectors, a resistance movement known as the Zealots, and acts of terrorism were taking place. In fact, if you read the story then you would realise it is so like today, it is so up to date. The whole situation was crying out for the right man to come. And if I ask what was the real meaning of the triumphal entry in the eyes of the crowd, one word will answer it: nationalism. It was a nationalist demonstration. It was a crowd of people who were fed up with others ruling their country, fed up with being a colony, fed up with not having their own land to themselves and their own ruler over them. It was a protest movement, a march. That becomes strangely relevant. In their eyes they had found the right leader. They had tried some months earlier, up in Galilee, to make him king — and he had refused. Now they thought: he is willing. What a king to have! Imagine finding a king to rule over your land who is a wonderful teacher, a friend of everybody no matter what their class or background, a man who can heal and work miracles, a man who loves the common people, a man who is fond of children, a man who is fair and wise and just and merciful, a man who puts hypocritical religious rulers in their place, a man who can even raise the dead. Would you want a man like this to reign over your country? That was the man they had found, and when he came riding over the brow of the hill, with all the crowds waiting there, they thought this was it: he was going to be king; it seemed he had accepted the offer! No wonder they got excited. So there was no doubt in the people's minds as to what was happening. The throne of David was not going to be vacant for another twenty-four hours. It was a tide of nationalist feeling, the end of foreign domination, the end of a divided country. You may think: how does he know it was nationalism? Isn't he just trying to update the Bible by linking it to a modern newspaper? No, I am not. Look at two things and this will prove to you that in their minds it was a nationalist demonstration. First look at what they *said* and then at what they *did*.

Every single word they said and every act they did on that day was sheer nationalism. What did they say? They said, 'Hosanna!' What does that mean? If you think it means a kind of glorious 'hello', or a great 'hail', some greeting, some act of praise, then think again for it means nothing of the sort. In modern Christian worship 'hosanna' now means 'praise him', but it did not then. It is a Hebrew word meaning 'save us now'. It is an expression of impatience. It is saying get us out of our troubles now, now is the time to fight, now is the time to meet the enemies and tackle them — save us now! Shouting 'hosanna' was just like singing a freedom song. It was a military expression.

Look at what else they said. Notice how the name David comes in again and again: Son of David, kingdom of our father David. There are the words. You can see that they are thinking of a political coup. Look at even the phrase *Blessed is he who comes in the name of the Lord!* It is from a Passover psalm which was about the defeat of the Egyptians. Read Psalm 118, it is all about cutting off their enemies. When they quoted that psalm they were shouting a political, nationalist, militarist term.

Now look at what they did. We think it is lovely that they

took down palms and waved them and strewed the road with them. We think it is wonderful that they took off garments and they put them down in the dust. What did those actions mean? The clue lies in their own history. They had done both these two things on two separate occasions. I wonder whether you have read of the time when they actually took their garments and put them in the road outside Jerusalem. They did it once for a man called Jehu, and he was coming to throw Ahab's house and Jezebel off the throne. He was coming as a resistance leader, a terrorist, and he was coming to liberate the children of Israel from the domination and exploitation of an evil royal family. So they took off their garments and they put them in the road for Jehu. He was the man who drove furiously! He was coming at a great pace in a chariot up that road and they threw their garments in front of him, and the chariot wheels went over. It was a military action.

What about the palms? This is not in the Old Testament but in the Apocrypha. In that period of four hundred years between Malachi and Matthew there was one — and only one — occasion when they got the throne back, and it was under a family of brothers who were very skilled resistance fighters. They were called the Maccabees. Perhaps you have heard of this family of seven brothers who fought the Greeks and who managed for a very few years to put one of their own number on the throne again. When Simon Maccabeus came to Jerusalem, the people waved palm leaves to welcome this resistance leader who was going to set them free. I hope I have not spoiled Palm Sunday for you, but that is what it was. That was why they shouted 'hosanna'; that was why they took off their coats and put them in the dust. They thought this was a military leader who would set them free, and it was a nationalist uprising. The people were thrilled, bursting with excitement and pride. Imagine the disciples! This is what we left the fishing for, this is what it is all about. Isn't it great! See them looking at us, and we are near him. You can sense what they thought was happening.

But when they look at our Lord he is crying. They think these are tears of joy, they think that he must be so happy with it all that he is overcome with his emotions. But he looks at that crowd who think it is a day of triumph and he sees it as a day of terrible tragedy. Why? What had gone wrong? He loved this place, he loved this people, and his heart ached for them. He could see that this kind of nationalism would lead them to utter disaster. Indeed, if we study his words on this occasion in the other Gospels we find that he predicted to the people at that point: *"The days will come upon you when your enemies will build an embankment against you and encircle you and hem you in on every side. They will dash you to the ground, you and the children within your walls. They will not leave one stone on another, because you did not recognise the time of God's coming to you"* (John 19:43f., *NIV*). Nationalism leads to that. Jesus said, *". . . all who draw the sword will die by the sword."* (See Matthew 26:52, *NIV*.) In the year AD 70, only forty years after Palm Sunday, what Jesus saw would happen did happen. They rose against the Romans, and the Roman might under Titus crushed that city and killed more than a million inhabitants. During the siege they were so reduced that they were eating dung and even cooking their own children's bodies to eat. It is an appalling story which you can read in the history of Josephus. Jesus saw all that. He saw that if that is the kind of kingdom you want, if that was the kind of feeling that was going to stir them, it would lead to utter ruin and disaster, and he wept over them.

The thing that they had not noticed, which Jesus had deliberately chosen, was the animal on which he rode. That is the tragedy of Palm Sunday. All their eyes were on him, they had no eyes for the animal on which he rode, and that is the key to it all. If you are coming as a military leader you come on a horse, or even with a chariot as Jehu did, or as Simon Maccabeus did, but Jesus came on an ass and it is the one animal you do not use in battle. He had deliberately chosen this animal. If they had known their scriptures (and he was often telling people that the reason they got wrong ideas was that they didn't know scripture), in Zechariah it said that the king would come to Jerusalem humble, meek, —not a fighter, but as a prince of peace riding on an ass. When General Allenby in the First World War liberated Jerusalem, he rode up to the city on a war charger of a horse and then, when he came within sight of the gates, he realised he should not come like that and he dismounted and took his military cap off, and he walked bare-headed into Jerusalem. He could not enter that city as a man of war. The word 'Jerusalem' means the city of peace — the suffix 'salem' is the same as the word 'shalom', the greeting 'peace' that you give to Jews in Israel today. It was always meant to be the city where peace would be, from which peace would flow to the whole world — this was God's intention. It was not meant to be a city of war, but instead the city from where peace was made and from which peace could reach the whole earth. Jesus came to bring peace to the whole world from that city, and indeed he has done, he has made peace by the blood of his cross. That was why he came; he was coming for peaceful purposes — to bring the peace of God to a world that needed it, and they misunderstood because they did not see the donkey, they only saw him.

Their disappointment with him was great. Imagine the scene. You come down from the Mount of Olives, past the Garden of Gethsemane, over the Kidron brook up the other side towards the magnificent Golden Gate — which, by the way, has been bricked up ever since; it is the only gate of Jerusalem that you cannot go through now, and Ezekiel had said it was for the king, not for anybody. Now it was wide open, and when Jesus got through it they would expect him to turn right, because at the corner of the temple area was the Roman garrison.

To their horror, when he came through the gate he turned left and made for the temple. That was shattering. He did not even take one look at the Roman garrison or at the soldiers. He went right into the place of worship and began to look in every cupboard and back room. He wanted to know everything that was going on there. This shook them. They thought he was coming to deal with the Romans, and here he was dealing with them! There were things in those cupboards and those rooms that they did not want him to see, and it was profoundly disturbing. It was getting late and he went out down the valley, up the Mount of Olives, over the hill and away. It is a most disappointing anticlimax. They were so disappointed with him that within days they were shouting 'Crucify him', and the mob psychology of it is utterly true to life. If you have once roused a nationalist mob and then do not do what they want you to do, the mob will turn right around, and that is precisely how the cross took place within the week. Only days later, where were the people who had shouted 'Hosanna'? They were still in Jerusalem, yet no-one would lift a finger to help him. Why? Because they were disappointed with Jesus. They did not understand the things that belonged to their peace. They had failed to understand how peace comes.

I want to apply this practically, first at a political level and second at a personal level. What does all this have to do with us? Simply this: the crowd was made up of ordinary people like you and me, and in them we can see a mirror to ourselves. Here is the political application. The nationalist spirit is characteristic of our times. The desire to protest, the desire to have big demonstrations, the desire to overthrow those who oppress, the desire to use force, is a desire that is rampant in our world. This world in which we live is an old world. In every continent, this spirit is abroad. And one wants to say to such people again and again: would that you knew the things that belong to your peace. May I say that I do not think it is possible for Britain to be a peacemaker and a world leader in peace because we do not understand the things that belong to our peace. What does belong to our peace? I will tell you. Righteousness exalts a nation, but sin is a reproach to any people, and if Britain is ever going to be a peacemaker in the world we shall need to be prepared to let Jesus come and inspect every cupboard in Britain and look at our life in all its aspects, and begin with us. Some say, 'It's always that nation, it's always that race, it's always the *other* people', but Jesus comes to look around *our* lives.

The other thing we need to say is personal. It is easy enough to welcome Jesus as the answer to our troubles. It is easy enough to say, 'Jesus, come into my life, I am unhappy and I want to be happy; Jesus come into my life, I'm bored and I want to be interested.' But Jesus can weep over that and say: I want to come in and put right what is wrong with you. I have not just come to deliver you from your troubles, I have come to deliver you from your sins, that is what belongs to your peace. If we want the peace of Jesus then we must welcome him and say, 'Jesus, come in and inspect every part of my life — that is what belongs to my peace.' That is why he comes riding on an ass. He is not coming to get us out of our troubles but out of our sins. That is the heart of all true peace.

13

JESUS AND JEWS
11:12 – 12:12

At the beginning of this book, I told you that Mark's
Gospel is like an express train slowing up. In the first few
chapters we race through months, and the favourite phrase
of Mark is 'and straightway', and we tear around Galilee at
a tremendous speed. Then the months become weeks and
the weeks become days, and the days become hours, until
finally we stop at the cross, as if we can go no further, as if
that was what it was all leading up to. We have now reached
the place where it becomes days. Mind you, we are all mixed
up in our chronology of the last week in the life of our Lord.
I am personally convinced that Jesus died on a Wednesday
and rose on Saturday night (which would be the Jewish
'first day'). If this is so, then he did not enter Jerusalem on
Palm 'Sunday', and probably it was a day or two earlier. It
does not really matter that we have not got the exact dates,
except, of course, if we do think he died on a Friday people
still ask, 'How do you fit three days and three nights in before
the Sunday?' and the answer is, you can't possibly. But the
important thing is that we should remember the events.

Jesus had a problem and he slept on it. That is a very
wise thing to do. If you are worked up about something and

you feel something is terribly wrong, and that you must do something about it, the best advice I can give you is to do what he did: go to Bethany and sleep the night, or wherever your 'Bethany' may be, and come back to deal with it the following morning. Again we remember that he rode into Jerusalem and instead of turning right after he went through the Golden Gate and going to the Roman garrison as the people expected him to, he turned left and went to the temple. When he got there he simply went round the whole temple and *He looked around at everything* —and what he saw horrified him. In the very place that people should have been thinking about God and praying to God he found just the opposite. He found people counting the money and people planning evil; he found crowds, he found noise, he found everything that you would find in the middle of a town, but not in a place of prayer. He was obviously terribly angry about everything that he found in the temple, but he went out to Bethany, slept the night and came back in the next morning — the wonderful control of Jesus! I have made enough mistakes flying off the handle at something I have felt was wrong at the time to know that he was absolutely right in doing this. But he did come back the next morning. He may have cooled off but he soon warmed up again. But the important thing is that he came back quite deliberately in the cold light of day in order to deal with something that was terribly wrong.

At this point we have the strangest story, a story that at first sight seems so incongruous, so unlike Jesus, that I have met people who mistakenly believe that it cannot possibly be true. Here is the story in its utter simplicity. Jesus was hungry and he came to a fig tree. It was not the time of year when there should have been figs on it, there were none, so he cursed the tree and it died. That seems the most extraordinary thing for our Lord Jesus to have done. If we only look at the story superficially I think we could easily gain the wrong impression that this is a mistake, a story that could not possibly be true. But when we look at it more deeply we find a wonderful story. It was not a childish act, he was not in a bad temper and working it out on this tree. Mind you, I am a bit puzzled as to why he was hungry. I am not quite sure what had happened to Martha who was always so busy in that kitchen at Bethany. He had set off in the morning — had he not had breakfast?

We need to remember a number of things if we are to understand this story.

Firstly, our Lord was prepared at times to do a destructive thing to nature when there was a purpose in it. Do you remember all the pigs that ran down the hill into the sea to save one man's sanity? Well, he was prepared to do something like that then, and there is no real contradiction between this and the pigs, except that the pigs did feel something and the tree did not.

Secondly, in fact, though it was not the season for figs anybody who grows fig trees (and that does not include me) knows that in the spring when the leaves first come there is a small crop of what are called 'first ripe figs', which are not normally good enough to use for any good purpose so they are not harvested, and then later in the summer comes the main crop. So our Lord was right in expecting at least something there. The leaves had come, there should have been a little something to eat with them, and that is characteristic of a fig tree.

Thirdly, if you remember *when* he did this you will begin to understand *why* he did it. It was between inspecting the temple and coming to turn out the money changers. This gives the meaning to the curse — 'nothing but leaves', all show. Are you beginning to see some meaning in this? He came to the temple and it looked tremendous — it was a wonderful building with gold, marble, the lot. It was so impressive and it was crowded. Yet when you looked at it closely, it was all show, there was nothing but leaves, no fruit; there was nothing really about God in it all, it was just man the whole way through. That is one of the meanings.

But I can go even further. You will never understand the New Testament until you know the Old Testament well. People who never read the Old Testament miss a great deal in the New. Someone has said: the Old is in the New revealed, the New is in the Old concealed. When you read the whole Bible as one book you get the clues, and here are some of them. Prophets like Hosea, Jeremiah and Isaiah quite often talk of Israel as first ripe figs; it is a favourite phrase — the first little bit of a harvest that is going to bring in the whole world one day. The prophets also say that if they are not careful they will not even be able to produce first ripe figs and the fig tree will become barren and withered. In other words, the fig tree was used as a picture of the whole nation, the people of God. The prophets Jeremiah and Hosea both say God will one day come looking for some fruit from you, and if he finds nothing but leaves then your fig tree will wither and become barren and nobody will get any benefit from you. Once you know that that was a familiar picture, and something the prophets had said already, you can begin to see what Jesus was doing — he was acting a parable.

Remember when Isaiah took off all his clothes and walked naked through Jerusalem? Why did he do that? He was acting his message. He said that you will be stripped as naked as I am unless you repent and turn back to God. Or perhaps you remember the story of the day that Jeremiah got hold of an ox yoke and put it round his neck. He staggered around Jerusalem with this ox yoke round his shoulders. He said as certainly as I am wearing this yoke, the Babylonians will come and put a yoke on you and lead you away into slavery unless . . . . The Jews were familiar with this kind of acted message, and Jesus was doing something the disciples would never forget. He came to the tree hungry. He should have found something to satisfy him and yet there was nothing. So he said to it, *"May no-one ever eat fruit from you again."* It is precisely what he was doing with the temple that day. He came to it, he looked in every room. What was he looking for? I think he was looking for someone praying, and all he could find were people changing money, people buying and selling things, the temple crowded with people but nobody praying — that was what he was looking for in the house of prayer. He found nothing but show, nothing but leaves.

Jesus comes to churches and he looks for fruit and he looks for some result of all the activity, he looks for something that will bring glory to God, he looks for people praying, he looks around in private rooms to see if anybody is praying to God in a house of prayer. All he found in the temple was show. The outward signs of prosperity were there: a very expensive building, a lot of busyness, a lot of activity, but nobody loving God. He found nothing but leaves. And when he cursed the fig tree he was damning the temple, and indeed God was going to rip up the veil of the temple in just a few days' time and the temple was going to cease to be the place where people met God. I can see now why he did it. He was showing the disciples something in an unforgettable way, and in fact they did not forget it because we have it recorded in the Gospel of Mark, which was not written down until years later.

Jesus' action impresses a lesson on us, too. God comes to our lives and he comes to our churches, and he looks for fruit, he looks for some result, he looks for something that will bring glory to his name. He may find a nice building and a lot of busy activity, but if he does not find what he is looking for then his Spirit can use some other church and some other people to do his work. We can be cast away in that sense. That is why Paul said, *'I do not fight like a man beating the air. No, I beat my body and make it my slave so that after I have preached to others, I myself will not be disqualified for the prize'* (1 Corinthians 9:26., *NIV*). He does not mean that he should lose his salvation, he means that God should cease to use him as a preacher. This can happen. Nothing but leaves, all show, nothing real.

They passed the tree and they got into the temple. Jesus shows up in this chapter in quite a different light. Here is a Jesus who is angry, who does extraordinary things. We know the outline of the story well enough. I am just going to run through the four things that were wrong with the temple that he put right, each getting more and more serious.

Firstly, it had become a thoroughfare. It was a handy short cut from the town through to the Mount of Olives, so people were cutting through the temple just to save a few more yards walking. They were not only cutting through it as a thoroughfare, they were carrying baggage through it, because there was always a lot of baggage to take from the shops in town to the Mount of Olives where two million people were camping out for the Passover. So they were coming straight through the middle of the temple in this way. Suppose this happened in your church. If the door opened and somebody came in loaded with shopping bags and walked across the church and out through another door while the congregation was seeking to worship, what would you think? You would probably think wrong thoughts about the person. And if you asked them afterwards why they did it they would say, 'Well, because I was coming from the supermarket and it was the quickest way to the bus station!' But something like that was happening in the temple, the place of prayer. We notice that it says that Jesus *would not allow anyone to carry merchandise through the temple courts.* That was fault number one and he stopped it.

Secondly, they had actually brought business right inside the place of prayer. There were two things you needed if you wanted to worship God at the temple: you needed your temple tax to get into the place and you needed a sacrifice once you got in. If you were poor it would be a pigeon, if you were rich it would be a calf or sheep or something like that. Formerly, you got your sacrifice outside, but they had now started doing this. First of all, the priests had ordered that you must pay your admission in special temple money which they would make, and you would have to exchange your money for theirs. The charge on the exchange was half a day's wage. Imagine that! Supposing when the collection was taken in your church they said, 'We won't accept your money, we've got special money, so you'd better get it changed in the porch before you come in.' And supposing you were charged, say 60%, before you got in. I guess that not many people would be back soon. It would get around town quickly. But if it was the only church and you had to get to church, it would have a monopoly. They could charge you the earth in the vestibule.

Let me tell you something else. If I were poor and I needed a couple of pigeons to offer as a sacrifice to God for my sin, I could buy them outside the temple for a certain sum for a pair, but inside the temple they would cost more. Why buy them inside when you could buy them outside? For the very simple reason that there were inspectors at the door and they inspected your pigeons. They said there must not be the slightest flaw in a pigeon used in worship, and they would look around for one little blemish and say: sorry, no good, you bought them at the cheap shop down the road; come inside, we have got perfect pigeons inside, such and such an amount for the pair. You may think this is ludicrous but it was going on. We have the facts and figures and we can compare the figures with the wages of those days. Jesus saw this in the house of God: exploitation on a wide scale. He whipped them out and it was not a punishment bad enough for them. He threw their money on the floor, those temple shekels. Why could God not accept their ordinary money? Of course he could. He threw it all out, and he turned out the animals and let them loose.

The third thing that they had done to the temple was to make it into an exclusive club. The outer court in which all this was happening was the only part of the temple that you could go into if you were a Gentile, a foreigner. When the temple was built, the innermost court was for the priests, the next part for the men, then for the women, and then came the largest court of all, the court of the Gentiles. If you were a foreigner that was the only place you could go to pray. But it was meant to be a symbol of the fact that the Jewish God was the God who loved the world and anybody could come and pray in that place — and the one place you could not pray for the noise that went on was that court. In other words, they had virtually said by their actions: we don't care about the outsiders as long as we have the temple for ourselves; we don't care if anybody else comes in, we want this to be a club for ourselves. That again can happen to a church. We can treat the church as a convenience, we can exploit the church, we can make it an exclusive club that says to people outside: we don't want you here, we are just here in our own church to pray.

The fourth thing was the most serious of all. Jesus said of the temple, *". . . you have made it 'a den of robbers.'"* What did he mean? He did not just mean the exploitation that was going on. Once again the clue is in the Old Testament. Isaiah talked about this being *a house of prayer for all nations* (see Isaiah 56:7). And Jeremiah in his day said the temple had become *a den of robbers* (see Jeremiah 7:11) and he tells us what he means.

If you went to the temple from Galilee, you went down the Jordan valley, then you went up from Jericho, up to Jerusalem four thousand feet higher, and you went up a very barren wilderness area with caves on either side of the road. And lurking in these caves were people who sprang out at you. That is why the man fell among thieves on the road from Jerusalem to Jericho. And a 'den of robbers' refers to the place they hid, waiting to trap you. Jesus' words mean that these pilgrims have passed all the dens of robbers all the way up and thought they were safe in Jerusalem, but when they came into the temple there was just another hideout of crooks waiting to take their money. It is a most telling phrase. They think they have got past all the bandits, yet all they have done is come into the biggest lot of all. Jeremiah was highlighting their use of the temple as a cloak for sin, for crime. They put on this cloak of religious respectability and because it was the temple they thought that selfishness and greed were alright. The voice of Jesus comes down to us today warning us to never use religion as a cloak to hide sin, never to use the respectability of churchgoing to hide greed. That was what they were doing, so Jesus cleansed the temple.

I think it is very interesting that three years previously Satan had suggested to Jesus that he go to the temple and climb the tallest tower, the pinnacle. Then from the top to launch out into space, float down in front of the crowds and they would be his. Jesus did go to the temple but he did not come concerned with the miraculous he came concerned with the moral. He did not come floating down from the pinnacle, he walked in quietly at the door. And he did not come to dazzle people, he came to cleanse them, he came to put them right. Time and again, people are more interested in the spectacular than the moral issues; time and again we pray for great things to happen when we should be praying for forgiveness.

We move to the third incident on the following day. They had been back to Bethany and now they are coming in again to Jerusalem. Each day Jesus goes out to Bethany — until the last night — and this is to avoid arrest until the time has come. So he comes in the next day, and as they pass by in the morning Peter points out the tree which is now a poor old, dead, withered thing, with not a bit of sap in it anymore. I find people today, in the twenty-first century, who think that it is only in the last hundred years people have found miracles difficult to believe. But the people who were there found them difficult to believe, so this is no new problem! A scientist cannot tell a piece of matter to do something and have it obey him. We say matter cannot obey because it has no intelligence to understand what is being said to it, but God can do this. Peter exclaimed, *"Rabbi, look! The fig-tree you cursed has withered!"* By nature we find it terribly difficult to believe that God can control matter. That is why very few Christians in England today pray about the weather. They believe that it is fixed by natural laws and that God cannot do anything about it. But Jesus taught that if you have faith you could pray and things would happen.

There are two conditions for such power that Jesus laid down. The first is the condition of faith. Notice how he defines faith as not having the slightest doubt in your heart. I heard of one lady who asked her minister about this and she said, 'Do you mean that if I have faith I could move that mountain behind my cottage?' The minister replied, 'Well, it seems to say that.' So she prayed that God would move the mountain and she got up the next morning and she threw back the curtains and it was still there. She just muttered, 'I thought so'! What is faith? Do you think the amazing thing that Jesus is saying here is true? There are two things of which you would need to be absolutely certain to be able to pray in this faith: one is that God *could* do it and the second is that God *will* do it. If we can pray in faith with no doubt that God could do it and no doubt that God will do it, we have the promise of Jesus that it will happen.

Let me underline both those points. In our scientific twenty-first century it is hard enough to believe that God *could* do it. But the second question is equally important because it does mean that we are quite sure that it is God's will that he *will* do it. Otherwise we are going to have Christians shifting mountains around so much that the National Geographical Society will get completely lost! In other words, this is not just a test — going around proving things to people.

If faith is the first condition, forgiveness is the second. Jesus said, *"And when you stand praying, if you hold anything against anyone, forgive him, so that your Father in heaven may forgive you your sins"* (Mark 11:25, *NIV*). So you can never ask for a miracle if you are not forgiving other people in your heart, if there is any resentment, any bitterness, anything you have against anyone else because of their attitude to you. Whenever we pray we ask for forgiveness ourselves, because we are not just concerned with the miraculous, we are concerned with the moral; and we need to forgive others, because we cannot ask for forgiveness ourselves, or even be able to receive it if we cannot forgive someone else.

Here then are the two conditions: that you be forgiving to others and that you have such faith as has no doubt in your heart. Have I said enough to show why we do not see more miracles? There is no fault on God's side, the limitations are on ours.

So they came to Jerusalem again, and now they met the enemy face to face because the people whose pockets had been touched (and all the business in the temple was for the profit of the priests and the Sadducees, they got all the money from that business) came up to him and said, *"By what authority are you doing these things?"*

My advice is: never challenge Jesus, he has a way of putting the ball back in your court with a very disturbing question. They asked, *"And who gave you authority to do this?"* With one of his brilliant and wise answers Jesus said quite simply, *"I will ask you one question. Answer me, and I will tell you by what authority I am doing these things. John's baptism — was it from heaven, or from men? Tell me!"* (Mark 11:29–30, *NIV*) That put them in a terrible dilemma because officially they had not recognised John. So the official religious leaders kept at a cool distance from the Baptist. The crowds went to hear this preacher but the official religious leaders kept neutral. Jesus is now putting them on the spot and urging them to take sides. Did they think that John was from God, or did he just decide himself to be a preacher? They were going to upset somebody whatever they said; it was again a question like, 'Have you stopped beating your wife?' If they said he was from God then Jesus could say: well then, why didn't you recognise him? If they said he was self-appointed there would be a riot — the crowd would not stand for that. But notice that they do not then ask about the truth of the question, they are only concerned about their own position, —how it will affect them — whatever they answer. So Jesus refuses to tell them by what authority he was doing what he did. But the wonderful thing is that he had really answered their question. If they had only listened to the question he asked, then they would have got their answer. They knew perfectly well how close Jesus and John were to each other. They knew perfectly well that John had spoken of Jesus. They knew perfectly well that John's ministry and Jesus' ministry were one. And if they believed that John's ministry was from God, so was that of Jesus, as they shared the same authority. But if they believed that John's was of men, then Jesus could not tell them whose his was either. He had answered the question. Now he went on to tell them a story and to answer the question even more fully — a story about an absentee landlord. That was a very common feature in their social life, so they would understand.

Centuries earlier, the prophet Isaiah had used the picture of a vineyard to portray the nation of Israel. They would get the message and you can see the meaning of every detail in the story. The owner of the vineyard quite clearly represents God. The vineyard is his people Israel. The tenants are the high priests and the rulers who have been given charge of it to bring fruit for the glory of God. The servants are the prophets who have been sent to this vineyard to tell them about the owner and to have something for the owner, some glory. And every time a prophet came he was disliked, he was put in prison, beaten or killed. So the owner of the vineyard, seeing that they had dealt this way with all his servants, decides to send his son. When the son comes, the tenants realise that if they kill this man they will have the vineyards to themselves. They can hold off the owner and there will be nobody left to inherit it. The first meaning of the story is pretty obvious: God does not let people get away with things forever — he will come. Our Lord appeals to the justice of the situation and says, *"What then will the owner of the vineyard do?"* The answer is, *"He will come and kill those tenants and give the vineyard to others"* (Mark 12:9, *NIV*). What ought the owner to do? What ought God to do about you? The answer is to come and hand your vineyard over to someone else.

The other thing is this. Jesus was communicating to them that he is the Son of the owner — that is his authority. Why did he clean up the temple and turn out the money changers? Because he is the Son of the Owner. As a boy of twelve he had stood in that temple and said to his mother, *"Didn't you know I had to be in my Father's house?"* (Luke 2:49, *NIV*) Jesus was doing his business. Now, at the end of thirty-three years, he is saying that he is still doing his Father's business, that he is the Son of the owner — that is his right. His Father owns the place and he has been sent to clean it up, to get the fruit. Furthermore, Jesus is telling them that he knows perfectly well that they do not want him there, that they do not want his Father there, but want the temple to themselves, so they are going to kill him for it.

Now he switches the story and the illustration to get an important point across. He suddenly starts talking about buildings. The head of the corner in a building is this: at one corner of the building they will place a very big stone and then the other stones are built up on the corner. The biggest stone at the bottom holding the whole thing up is the head of the corner. We still talk about a brick end ways on. Some of these bricks are headers — the ones that only show their ends every other course up the wall. This header, this big stone, really held up the building, and if you pulled that stone out the whole building would collapse. Jesus now switches to this picture and he describes some builders putting up a big building, and they are looking at a stone and they decide not to have that stone for the head of the corner because they think it does not fit, and they throw it out. Yet a later builder comes along and tells them that they have made a mistake, that the stone is ideal to hold the whole thing up. It is a quotation from the very psalm (118) from which they shouted on Palm Sunday, *"Blessed is he who comes in the name of the Lord"*. And Jesus had to switch the story because the story broke down at one important point. Once the son in the story was killed, that was the end. Now he tells them the rest of it by using another illustration. The very stone which they reject (Jesus himself) will become the head of the corner — God is going to build on him. I have seen some of the stones that held up the temple, and one of them weighs 110 tons — a massive stone holding up the corner of the temple. How they got it there I don't know — that is the head of the corner. Jesus virtually says here that this temple is finished, this vineyard is fruitless, it is going to be given to someone else. I will be the new corner, I will be the new foundation, God will build everything on me from now on. You throw me out and say you cannot fit me in; God will put me in the most important position. They got the message so clearly that they went away and plotted to kill him. They could see that he meant this: you are so envious, you are so jealous for your temple, you are so greedy for the money you are making here, you don't want me at all, you are going to kill me, but you won't get rid of me. I will come back as the head of the corner.

What has all this to say to us? Simply this: the tragedy of Easter is that the real people who put Jesus to death were the religious people. The people who hated him were those who were right in the middle of the temple, those who should have been the first to welcome him. I would sum it up like this: *religion and Christianity do not mix*. Religion has always been the enemy of Christianity. Much religion is what I would call 'churchianity' — it can become what the temple had become then, a religion of convenience. A large percentage of people in Britain are buried by a minister or religion —we have a religion of convenience in which to be 'hatched, matched, and dispatched'. There can also be a religion of exploitation. People can get power and other things out of it. When I saw St Peter's, Rome, that magnificent Baroque building, I remembered it was built on money gained by selling indulgences all over Europe. A few pounds and you could supposedly get a relative out of purgatory, and that would build St Peter's. Religion can also become an exclusive club in which you are not interested in people outside the church. Religion can become a den of robbers, it can become a cloak of respectability over things inside — envy, jealousy and greed that are still there, and people cannot see them for our religion. Such religion crucified Christ. When Jesus comes to face that kind of religion, either he goes or it does. Therefore, it behoves us to say, 'Lord Jesus, here is our church, hosanna, come to us; come and look in every room in our church, come and look in every room in our lives, and if there is anything there that should not be there, cleanse us, make us a temple worthy of your name. Will you come and make us a house of prayer, a temple that reaches out to everybody in the world to bring them in, to welcome them to your house? Will you come and make us what you want us to be, lest we too become a barren fig tree or a fruitless vineyard that has to be discarded?'

14

CUT AND THRUST
12:13 – 44

Our Lord has laid down a challenge, and in this chapter we see others come out and challenge him. They are fighting him only verbally at the moment. 'Sticks and stones may break your bones, but names will never hurt me' used to be a well-known saying, but actually, words can hurt much more than sticks and stones, they can cut very deep. Words were the first weapons used by our Lord's enemies.

One gets the impression that the enemies of our Lord — the Pharisees, Sadducees, scribes, priests, elders, and even the Herodians — all team up against him as one. The two things they are aiming at in this verbal battle are: firstly, to discredit him in the eyes of the public and get the crowd on their side; secondly, to try to get a charge with which they can accuse him to the authorities — which meant Pontius Pilate. Everything they say to him has this double object. They have some pretty acute questions worked out, which seem at first sight to force Jesus either to lose public support or to fall foul of the authorities.

Six little conversations are recorded, and they can be grouped into two sets of three. In the first three questions raised in chapter twelve, those who oppose Jesus attack him, but none of their attacks defeat him; then in the second half of the passage we have three more conversations in which

Jesus now comes on to the attack, and he delivers three telling sayings to them.

The first question is a political one. The people involved are the Pharisees and the Herodians. As we noticed above, in our discussion of Mark chapter eight, they were a strange alliance. Normally they would not have spoken to each other. The Herodians were not Jews, they were political puppets in the hands of the Romans; they belonged to the hated line of Esau, they were Edomites, and the Herodians were hated by the Jews because the Romans had set the Herodians over them. The Pharisees were about the most exclusive religious people in the whole land. To see exclusive, religious people, who normally see politics as a terribly dirty business and will have nothing to do with it, lining up with Herodians who are just up to their eyes in dirty politics, is to see an amazing coalition. When we read the scripture carefully we find that somebody else put them both up to it: *Later they sent some of the Pharisees and Herodians to Jesus to catch him in his words* (Mark 12:13, *NIV*). Note the word 'they'. It is a remarkable intrigue, and it simply shows that when people hate God they will make extraordinary alliances. So 'they' — the priests — set up the Pharisees and the Herodians with a trick question.

I remember at school two large schoolboys got a little boy and asked, 'Which one of us do you like best?' The two big bullies had this poor little lad right in the middle, and there was nothing he could say. Whichever one he said ,'You' to, the other one was going to beat him up. It is that kind of question they had managed to think up. The Pharisees represented the Jewish side and the Jewish feelings, the Herodians represented the Roman feelings, and the answer to the question was bound to offend one or the other.

The question was a most offensive one. Israel was an occupied country at this time — the Romans were an enemy occupying power — so this is an appalling trap. Either Jesus could say: No, we shouldn't pay these taxes to Rome and let this money go out of the country to Rome and Caesar, in which case they could accuse him to Pilate straight away as a traitor, or he could say: Yes we should, in which case he would be so unpopular with the people that that would be the end of his public ministry. It was a cleverly worded question. But my advice to anyone is never try to get the better of Jesus. Many people have tried and nobody has ever done it. Never try to be too clever for him. Jesus saw straight through their question. They were not bothered about taxes at all. Jesus knew their hypocrisy (see 12:15), and that means they did not want an answer, they just wanted to trap him. Seeing straight through it, Jesus asked them why they were trying to trap him and since, presumably, they did not reply, he went on to give them an answer, and it is a brilliant one.

He asked for a coin. I have heard it said that Jesus was so poor that he had to ask someone to give him a coin. I do not think that is the reason that he asked for one. Judas, the treasurer for the disciples, had some money and Jesus could have asked for one of their coins, but he did not. Why? Because he wanted something out of their pockets, something that they were already using, something to which they had already committed themselves. So it was made clear they were willing to use this money and accept it at its face value. They bought their food and clothes with it. Whose money is it? In other words, you are already committed, you are already involved. It is a very clever answer.

To go a little further, here is something that is not in the Bible but which will help you understand. In AD 6, Jerusalem was under Herod's son Archelaus, who was a thoroughly bad lot. The people got so fed up with him that they petitioned Rome (which had put Archelaus on the throne, and the Herod who had killed the babies at Bethlehem), asking for a Roman governor instead of Archelaus. They thought that even a Roman governor would be better. So they had actually asked the Romans to come. They need not have had a Roman governor at all. And when the Roman governor came, he introduced Roman coins and Roman taxes. Our Lord's hearers were being reminded that they asked for the Romans. They were quite happy to have them come, and quite happy to use their coins. They asked whether they should pay taxes, and Jesus said, *"Give to Caesar what is Caesar's"* and the word used in that reply means 'repay'. So they had asked whether they should pay taxes and he told them that they should repay taxes, and that is a different matter altogether. This puts it all in a very different light. Of course, they could not say anything about this because they had benefited from the Roman peace — the 'Pax Romana' that for many years brought security to the whole Mediterranean world, a situation in which you could travel around the Mediterranean without a passport, protected by Rome.

But Jesus goes on to something more in the second part of the sentence: *". . . and to God what is God's."* You also have a duty to God for the benefits you get from God, and God has a right to expect something from you as well as Caesar. Therefore, a Christian is in a double citizenship. He is a citizen of earth and owes certain things to the earthly country to which he belongs. He is also a citizen of heaven and owes certain things to the kingdom of heaven to which he belongs. The problem arises for a Christian when Caesar begins to claim something that only God can claim. Then the Christian has to say, 'No, I can't give it to you.' There would come a day when Caesar said, 'I am God. You must worship me as Lord', and the Christians responded: that is something that isn't yours and we can't give it, and we'd rather go to the lions than give it. But in this case it was a simple issue: give to Caesar what is Caesar's. You are using his money; why shouldn't you give him his money? If you really want to be logical you should not touch his money.

Of course that was a real dig at the priests because they were fairly wealthy and they were rather fond of the Roman cash. They were also to give to God what is God's. I use the money that I have with the image of an earthly sovereign on it — Queen Elizabeth. I am using her money, she has a claim on it. But what is it which has God's image on it? The answer is: every man and woman on earth. What I must render to God that he deserves is *me* — he has a right to me. If the money that we use has the image of an earthly ruler who therefore has a right to it, we are made in the image of a heavenly king, and he has a right to us. This is what Jesus' teaching here tells us. In this way he turns it very cleverly back on them and, in effect, asks whether God is getting from them what God should have from them — that is the biggest question. Pharisees and Herodians retire. It was a wonderful exchange.

The next encounter is concerned not with the political question but a philosophical one. Now the Sadducees come. They are the wealthy, aristocratic priests of Jerusalem. They run the temple, getting most of the money from it. They are somewhat anti-supernatural in their views — they would be called the liberals of their day. In particular, they said the only part of the scriptures to take notice of is the first five books — the law of Moses, the Pentateuch as it was called: Genesis, Exodus, Leviticus Numbers, Deuteronomy. You had to prove a thing from those five books before they would believe it. One of their strange views was that unlike the Pharisees they did not believe in a personal resurrection from the dead after this life. The Sadducee believed that you lived on in other people's memories and in the good that you had done (which is what a lot of British people seem to believe about the future).

They came along to Jesus, and this time they were trying to get him discredited in the eyes of the public by making him look silly. Some people love to do this. I had some sessions at a university and I could pick out the students who just wanted to do that. They had their clever questions; they did not want to know the answer, they just wanted to make the speaker look silly in front of the others. And if you can make a speaker look utterly silly then of course he is not going to have any effect on them.

So the Sadducees came with a very funny question. In the book of Deuteronomy, which they did accept, there is a law that if a man died without children his brother has to marry his widow and produce a child for him, and so on down the line. The reason was two-fold. The land was divided up and a parcel of land was given to a family forever. Therefore, the family name needed to be kept alive and there had to be a continuity to the family to keep that land. And it was God's law when the land was so tied to families that this family name be kept alive this way.

Here was their question. It is not a living issue really, it is one of these logical puzzles. They said that a man died with no children; his brother took his wife and he had none, then his brother took his wife and he had none, seven times down the line. They suggested that there is going to be an awful situation in heaven because all these seven men are going to fight over this woman, each claiming her as his wife. If you think this is a silly question let me put it to you in the form in which it has most often been put to me. I have often had the same basic question in my ministry. People have said to me, 'How could I ever be happy in heaven if any of my family were in hell?' It is the same basic question; deep down it is the same basic principle, and the answer Jesus gave would be applicable for both questions. So before we dismiss the Sadducees too lightly we must realise that it is a problem. The basic problem to people is that they cannot imagine how heaven can be different from earth, and they imagine that everything we know here will be the same there, including our relationships, and we are told quite simply they will not be, that heaven is different in many ways.

Jesus tackled them head on. They had asked the wrong question, and if they had known their scriptures they would not have asked that question. He points out two very important things of which they are ignorant. He says, *"Are you not in error because you do not know the Scriptures or the power of God?"* (Mark 12:24, *NIV*.) So many of our trick questions show an ignorance of the Bible, and I am more and more impressed with the fact that the more I read it, the more every question is answered. Ignorance of the Bible is one sure way of getting tied up in such knots. The second thing Jesus says they do not know is 'the power of

God', meaning the power of God to change things, to make things different (here, to raise the dead).

He goes on to question whether they think that heaven will just be earth *ad infinitum*, just continuing what they have got down here. The answer is: it most certainly will not. Quite frankly, that would not be heaven for most of us. That is not a reflection on my married life, so please do not jump to conclusions! But for my wife to have to live with me as I am now forever would not be heaven! And for all of us to have to live with each other forever as we are now would not be heaven, but we believe in the power of God to change people. Sometimes at a funeral when we have been burying someone who was known for being a bit awkward, I have said quite openly, 'One of our hopes for the future is not just a glorified body but a glorified character, and the next time we meet so and so they will be perfect' — and that brightens up the relatives no end, and has given them something to look forward to! But the relatives will be perfect too if they die in Christ. In other words, life in heaven will be so different from life on earth, and we need to remember the power of God to change things and people.

The answer to the Sadducees' question was this: *"When the dead rise, they will neither marry nor be given in marriage; they will be like the angels in heaven"* (Mark 12:25, *NIV*). When my wife and I got married we said, 'Till death us do part', and we recognised that the particular relationship into which we entered on our marriage day was a relationship for this world only. That is not to say that we do not expect to be in heaven together, but when we get there it will be a different relationship between us. To put it as I imagine it, it will be a relationship of brother and sister in Christ. We shall all be as closely related to each other; that will be an even more wonderful relationship than we could have known here. Jesus reminded his hearers that this is how the angels live — the angels do not get married, nor do they reproduce and have children. Angels are created, each one. Incidentally, that is the answer to all those who believe that all life must come from evolution — you could not possibly believe in angels if you believe this. The angels were created distinctly, separately; they do not die, they do not grow old, they do not marry, they do not have children, and that is precisely what life will be like for us in heaven, difficult though it is to imagine. Therefore, the answer to those who have said to me 'I won't be happy in heaven if all my relatives are not there' is that relatives will be there, but the people you will count relatives there will not be the people you count relatives here. Our relationships will have changed. All your brothers and sisters in Christ will be there, and it is one of the things that God has the power to change. Lest that seem a hard or callous thing to say, let me add straight away that as long as I am in this life my physical relatives are my concern and my burden and my prayer, but in the next life the only relationships are in Christ, and those are the important relationships.

So the Sadducees had gone wrong because they did not know their scriptures well enough and they did not know the power of God to change things. On the positive side, knowing that Sadducees always wanted to prove a thing from the first five books of the Bible, and wanted to know where in there resurrection is mentioned, Jesus says, *"Now about the dead rising — have you not read in the book of Moses, in the account of the bush, how God said to him,*

'I am the God of Abraham, the God of Isaac, and the God of Jacob'? He is not the God of the dead, but of the living. You are badly mistaken!" (Mark 12:26 ff., *NIV*). Jesus points out that God said, 'I am' — not I was. That is a very important difference, and perhaps you could read that story and never notice it. Think of your father or grandfather or great-grandfather, someone who knew the Lord. Do you realise that God, if he spoke to you at this moment, would not say, I *was* the God of your great-grandfather, he would say to you, I *am* the God of your great-grandfather, which implies absolutely certainly your great-grandfather is still alive. These people are still alive and God is still their God, and you are just joining this wonderful company. This is a tremendous thought.

I remember going to Hebron to look at the cave of Machpelah and the tombs of Abraham, Isaac, Jacob and their three wives. The centuries seemed to roll away as I looked at their graves. Yet as I stood there I remember saying to myself aloud — I could not help it: 'They are not dead because God is still their God; whatever has happened to their bodies they are alive, because he is alive.' Could I put it this way: If you believe in a living God then you must also believe that he is the God of the living.

Now we come to a scriptural question, but this time the question is utterly sincere. It is wonderful in a discussion when somebody asks a question about the meaning of something in the Bible and really wants to know, and is really concerned about the truth. There has been a scribe listening to all this, and in his mind he believes that Jesus knows all the answers, knows what it is all about, and he decides to ask a question.

In those days, scribes had long theological discussions and they greatly enjoyed them. They used to discuss two things. First of all, they used to add a lot of laws to the law of God — all the detailed application of it, what you could do and what you could not do on the Sabbath; what new laws they could make that would help people to fulfil the ten commandments. But the other sort of discussion they enjoyed having was setting each other the question, 'Can you summarise the law in one sentence?' In fact, one rabbi said to his student, 'Stand on one leg and summarise the whole law of God.' This was to try and make them condense it, abbreviate it, get it summed up.

So now a scribe comes to Jesus, and he asks him this question: *"Of all the commandments, which is the most important?"* (Mark 12:28, *NIV.*) Our Lord quoted two texts, one from Deuteronomy, one from Leviticus, and he put them together and said: *"'. . . Love the Lord your God with all your heart and with all your soul and with all your mind and with all your strength.'"* He then said, *"The second is this: 'Love your neighbour as yourself.' There is no commandment greater than these"* (Mark 12:30f., NIV). So he summed it up in those two. Some people have said that Jesus was saying nothing new — there it all is in the Old Testament. But there are at least two things that he was doing that were quite new. The first is that nobody had put those two texts together before; teaching that love is the key to the law of God: loving God, loving your neighbour, the two relationships. The other thing is that he did not qualify the word 'neighbour'. In Leviticus your neighbour was your fellow Jew, but here it is as wide as the world.

First of all, if you read this summary you get the idea

first that love is not feeling. The trouble is that nowadays if you say the word 'love', everybody thinks of emotion. If you listen to the pop songs about love it is always about emotional love. But Christ makes it quite clear that real love is a response of the whole personality. You can love someone with all your heart but you can also love them with all your mind. That is a notion that you will not find in a pop song — that your thoughts can love people. You can love them with all your physical strength, and that is a thought you will not find in a pop song. You can love them with all your soul, and that is a thought you will not find. What Jesus has done is to define the word 'love' as something that your whole personality is involved in — all your thinking, all your strength, all your heart and feeling, all your soul — all of you.

Furthermore, he is teaching that before you love your neighbour your first duty is to love God. This is what gives the lie to the idea that you will find many better Christians outside the church than in. When anybody says to me, 'So and so is a good Christian and they don't go to church,' I will say to them, 'Now tell me why you think they are a good Christian,' and the answer is invariably in terms of the second commandment here, because they love their neighbour. One may then go on to say, 'Do you think that person loves God?' — because that comes first. Loving your neighbour is fine, it is good, it is part of the whole law, but it is the second thing, not the first. I remember in one house group a lady said, 'Well, how can you love God? The only thing that you can do is to love your neighbour.' But Jesus taught that loving God comes first. In fact, I do not think you can really love your neighbour until you love God — not in the fullest sense. Mind you, I think that to love God without loving your neighbour is just as one-sided and just as much a caricature. So Jesus' teaching meant that love is more than just our feelings, it is our whole personality; and love of God comes first.

The next thing we need to notice is that there is only one God and he demands *all* our love. Notice the word 'one' and the word 'all'. " *'Hear, O Israel, the Lord our God, the Lord is one'* " (Mark 12:29, *NIV*). Therefore he has a right to all of you. If you believed in a dozen gods then you might have to give each a twelfth of yourself. That may sound a bit funny but this is what missionaries find. They go to a country where people believe in a whole lot of gods, and there they are, a whole row of idols, and they give a little bit to this, a little bit to that, and a little bit to the other, and the people have to dish out among all their gods what meagre resources they have. But here the commandment tells us that the Lord our God is one — there is no other. Therefore he has the right to *all* your heart, *all* your strength, *all* your thoughts, *all* your feelings, *all* of you, and that was something wonderful.

Notice, too, that it is alright to love yourself. That may sound a bit heretical but let me tell you what I mean. He did not say love your neighbour instead of yourself or in spite of yourself, he said *as* yourself. This means that it is perfectly valid to have a care of yourself. We are to care for our own bodies, to look after them properly. But he is saying that you should take as much care of other people as you do of yourself — that is the standard. Anything that you would do for yourself you should do for them. That makes life very simple, yet very demanding.

The scribe listened to Jesus and said, *"You are right in saying that God is one and there is no other but him. To love him with all your heart , with all your understanding and with all your strength, and to love your neighbour as yourself is more important than all burnt offerings and sacrifices"* (Mark 12:32–33, *NIV*). And Jesus said to him, *"You are not far from the kingdom of God"* (Mark 12:34, *NIV*). I wonder what would have brought that man right in. He was not quite there in saying that he could see that it is love. The answer is very simple — there are two steps. There would be acknowledgment that he had not done either of those two things. The first step is to realise that you have not done what God wanted you to do. Once you realise what God has a right to expect of your life, the first step towards the kingdom is the step of repentance, with heart and soul and strength: 'Lord, I have not loved you with all my heart and soul and strength; Lord, I have not loved my neighbour.' Step number two into the kingdom is to say: 'Lord, even if you forgive me for not doing this, I will never be able to do this in the future without your help.' That is faith. That would have brought him right into the kingdom. He could see what was needed, but as far as we know he did not admit that he needed this, and he did not admit that he could not do it by himself. But he was very near to the kingdom, and a man who is as sincere as that is very near. From then on nobody asked Jesus any questions. Who would, after that? He could tie you in knots for one thing, he could judge you for another. You think you are tying him in knots and he ends up tying you in knots by facing you with the truth.

Having defended himself three times, Jesus now goes round to the attack. The first attack he makes is on a spiritual basis. It is quite complicated and rather difficult for us to understand today. He attacks their idea of the Christ, or the Messiah, or the Saviour they are expecting. They are expecting a purely human figure from the line of David, a descendant of David. And they keep calling him the son of David; they called him that when they welcomed him with palms. Jesus challenges them on this idea that they have. They are looking for a purely human descendant of David to come and reign over them, and he challenges them to look at what David himself said about this Christ who was coming. Do you notice, Jesus is pointing out, that David applied the same word to this Christ coming as they apply to God — the word 'Lord'? In other words, David knew that the Christ who would come would be far more than a human being. He would be divine. So our Lord attacks their idea of the Christ. All they want is a political messiah, a leader, an agitator, a resistance leader, an insurrectionist, and the triumphal entry to Jerusalem showed that so clearly. But Jesus challenges them to think again. They ought to be looking, as David did, for a divine person, someone they could call Lord, someone who is in fact far higher than David. It was always considered in those days that a descendant of someone was lower, that in a sense a grandfather was superior to both father and son. Jesus is teaching that the one who was to come is far above David. David said,

> *" 'The Lord said to my Lord:*
> *"Sit at my right hand*
> *until I put your enemies*
> *under your feet" '*

Mark 12:36, *NIV*

But it is 'Lord', not just a son of David. That was a technical point, but it was an important one. Jesus was attacking them and their understanding of scripture. Notice in verse 36 our Lord's view of the psalms. David wrote them, but the Holy Spirit inspired them, and therefore they could be appealed to as truth and as proof of truth.

Now Jesus knows that the common people are enjoying all this. There is nothing a crowd likes more than seeing hecklers put in their place. The crowd at the end of v. 37 are enjoying him greatly. *The large crowd listened to him with delight.* Jesus is only too aware of this. And he warns them in v. 38. He moves now to an ecclesiastical question and he says, *"Watch out . . . ."* Of what? There is a danger of being in religion for what you get out of it, of covering up greed, pride and hypocrisy with religion. And Jesus now says some very severe words which I find terribly disturbing and challenging. Those of us who have been called to full time Christian service need to read this again and again and examine our own hearts. But I think all Christians need to do so too.

First of all, the teachers were getting prestige out of it, and that is a most subtle thing. They liked wearing long robes. That of course made them distinctive anyway, and different from others. You cannot do any manual work in them and you cannot hurry in them, so it gave the impression of a leisured scholar. They loved special greetings like 'father'. Jesus taught that you should not let anybody call you father. Incidentally, I found out too late, after three years in the services, that padre is of course precisely that. It came from the Italian army originally, and it was simply the word 'father' put into Italian for the priest. Papa (Pope) — it is the same word. 'Father' and 'master' are terms that imply you are above others, and this is something you are not. The teachers loved titles. They also loved the chief seats, and if there was a feast they liked the best room in the house where they were staying. They were in it for prestige.

The second thing they were in it for was greed. Widows were easy prey because they had no man to defend and argue for them. I have noticed, again and again, how often cults and sects get hold of women and persuade them to accept their strange teachings, especially if there is no man to argue with the one who has come to the door. There is evidence that many widows lost their money to such people. Jesus pointed out that all this greed, as well as pride and desire for prestige, was covered up with long prayers. I find it very interesting that Jesus did not like long prayers — he mentions this so often. If there is one thing that kills a prayer meeting it is long prayers. Mind you, Jesus could spend all night in prayer without other people around, but he was thinking of public prayer. It is very interesting that in the Book of Common Prayer (a lovely book, and the more I study it the more I feel it is a wonderful book of devotion), the Collect was quite deliberately made a prayer of two or three sentences because it was meant to be *common* prayer, prayer that people could follow. If a prayer in a meeting is too long we so easily start thinking of other things. The people Jesus was referring to were professional pray-ers, and because of their privilege, their responsibility, their position, they would receive a greater condemnation. It is quite an attack on some professional religious people, and as I have said, those of us who are called to full-time service need to examine our hearts all the time lest we ever begin to be greedy for prestige or to be thought of too highly by others.

But it is a warning that our Lord gives to all the people so it is relevant to all Christians.

Now, like a breath of fresh air, we come to the loveliest little incident. Our Lord sat down and watched the collection. There were huge metal vases set up on end at the gate into the treasury, and as you went in you threw in your money. It usually made a nice 'ding' as it went in! I was in the Albert Hall for a Christian meeting and the American chairman of it said, "Well now, friends, I think we're going to have a silent collection tonight." I thought: now what is that? Then he pulled a dollar bill out of his pocket and said, 'Paper only!' So we had a silent collection. But they did not have silent collections in the treasury, and the bigger the coin, of course, the bigger the 'ding' it made as it went into the trumpet. So of course you threw in the big coins, and you made a nice 'ding'! There may be some connection here with 'blowing your own trumpet' — when you give alms blowing your trumpet before you. In fact, they probably did blow trumpets as well. In any case, there were certainly these large trumpet receptacles, and you tossed your money in as ostentatiously as possible if you wanted to — and that is why Jesus said that when you give you are not to let your right hand know what your left hand does. I have often wondered how Jesus knew those coins were two mites. They would only have made a tiny little 'ping'. He sat over against these trumpets and this poor little woman came along looking as if she could not rub two tiny coins together — she could in fact, but that was all. She just put two little 'pings' in. It is a most dramatic scene. For the first time we get a glimpse of real religion; for the first time we catch a glimpse of someone who loves God with all they have got. I am sure that this is why the Holy Spirit wanted it in Mark's Gospel. This note of a poor woman giving to God all she has is a lovely finish to the public ministry of Jesus —it is real religion. It tells us that when Christ looks into the collection he does not ask what that gift will buy but what it cost. That is a very different way of adding up the collection. Of course, we cannot announce in the weekly bulletin what last week's offering cost. We can announce what it will buy, we can say how much was given and we know roughly from that what it will get. It may have cost some very little and it may have cost some a great deal, but in God's weekly bulletin what goes down is what the offering cost, not what it amounted to. To put it another way, he looks not at what was put in but what was kept back.

Notice that Jesus called his disciples together to tell them something. He said, *"I tell you the truth, this poor widow has put more into the treasury than all the others."* Maybe they had thought she was one of those who had plenty of money, for the Lord to talk like that, and that she was just one who did not spend it on herself. But no, he said, *"They all gave out of their wealth; but she, out of her poverty, put in everything — all she had to live on"* (Mark 12:44, *NIV*). The other people he had watched throwing their collection in on that day gave from what was left over — that is the literal meaning of the word — and she had given all that was left. The way to apply this to ourselves is not necessarily to go away and draw out all our bank balance and get rid of it, nor to put it all in the collection next Sunday, it is to go home and say, 'Lord, do you have all that I have got?' There are different ways of giving all that you have got — that was her way, and there are other lovely ways as well.

You probably already know these stories well, but maybe you have seen something fresh in them. There are two things that I am left with, and they are really one. Firstly, if we think we are testing Jesus and testing Christianity with all our questions and all our puzzles, we shall very quickly find that sooner or later it is Jesus who is testing us and the thing is reversed. I have known this happen so often. People are argumentative, and they try to argue about the miracles of the Bible, saying, 'You don't still believe this, do you?' — and they are trying to discredit the Word of God. If they go on doing that there will come a point where the Word of God will begin to discredit them — it kind of rebounds on us. We can criticise the Bible and then we find the Bible criticising us; we can say things about Christ that we don't like — but sooner or later Christ will tell us something in our lives that he does not like. The second thing that strikes me about this chapter is Christ had a way of stripping off what hid real people from others. He could do it both ways. He could look at those public figures who were pretending to be religious, and he could strip it all away and say: look at them, greedy, proud people, hypocrites; and he could say that about us. Then he could look at a simple, unnoticed little woman and show that she was wonderful. He could immortalise such a person. We have not even got her name yet she is still talked about by millions of people two thousand years later — isn't that amazing? Perhaps she never knew what Jesus had said about her. There is coming a day when God will judge the world by a man, Christ Jesus, and Jesus will say about everybody in the world what he said about people here. About some he will say: Depart from me, I never knew you. Oh you used my name, but I never knew you; it was all pretence; it was all long prayers; it was all outward religion, but it was not love for me. Then, of some simple people whom the world will have forgotten, if the world ever thought of them, Jesus will say: Now look at this person. This person loved me so much, they are so important to me. There will be such a reversal. Many who are first will be last; many who are last will be first. But people who do not like being shown up will not like Jesus, and that was why this argument led to the cross; that was why within three days they were planning his death and crucifying him. Because a man who comes to me and says, 'Your life is hypocrisy, it's religious on the outside, but it's dirty on the inside,' I will not like — that man I will want to get rid of; that man I will want to put out of my life, and that is precisely what happened. The shadow of the cross was already beginning to fall across the scene.

15

TRAGEDY AND TRIUMPH
13:1–37

Mark chapter thirteen has been described as the most difficult chapter in the whole New Testament to understand. I think that is an exaggeration. It is certainly not easy, but if you are prepared to study it hard you do find a lot in it that you can understand. Some people say it is a jumble and that Mark seems to have collected a whole lot of things that Jesus said at different times and put them together. I do not believe that because it all hangs together so wonderfully that I am sure Jesus spoke the words at the one time to the four disciples.

It all happened so innocently, so spontaneously. They just made a remark about the temple building and they got an answer as long as this chapter, and so deep and complicated. In fact, they did not even ask a question, all they did was make an observation and this is what they got. That sometimes happens, especially with preachers. You just ask them a simple, short question and get a sermon back! But our Lord had so much to tell them, so much to teach them, that he took the opportunity to say all these things.

The temple to which they were referring was the most wonderful construction, I suppose, that has even been put up. In those days it was the largest in the whole world. It was far larger than any Greek temple; it was about the size of York Minster. Imagine that stuck in the middle of the

Judean hills — a magnificent thing. York Minster is made of stone, imagine it made of white stone and covered with gold. Just think what that would look like in the morning sun. The stones with which it was built were so large, one of them measures forty feet long, four feet wide and four feet high — just one stone!

The temple to which Peter, James, John and Andrew referred when they said to Christ, "*Look, Teacher! What massive stones! What magnificent buildings!*" was not the temple built by Solomon and it was not the temple built when Ezra and Nehemiah came back, it was a brand new one being built by Herod — or at least by his family. He was determined to build for the Jews the biggest and the best temple they had ever had. He was trying to get them on his side and he thought this would be a good way of doing it. He began building it twenty years before Jesus was born. It was not finished until thirty-four years after Jesus died, and it was finished only just in time for the Romans to pull it down stone by stone until there was nothing left. It is the most extraordinary story. But while Jesus and the disciples were walking through the temple at this point it was still being built, the scaffolding was still up. Even so, it was already the most amazing building that had ever been constructed by man and we read just how impressed they were by it. But Jesus replied, "*Not one stone here will be left on another; every one will be thrown down.*" That came true literally. It would seem impossible for it to happen. It took hundreds of people many hours to get one of these huge blocks which weighed many tons into place. But Jesus knew that it would only just be finished in time for it to be pulled down.

Some time later, as they sat on top of the Mount of

Olives, having crossed the Kidron Valley — a place where you could gaze for hours on end at Jerusalem set out before you — they were chatting, and four of the disciples came to Jesus and said, *"Tell us, when will these things happen? And what will be the sign that they are all about to be fulfilled?"* (Mark 13:4, *NIV*). Our Lord then tried to tell them a great deal about the future.

There is something we need to understand about every part of the Bible that deals with the future. Imagine looking through a telescope at two mountain peaks in the distance. The one thing the telescope does not tell you is how far apart those two mountains are. Looking ahead through your telescope you simply see what lies ahead. It will tell you what is there but it will not tell you how far from here to there, how far from there to there. Indeed, the further you look the more difficult it is to see, and you might think that a few mountain peaks in the distance are all in one big jumble, until you get to them and then you might find there is a great valley between. One of the problems in what we call prophecy, especially in that part of prophecy that is concerned with prediction, is precisely this: that all those in the Bible who look to the future, the true prophets, could see what was going to happen, but they do not usually give any indication of various distances between the events, they just see them all together as they look into the future. By the Holy Spirit they get a kind of spiritual telescope.

Here are some examples from the Old Testament. The true prophets in the Old Testament saw, as they looked through the 'telescope' the Holy Spirit gave them, the first coming of Christ and the Second Coming of Christ, and the prophets of the Old Testament predict that Jesus will visit the earth twice, but they give no indication whatsoever that there would be a gap of time between the two. Therefore, when you read some of their prophecies you discover that they talk of both comings in the same sentence; they are just describing what they see in the future — two future events. So they describe them in Old Testament language almost as if they are going to happen together. We now know, of course, that there is a long gap of at least two thousand years between those two events.

In this chapter, Jesus is looking into the future, and he is now looking at not one but two events. The disciples think he is referring to one event, the end of the world, when he talks about this temple collapsing and not one stone being left on another. They cannot imagine that temple being pulled to pieces before then; it will surely last. But, in fact, Jesus can see the end of the temple very much earlier, and throughout the chapter he is describing the end of two things. He is describing the end of the temple and the end of Israel as a state — at least for the time being — and he is describing the end of the world. The disciples had got the idea that the temple would last right until the end of the world, so they asked Jesus to tell them when this would happen, and how they would know when the end was coming. But Jesus has to tell them much more than that. He describes, on the one hand, the end of the temple, which actually took place in the year AD 70, about forty years after he died. But, looking through the telescope as it were, he looks through the end of the temple to the other end, the end of the world, which cannot be dated. Indeed he told us that we are never to try to date it, and that even he did not know the date of that one.

Throughout the chapter it is comparatively easy to see

which he is referring to because he talks about the end of the temple as 'these things' or as 'this', whereas he talks about the end of the world as 'those things' or as 'that'. If you can imagine sitting on the Mount of Olives you can hear him saying 'this', pointing to the temple, will happen in such and such a way and you will know when it is going to happen. But of 'that', the end of the world, I do not know when that will come. So you will find him talking about such things as this: he said, *"**this** generation will certainly not pass away until all these things have happened"* —and, of course, he was right, it happened within forty years. There were people alive when Jesus said it who saw the temple pulled down stone by stone. But then he said, *"No-one knows about **that** day or hour, not even the angels in heaven, nor the Son, but only the Father"* (Mark 13:32, *NIV*). Once you have got the clue like that the whole chapter becomes quite straightforward and understandable. It is because he is talking about two events, and because also he jumps from one to the other, that so many people have got so confused.

Why did he talk about them like that, instead of dealing with it simply? I nearly wrote, 'as I would'! Because he had much more understanding than I have, and he knew what he was doing, and what he was doing was this: he was indicating that even though these are two separate events, and there will be a gap of time in between them, *this* one is very like *that* one; the same kind of catastrophe that will hit this *city* will one day hit the *world*. And, in fact, if you study this one you will be able to know quite a lot about that one, and the same kind of thing that happens before this will happen before that. We can see now why he put them together. The two ends are so similar. The end of the temple was so like the end of the world that Jesus could see them both at the same time. They had the same character, the same kind of signs would be the beginning of both.

Let us go back to the question of the disciples. They asked Jesus to tell them about the future. Of course, it is amazing that Jesus knew; no-one else knows what the future holds; no-one else could have predicted that temple would be taken down stone by stone within a generation, for only God knows the future like that. But what Jesus does is to spend some time speaking to them about the general future in the valleys — the valley before the first event and the valley before the second event. He describes the kind of life they will live before the end comes — either of the ends. We now look at this.

The general picture is rather depressing. This is no bed of roses. Jesus is so honest with them and he lets them know that they are going to have a tough time. There are three things that he tells them. First of all, their minds are going to be very disturbed by false prophets, with whom they are going to have a very difficult time, and false Christs misleading people, who do not come with the truth. It is very interesting that just before AD 70, when the Romans were pressing very hard on the little land of Israel, man after man stood up and said, 'I am the Christ, I will save you', and there was a rash of false messiahs just before the end. One of the best known ones, who was crucified by the Romans, was a man called Bar Kochba. He said, 'I am the Christ, I'll get you out of this trouble' — and they were so desperate and so afraid that they believed him. Jesus warned them so that when it happened their minds would not be disturbed. I believe that before the second end, the end of the world, the same thing will happen: there will be an increase in people making messianic claims. So Jesus warns that when somebody claims to be the Christ we are not to believe it. I am afraid we are already seeing something of this, and we have heard in our lifetime of people who have claimed to be the messiah, and we will hear more and more. It happens before the end, and people's minds can be deceived. Jesus said that if possible they will even try and deceive God's chosen people. It happened before the end of Jerusalem, it will happen before the end of the world, and we must not believe such people.

How do we know? If somebody says, 'Come to Manchester, the messiah is there, he has come', how do we know that is not true? The answer is that when Jesus actually comes, every Christian in the world will know it immediately. We will not need anybody to say, 'Catch the train to Manchester, he has come'! We shall all know as soon as Jesus has come back, and we are not to believe anyone who tells us that Christ has come. It might be that in our lifetime this kind of rash of false prophets and messiahs could break out. If it does then it could make us very excited because it means the end is near. But if it does our minds must not be deceived, and we must not start running after false people. Jesus even said that they will perform miracles to try and prove that they are the Christ; don't believe them, the devil can do miracles as well.

Second, Jesus tells them not to be alarmed. They will be disturbed by frequent perils, and he lists some. He warns them that they will hear of wars and rumours of wars, and that is precisely what happened before the end of the temple. There was a rash of rumours of war and petty outbreaks of war, and people thought the Roman empire was being swallowed up in war. Jesus also warned them they would hear of widespread famines. Their hearts must not be disturbed by these. He is not saying you must not feed the hungry, he is teaching that you must not let your hearts be taken away from your faith because of famines. He was predicting that towards the end of history there would be increasing famines — and that is something that is coming true. He added earthquakes.

These were precisely the things that happened before the end of the temple, and will likewise happen before the end of the world. He said, 'do not be alarmed' and this is the same word that he was to use one night later. I know of many people who are very troubled by such things, so troubled that they feel they cannot believe in a good God, so troubled that they believe the world is not heading for the fulfilment of God's purpose. But Jesus told you beforehand so that you will not be troubled. It does not mean that you will not be concerned, it means you will not be thrown off balance by them; those things are going to happen.

Thirdly, he taught that your will is going to be under severe pressure because of fierce persecution. The nearer you get to the end, either of Jerusalem or of the end of the world, the more fierce the persecution of Christian believers becomes.

Here, then, are three very severe tests. Peter, James, Andrew and John went through all this before the end of the temple. Christians who are alive when the end of history comes will likewise go through these three pressures. See what kinds of persecution Jesus mentions: religious persecution (the elders, the synagogue); political persecution (kings and rulers); domestic persecution (your own family may be against you and betray you), and universal persecution, because you will be hated by all men. In other words, it will come at you from every angle. He was warning them, and I am afraid it all came true in the Acts of the Apostles, which covers the period up to the end of the temple. But you can be quite sure that in all this pressure the end will not come yet. Or, to put it in very simple English, however bad all this gets you will know absolutely certainly that this is not the end, by one thing: *". . . the gospel must first be preached to all nations"*. That is why I know the end could not come tomorrow. The gospel has not yet been preached to all the nations. One of the things that will tell us that history is drawing nearer to its conclusion is when every nation, every kindred, every tribe, every tongue has heard the gospel of Jesus — then we will know that it could happen.

Then Jesus gives a word of encouragement – it is not a word of judgement: *". . . he who stands firm to the end will be saved."* As we persevere, the end is not bitter but glorious.

Now let us return to what we were looking at in the beginning, the two events: the end of the temple in AD 70; and the end of the world. Just as we are coming up to each, this is the kind of thing that we will go through. Forewarned is forearmed, and all Christians need to have these things clear, so that if they should be alive when this pressure comes then they will realise what it is all about and will not be thrown off balance but will endure to the end. It happened most certainly in that period, and it will certainly happen again. There is a parallel between the two events.

We take the first in AD 70 — the end of Israel. We know that God had not finished with them finally, of course. Our Lord knew perfectly well it was going to happen; it was inevitable because God could no longer protect them. They would be at the mercy of their conquerors from now on. There would be dreadful suffering, even for women and children. And he did not tell the Christians to pray that it would not happen because it had to, he told them instead to pray that it would not take place in winter, and it did not, which means that Christians must have prayed hard. That would reduce the suffering that must come. He was especially thinking of the children and of the women who were expecting children when he said this. What was going to happen? What did Jesus see? He said, *"If the Lord had not cut short those days, no-one would survive. But for the sake of the elect, whom he has chosen, he has shortened them"* (Mark 13:20, *NIV*), and we know of course that many did indeed survive. What will be the sign that this is about to happen? Jesus now said something that was a kind of clue, something that only certain people would understand. *"When you see the abomination that causes desolation standing where it does not belong. . . ."* It is very puzzling, and Mark adds the words *let the reader understand*. There is a dramatic piece of history behind that, because Mark's Gospel was written between AD 60 and AD 64 and he was communicating this: read this and understand what I am saying; I am giving you the sign that this is going to happen. Speaking of this time, Jesus says, *"then let those who are in Judea flee to the mountains. Let no-one on the roof of his house go down or enter the house to take anything out. Let no-one in the field go back to get his cloak"* (Mark 13:14b, *NIV*). When they see that sign they are to get out of Jerusalem, otherwise they will go down with the temple. We are not talking about fancy ideas now. Did you know that thousands of people were saved from the fall of Jerusalem because they understood what was written in Mark's Gospel? If they had not remembered our Lord's words and got out when this happened they would not have survived. If the Jews had believed what the Christians had said, they could have been saved too, but they would not listen, and because Jesus had said it they would not believe it. It is a most dramatic story. We now look at what it means.

This phrase 'the abomination that causes desolation' is a phrase that comes from the book of Daniel where it occurs three times. Anybody who knows their Old Testament will understand the New, and the clue to this phrase lies in the Old Testament. Daniel was a man who suffered under foreign powers. We read of this 'abomination of desolation', or the abominating sacrilege, or desolating sacrilege. Sacrilege is the most apt word because it means something that is absolutely defying God, something that you can see that is set up in the wrong place. Years before, this thing had come true once, when the Greeks came into Jerusalem. When the Greeks came into the temple — in the time of Judas Maccabeus — they put on the very altar of the temple a statue of a Greek god, a graven image standing on the altar of the God who had forbidden graven images. They then killed and sacrificed a pig on the altar, an unclean animal in the Old Testament that God had forbidden them to bring as a sacrifice. Here was something absolutely abominable, sacrilege in the place where it ought not to be. So they would understand this only too well.

In fact, the sign was that the Romans marched on Jerusalem, and they brought with them their gods, their idols, their statues. It was quite clear to everybody they had every intention of putting them in the temple and of standing them where they ought not to be. But the interesting thing is that when the Romans came to Jerusalem they gave them a few weeks grace to surrender. For that time they did not interfere with traffic in and out of the city, they surrounded the city with their eagles, with their statues, and they waited. As soon as they saw that sign, and the things they were bringing to put in the temple, every Christian in Jerusalem got out. They told the Jews to get out too, but the interesting thing is that the Jews came in for miles around because they thought Jerusalem was safe. But the Christians did not even stop to pack. The Christians went over the Jordan river, to a town called Pella. Jesus had told them what to expect; they had seen the sign coming; they had seen the sacrilegious idols on their way — and they left. When Jerusalem fell, not a single Christian died, and not a single Jew need have died if they had believed in Jesus, and had believed that he spoke the truth — but they were determined not to believe a word that Jesus said; they thought of Jerusalem as a safe place and piled into it. What happened then is most terrible reading: 97,000 Jews were taken prisoner as slaves to Rome, 1,100,000 perished as the city fell. They either died by the sword or by starvation. Before they died many of them were reduced to the eating dung, sewage, cooking their own shoes and even their own children.

Jesus had said that the temple would be pulled down in that generation. He could see it coming and he gave them the sign of its coming, so that when they saw the sign they would know what to do. He gave them the time and the answer was soon, in your lifetime (see Mark 13:30). He also told them what to do: to watch and to flee. Those who did what he said were ready for the end when it came, and the Christian church was saved because they believed that Jesus knew the future and had told them the right thing. Within what was left of Jerusalem, false messiah after false messiah claimed to be able to get them out of trouble and the Jews were running around from one false messiah to another during those last terrible days.

Now we look at what Jesus said about the end of the world. The interesting thing is he says exactly the same type of thing about that. First of all, he said that you will see signs. Certain things will happen which you will notice. You will see things happening in the sky. You will see things happen to the sun, the moon and the stars. We can see when the switch comes. The sun will go out (it did on Good Friday of course, but it will go out at the end of the world; the moon will go out and the stars will fall; see Mark 13:24). These will be universal signs and everybody will see them. If somebody says, 'Christ has come and he's in Timbuktu', you can say, 'Well, the sun is still shining, it can't be him'. So he gave them these signs which have not come yet, of course. On the Day of Pentecost Peter quoted this. He said that the sun will be darkened and the moon turned to blood. That is the first sign.

Secondly, Jesus says, *"At that time men will see the Son of Man coming in clouds with great power and glory"* (Mark 13:26, *NIV*). That is the second sign, that you see him coming. I do not know how we shall all see him coming but I believe he can arrange that perfectly well.

The third thing will be the gathering of his elect, or his chosen. There is going to be a lot of travelling all at once. We shall not meet him on earth for there is really no place on earth that would be big enough for us all to see him at once, so we are told in the scripture that we shall meet him in the air — not on the ground. This, to me, is a most exciting thing to look forward to. Think of all his people coming from all over the world to meet him. What a meeting that is going to be! Frankly, those signs will be enough to tell us that something — the biggest thing of all — is happening.

What about the time? When will this take place? Jesus had indicated that the fall of Jerusalem would occur soon, before the end of the generation. This time he taught that only the Father knew the day and hour (see Mark 13:32). Reading church history I am impressed with the fact that every time someone has tried to date the Second Coming of Christ they have led people astray. What is Jesus' advice, since we do not know? In the first case it was to watch and *flee*; his advice in this case is to watch and *pray*. What are we to watch for? Firstly, we are to watch for signs. This does not mean that we walk around the high street looking up into the sky all day. A number of other signs are given to us in scripture, the kinds of things going on around us that you can read in your newspaper and in other media. We are to watch these things without panicking and without getting silly. Certain things are happening in our world that are so clearly parallel to what happened before Jerusalem fell that I am feeling that I am much nearer than my grandfather was — beyond that I will not go. The one thing I can predict is this: Jesus Christ is coming back, those who are dead will be the first to meet him, and we shall not be far behind. We can read all about it in 1 Thessalonians 4, and it is very exciting. We are to watch world trends and what is happening around us. One thing that I think is significant that we need to be watching is the spread of violence as a means of settling arguments, the resort to physical force in so many areas of the world.

Then Jesus told a story, and he said, *"Now learn this lesson from the fig tree: As soon as its twigs get tender and its leaves come out, you know that summer is near. Even so, when you see these things happening, you know that it is near, right at the door"* (Mark 13:28f., *NIV*). If you have a garden I am sure you notice the changes to the trees, especially when the buds come out each year. For 'the fig tree' read whatever trees you have in your garden. Jesus tells us that we can look out at our 'fig tree' and we can see that something is coming, something is about to happen soon. Why then can we not look out on the world and see that something is happening — something is coming soon, something is getting nearer — and get excited about it? He tells us to watch.

Why pray? Because you realise that the nearer we get to such events, the more the pressure on Christians grows. The pressure on our minds from false teaching, the pressure on our hearts from world disasters — and it is an awful pressure on your heart — the pressure on your will from persecution and from those who dislike you and even hate you because you belong to Christ. Because of these pressures we need to pray.

Jesus finished up by telling us a story about a man who went on a long journey, and he told the porter at the door of his mansion to get ready to open the gate whenever he saw him return. He did not say when he was returning, so the porter did not know whether it would be at night, the middle of the night, the middle of the day or in the morning. What could he do? All he could do was to be ready at any moment, to be ready all the time, so that if the man did come he would not need to change anything, he would not need to rush out of bed, he would just go on doing what he was doing. If we are doing the right things then we do not need to make any change; if we are doing the wrong things then we do.

Years later, some believers in Thessalonica would give up their jobs in case the Lord came back again, which was absolutely unbalanced and not right at all. We are to be found doing what he commanded us to do; we are to be found watchful. This does not mean that we should not go to bed and sleep, it does mean that we should go to bed remembering that one day the darkness will come, not because it is night but because Jesus is on his way, bringing the light of the glory of God to this old world.

All the disciples did was say to Jesus 'What massive stones! What magnificent buildings!' — and they got so much in reply! Why did Jesus take all this time to tell them about the end of the world as well as the end of Jerusalem? For precisely this reason: the more wonderful you think the things are that men build on earth, the more you are tempted to forget that it is all going one day. You look at the skyscrapers and the buildings people are putting up today in London and other major cities, and you think they are building as if they will be here for a thousand years. We need the constant reminder that this world is passing away, and everything that belongs to it is passing away; you have a different attitude to the world, which does not mean that you ignore it or that you do not contribute to it.

Perhaps I can illustrate this point like this. When I was pastor of one particular church we made plans to move to a new location, but we still had two years before we moved out. Therefore, we decided to redecorate the old building and make it nice, but we also decided not to spent too much on it because it was passing away quite soon. Have you got the balance? Because it was only temporary and we were only going to be in it for two years we needed to have a right attitude towards it. We said, 'Not too much. We're here for the time being, we'll make it useful and presentable for the time being, but are not going to kid ourselves that we are here forever.' When we got our new building the same attitude needed to prevail, because that building is certainly going to be pulled down too one day and it is going to be dissolved and finished with — so we were just building a temporary resting place for the church. If you keep this attitude you keep watching the right things — you watch the signs of God, not the achievements of men, and you look for the coming of Christ. That I think is something that every real Christian is constantly thinking about: Jesus is coming back. We are watching the world and we are seeing how it is all drifting. It is not drifting nowhere, it is drifting into crisis, it is drifting to a climax; it is moving to what a poet called 'the one far off divine event to which the whole creation moves'; it is all moving up to the moment when the trumpet sounds and Jesus descends from the sky and we meet him. It is going to be a great moment, and so Jesus took the opportunity of the disciples' comment to tell them there is going to be an end of the temple and there is going to be an end of the world. He wanted to tell them and us all we need to know about both so that we will be ready for both. Jesus' last word in the chapter is, *"What I say to you, I say to everyone: 'Watch!'"* (Mark 13:37, *NIV*), and that is what we ought to be doing.

16

ANOINTING AND BETRAYAL
14:1 – 11

Two things strike me as I read through this chapter. The first is how many practical, material things come into this account: a jar of perfume, a loaf of bread, a cup of wine, a sword. Each of these very ordinary things takes on a tremendous meaning because Christ had something to do with it. There is a profound lesson here before we go any further: very ordinary, everyday things become quite extraordinary when they are related to Jesus Christ. It is particularly striking that at each of the points at which something happened, one or more of the disciples did the wrong thing. It is humbling to look at those twelve men and see them doing the kind of thing that I might have done: the wrong thing, the weak thing, the cowardly thing. This is why we must study this chapter, so that we come to the Lord's table as penitent disciples, as those who are ready to say, 'Lord, if we had followed you two thousand years ago we would have let you down just as much as they did; and, Lord, we need your help just as they needed it.' The amazing thing is that though Jesus knew they were so weak he still kept on with them; they were his disciples.

The chapter opens with a note about the Feast that was

happening. It was a double Feast. It was the Feast of the Passover, going back through many centuries — and still to this day, thousands of years later, the Orthodox Jewish family celebrates the Passover. It is the Feast when they thank God for bringing them out of Egypt, out of slavery into freedom and into his service. I remember that in the road in which I was brought up, about four doors away a Jewish family lived. Every Easter we naughty children used to gather outside the house to watch them sprinkle the doorposts with blood. We thought it was an extraordinary thing to do, and I am afraid in our ignorance and childishness we used to laugh at this and mock it. But they were doing something that had been done every single year for centuries. The Passover is the greatest time in the Jewish calendar.

The gathering of some two million Jews around Jerusalem for the Passover ensured, of course, that our Lord's death would be public, known by as many people as possible. Indeed, it was the largest gathering of people in the then known world, so it certainly ensured that it would be a public death. But there was a much deeper reason for our Lord coming to die at the time of Passover. We get the impression that Jesus decided when to die, how to die and where to die, so that it might have this meaning. The meaning was that he was going to have another Passover, another exodus. As God had brought people out of slavery, he was going to bring them out of sin. As God brought them out with the blood of a physical animal, a lamb, he was now going to bring people out with the blood of another Lamb — himself, and the whole thing takes on deep meaning. The meal that we have at communion virtually was the Passover for the disciples that year. For Christians it has replaced the Passover; this is now our meal of remembrance, and what we do at the Lord's Supper (or communion service) has been done for two thousand years. It is much more meaningful even than the Jewish Passover. One of the texts in the New Testament which frequently comes back to me at Easter is this: 'Christ our Passover lamb has been sacrificed' (1 Corinthians 5:7b). That is why we come together in this way. A Jew would understand our doing this, though he would say there are some things missing from the table. There are the bitter herbs missing and the shank bone and a number of other things: the lettuce, the parsley, the egg. But we would say that we do not need all those things, we just need two things: bread and wine. They would have had those two things, and our Lord simply used the bread and the wine that was already there prepared for the Passover, to give Christians their memorial meal.

This then is the setting, and it is the lull before the storm. But what we are then told takes place not in Jerusalem but in Bethany, the little village just over the top of the Mount of Olives, out of sight of Jerusalem and out of the reach of the temple police. Every night, Jesus retired to Bethany. This is why they could not arrest him. During the day he was with the crowd the whole time and they did not dare to arrest him, fearing that the crowd would riot if they dared to touch such a popular teacher. Every night, when they looked for him and asked where he was staying, nobody knew. He slipped out to Bethany. The reason why Judas could betray him was so simple. Jesus said that they were going to stay in the city that night, and Judas saw his opportunity. That was why he was needed. The temple priests and the police needed to know when they could lay their hands on him privately, quietly. I once read about events in another part of the world that the secret police of that country always arrest somebody in the middle of the night because they know that they could not avoid public riots if they arrested people during the day. This is precisely what happened then — it has a modern ring.

So Jesus is in Bethany one evening, the last evening he is going to spend out of the city, and they are having a meal in the house of a man who is a leper. I wonder if that means that Jesus had healed him, because normally he would not have been able to eat with others. Maybe he was one of the lepers Jesus cleansed. They are sitting at the table and Mary brings the perfume. Here we have the first physical object that becomes so meaningful in this chapter. It was certainly a costly thing and it may have been an heirloom. If you are interested in the value of it, it was worth about a year's wages. A denarius was one day's wage and it was said to be 300 denarii worth of costly perfume. It would be kept in the bottom drawer, not for a wedding but for a person's funeral. In those days, if you could afford it, you bought some very costly perfume and you put it away for your funeral, for the anointing of your body. That was the only justification for using such an expensive thing. (Of course, it is so often the case that at a funeral we do not count the expense. I remember an undertaker telling me many years ago that he had arranged a funeral in which he estimated that £1,000 worth of flowers had been sent — it was a very large and prominent funeral.) So down in Mary's bottom drawer was this costly jar of perfume, kept for her own funeral, or perhaps her mother's funeral or her brother's. She brought this into the house. It was the custom to anoint the guest with a few drops of perfume when they came in. We would show someone to the cloakroom or ask them if they would like to wash; they would anoint them with a few drops of perfume — this was normal hospitality. But to use all of this was scandalous, and she came in and smashed the jar, which meant that it would never be used again. Then, scooping up the perfume, which must have filled the room with a powerful scent, she just poured it onto our Lord. It was a most amazing and moving act. And the commercial attitude of others was immediately revealed. Here we learn that others than Judas criticised her. *"Why this waste of perfume? It could have been sold for more than a year's wages and the money given to the poor." And they rebuked her harshly* (Mark 14:4f., *NIV*). This is sometimes how worldly people argue. I have on occasions heard this argument used about erecting a place of worship at considerable cost, and it may or may not be valid in that case. But here the valuable perfume was used rightly, yet they criticised her. They still had not learned the lesson of the widow's mite, and the lesson is when someone gives something you should not ask about the value of the gift but of what it meant to the giver. If they had stopped to ask why she had done this thing they would have understood and approved. I notice that it was the men who criticised her — I think the women would have understood.

Jesus said four things about her act. Firstly, he said it was a beautiful act. The nearest word in the English language to the word used is the word 'bonny'. It does not just mean something good, it means something beautiful, a most attractive act, a lovely act.

Secondly, he made it clear that she had done a very opportune thing: she had seized an opportunity that she would not have again. She could either have done this now or never. She saw an opportunity to do something that was unique — a once in a lifetime act. All of us have had opportunities to do something and, alas, some of us have missed those opportunities and wished, 'If only I had done that' —particularly when the opportunity was in connection with someone who died shortly afterwards. When anyone dies there is often some relative who wishes they had just taken the opportunity to do something. I remember a poor lady dying, and when she died and the news got around, a lot of her friends and relatives sent flowers, but somebody at the funeral with rare discernment said to me, 'Oh, if only they had sent her some flowers before she died.' I suppose we all have those moments when we say, 'Oh, if I had only known they were going I would have seized that opportunity, I would have done that thing.' Mary was seizing an opportunity to do something that she could never have done again, nor could anyone else have done. So Jesus told them not to blame her.

Thirdly, he was pointing out that she had done a most discerning thing, and here he points out the real meaning of the act. This woman, alone of all those in that room, knew first that he was going to die very soon, and second that no-one would have an opportunity of anointing his body as was the normal custom after death. She knew this, and how she knew it I do not know. If it was Mary (and it seems to be, as again from another Gospel we have this information), I guess it was because she had sat at his feet and listened to what he had to say, so she knew. But Jesus said, *"She did what she could. She poured perfume on my body beforehand to prepare for my burial"* (Mark 14:8, *NIV*). She was the one who knew that he was going to die and there would be no opportunity to anoint his body.

Normally when a criminal was executed on a cross his relatives were not allowed to bury the body. His body was thrown onto the rubbish heap of the valley of Gehenna on the south side of Jerusalem. So Mary must have seen that he was going to die a criminal's death and his body would be discarded and would not receive proper burial. As we shall see in the next chapter it was only because a man went and begged the Roman governor for the body that there was a burial, otherwise there would never have been one. This woman saw that here this man, at the age of thirty-three, whom she loved more than any other, was going to die so soon and in such a terrible way that there would be no proper funeral for him. She understood; it was a discerning act and Jesus asked them why they were criticising her. If she had done it in three days' time none of them would have criticised her, nobody would have criticised an expenditure of this kind on a dead body, but she had done it on a live body and that was why she was reproached.

Fourthly, Jesus told them that she had done a memorable act, and he predicted then that wherever the gospel was preached people would hear about this woman — and here we are thinking about her. This was a lovely thing to do, it was an opportune thing to do, it was a discerning thing to do and it was a memorable thing to do, so it should not have been criticised.

We step straight from this story into something terrible. I don't quite know the right word to use, so contradictory is it, such a contrast: a lovely woman doing a generous thing, to a dreadful man doing a greedy thing —the contrast is appalling. Here is the incident. Because he realises that

Jesus has virtually announced his forthcoming death, he has now seen what Mary had seen. One disciple now sees that Jesus is willing to die. Judas is going to cash in on this, getting out of the remaining situation as much money as he can lay his hands on. He backed Jesus thinking it was going to be wonderful, that he would be in a wealthy, prospering kingdom, and now he realises that even Jesus is going to let them kill him. So what can he, Judas, get out of it? This man can only think of going to betray Jesus and making some hard cash out of the betrayal.

It became fashionable in the twentieth century to try to whitewash Judas. In fact, there is a craze to try and turn the Gospel story upside-down. Have you noticed this? Newspaper articles, paperback booklets, everybody is on the bandwagon now. Why do people want to whitewash Judas? Why do they want to say that it wasn't the money, that really he was a good chap and he was just trying to force Jesus' hand and get things moving? Because Judas reminds us too much of ourselves, that is why. Because there is the same kind of covetousness and greed in us that was in him, and we do not like it. Judas is a mirror, so we try to smash the mirror. But the Bible is quite clear that the one reason why Judas did it was because he loved money. We know this from the earliest days. Indeed, away up in Galilee Jesus had sadly said to the twelve, *"One of you is a devil."* Judas was the treasurer, and he was dipping his hand in the money bag for himself quite early on. It was Judas who pointed out that they could have had a year's wages in the fund if that perfume had been sold. I have a feeling that he was already thinking of how much cash he could slip out. Here was Judas, and for hard cash he sold his Lord.

A thought strikes me at this point. What would those priests think of the followers of Jesus after that? They would say, 'You can buy any of them. Grease their palms enough and you can buy them out.' We notice that each time Judas's name is mentioned in this chapter, immediately after his name comes the phrase 'one of the twelve'. Here is a man who has lived with Jesus for three years, yet still he can be so greedy that he can do this. It is an amazing and wonderful story, terrible though it is. How can a man be as close to Jesus as that and not get rid of such covetousness? Well, how can *we*? It is the same problem.

Here is Judas, and he goes to the priests and agrees to sell our Lord for the price of a slave. In those days if you could buy a slave you were definitely 'one up'. If you wanted to move up the social scale a bit, the status symbol was to say, 'I have a slave now, you know', as you might talk about a swimming pool in the garden nowadays. Judas sold our Lord for the price of a status symbol that would move him up the social scale. Of course he more than regretted it later. Judas, like Mary, has been preached about in the whole world; wherever the gospel has gone, Judas's name has been remembered. What would we rather be remembered for: our generosity or our greed; our sympathy towards the Lord Jesus and understanding of his death or our hardness and callous attitude to it?

17

INDOORS AND OUTDOORS
14:12–52

Now the scene moves to Jerusalem and events begin to move rapidly towards their climax. The whole thing is building up to a terrible denouement. Let us look into the upper room. Again I am struck with the fact that throughout the whole of this last week our Lord is the master of the situation —he has planned it, he controls it, he decides when, how and where everything happens. He has made the arrangements for the upper room and the Last Supper. At some time he has arranged the use of the upper room. He had even given a secret sign to find the room. Why these elaborate and secret precautions? Why a man carrying a pitcher of water on his head, which only women would normally do? It is rather like a man walking down the road with a woman's umbrella. Why such a secret sign? Why did he not tell the disciples exactly where they were going? Judas must not know where the upper room is. Our Lord must have one last evening with them, so he sends two disciples to meet the man with the pitcher of water, who will show them the upper room. So Judas still does not know Jesus' plans. Our Lord is controlling and timing the whole thing perfectly, so that when the time has come for him to give himself up he is able to say to Judas: what you have to do, do quickly.

So we come to the upper room. There are couches and a table, a basin full of water, and a towel for washing their feet, but no servant to do it — we know who did it in the end and who was reluctant to do it. There they are for the meal.

Now comes one of the most terrible things that Jesus ever said. During the middle of the meal he says, *"one of you will betray me — one who is eating with me"* (Mark 14:18, *NIV*). The amazing thing is that he had already said five times that he was going to be crucified, and the disciples were puzzled but not upset. But as soon as he states that one of them is going to betray him they get terribly upset. They begin to be sorrowful. Is is not astonishing that they are not sorry for him? There is no word of their sorrow about the cross right until this point, but as soon as he tells them that one of them is going to be involved, that is when they immediately begin to say, 'Surely not I?' One could put two interpretations on that phrase. If you were going to be kind and generous to the apostles you would say that each of them was prepared to examine his own heart. If we were to be more realistic, I think each of them knew perfectly well that they were capable of doing it. Immediately they all wanted to be let off the hook quickly. They wanted Jesus to say, 'No, it's not you', but he did not say that to any of them — he left them thinking that way. He just said that it was someone who was going to take the bread with him. Fancy Judas being able to go through with that. This last appeal of our Lord to him, ". . . *one who is eating with me"* said Jesus, and he handed the bread to them all — how could Judas sit there and accept all that? He must have had a heart of granite by this time, his feelings must have been so scarred that they were dead. But he took the bread. Then Jesus did the lovely thing that we do at communion, even in spite of the fact that one of them would betray him. That one was fully responsible for his act — we must not start blaming predestination or anything — and he said of that one, *"It would be better for him if he had not been born."* Jesus, knowing all that, knowing that the disciples would all run away, knowing that there was not one of them he could trust during the next twenty-four hours, took bread and broke it, and he took the cup and made them drink. The communion service is so full of meaning.

We notice five things about this simple memorial meal. First of all, he did not eat and drink, he gave them to eat; he gave them to drink, he did not. He told them he would not be eating and drinking with them again until the kingdom came. When we take communion, Jesus is not eating and drinking with us, although he is spiritually present. One day he will eat and drink with us again.

Secondly, notice they had to partake, as if he was saying my broken body and my shed blood is no use unless you accept it for yourselves. It is still true to this day that our Lord's death on the cross cannot save a soul until they will accept it for themselves. So he did not just take a loaf of bread and break it and say there, that's my body broken, he said, *"Take eat; this is my body"* — they were to take it into themselves otherwise it was of no use.

Thirdly, the bread and the wine were symbols. There was nothing magic about them, and Jesus' real body and blood were there before their eyes, so that there should never have arisen in the course of Christian history the confusion between the bread and the wine and his body and the blood — they are symbols, emblems, no more. His physical body and blood were there for them to see. You cannot confuse something on the table with something on the chair beside it.

Fourthly, this was the new covenant —the old one had been sealed in blood in the broken body of a lamb and in the shed blood of the lamb. Now a new covenant was to be sealed, a new relationship between God and men sealed in the body and blood of Jesus.

Fifthly, it had a forward look. Jesus said, *"I tell you the truth, I will not drink again of the fruit of the vine until that day when I drink it anew in the kingdom of God"* (Mark 14:25, *NIV*). So this meal looks back to the upper room and forward to heaven, back to the Last Supper and forward to the wedding breakfast, and it links the two meals.

Now Jesus foretells his death again and he adds to it the fact that when he is killed they will run for their lives —and they will not have any of it. It is strange how they have changed. They had been saying earlier, 'Surely not I?' (will betray you), now they were denying that they would ever desert him. Peter, voluble as ever, comes out with a most incredible slur on the other eleven, declaring in front of them (and they would not have liked him for this): *"Even if all fall away, I will not."* He is told that he would disown Jesus three times. This betrayal would be worse than the others —they were just going to run, but Peter would swear and deny knowing him. Peter has been remembered for what he did that night more than the others. Mary has been remembered, Judas has been remembered — and Peter has been remembered for his denial.

Jesus said to them: *"But after I have risen, I will go ahead of you into Galilee"* (Mark 14:28, *NIV*). Galilee is so lovely compared with the hot, noisy, smelly streets of Jerusalem that one can understand their hearts leaping when he said that. To get back to the good old days in Galilee, back to the sunshine, the lake and the open air, without these scheming enemies in back streets and in the shadows. They would have a new start afterwards, and of course Jesus did what he said, though they didn't believe it yet.

Now the scene switches to the Garden of Gethsemane. They are going to spend the night on the Mount of Olives, and Judas has known this — he has informed the chief priests of their opportunity to arrest Jesus. There is a delay of about two hours while they make preparations for the arrest and the trial, but soon they will be coming. Our Lord's time is now limited to just an hour or two. They go into a garden and Jesus wants to make sure that he has time and quietness to pray, so he asks the first few disciples to stay at the gate. He tells Peter, James and John, to come a bit nearer; then he goes a little further still —two lines of defence to secure his prayer time. Luke tells us that Jesus now begins to sweat drops of blood. The words used in the Bible indicate the most terrible anguish of spirit, something that he just could not face. It was not death from which he shrank. What was it? It was worse than death. What could be worse than death?

Twenty times in the Bible the word 'cup' is used metaphorically — not a literal, physical cup, but some experience that a person has to go through. It is expressed in terms of a cup that they must drink. Out of those twenty times, on seventeen of the occasions it is a dreadful cup to drink, the cup of God's anger against sin and an experience of being cut off from him. All through the scriptures this is what the cup means when it is used in a metaphorical sense. Do you realise that Jesus had never been separated from his Father? I know that he had left heaven, but he was still with his Father. He could talk to him at any time. He was always in direct communication. As the President of the United States, wherever he goes, is always in direct communication with the White House, our Lord, wherever he went, was always in direct communication with his Father. He had never known what it was to be away from God. We who have been estranged from God to a degree cannot understand what it would be like for Jesus to have been in perfect communion with his Father and to face not having that. I do not think we can realise what it would have been like. I do not think that anybody can fully realise what hell will be like because there is no hell on earth. I have heard so many people say you make your own hell, and hell is what you go through on earth — but nobody has been in hell yet, because nobody is completely cut off from God yet. But Jesus knew that if he was going to drink this cup what it would mean would be that for the first time in all eternity Father and Son would be separated. *"Abba, Father,"* he said, *"everything is possible for you. Take this cup from me"* (Mark 14:36, *NIV*). Jesus even used that intimate term in his prayer which is remembered and written down here: Abba, 'Dad' — that is what it means. Then the battle is won and he says, *"Yet not what I will, but what you will"* (Mark 14:36, *NIV*). Within hours he was going to cry out, *"My God, my God, why have you forsaken me?"* (Mark 15:34, *NIV*) Everybody else has gone, now you have gone. He was drinking the cup when he cried that. That is what hell is like — to be forsaken by God — and it is dark, thirsty and lonely. You understand the sufferings of Christ when you understand that on the cross for those few hours the Son of God was in the hell of experiencing separation from the Father. That is why he shrank. Three times he fought this battle, and each time he came back to the disciples and they were asleep. If you have ever taken part in an all-night prayer meeting you will know the truth of the words: the spirit is willing but the flesh is weak. You would love to see it through, but by about two in the morning you are beginning to feel heavy, and then you can get your second wind.

A minister friend of mine held a rather interesting Good Friday service. He announced, 'For one hour there will be complete silence in the church.' Everybody came and they sat in complete silence for one hour. It was the first time most of them had ever been silent for so long. One lady came to the minister afterwards and said to him, 'Well, I don't think I got much out of it.' He replied, 'What kind of thoughts passed through your mind?' 'Well,' she said, 'it's funny but I could only think of one text and I couldn't get rid of it, it just kept going through my mind. I really didn't think of anything else.' And he asked, 'What was the text?' She replied, 'It was the text, *"Could you not watch with me one hour?"'* The minister told her, 'Well then, you got a very great deal out of that silence.' How did anybody know what Jesus was praying if all the disciples were asleep? I will tell you the answer shortly.

Now comes the contrast. There were two gardens — the garden of Eden and the garden of Gethsemane: the first a garden of disobedience from which a disobedient man went out to die for his sins; and, here, the garden of Gethsemane, a garden of obedience from which one man went out to die for everybody else's sins. Can you see the connection?

Then comes Judas. I do not know how Judas could do it except I know that I could, and I suppose you could too. He used a token of the utmost affection, a kiss. Our Lord must have been horrified at this. How could Judas betray him in that way? Couldn't he just have pointed? How could he use a symbol of affection and friendship to do such a dastardly act? So low can a man sink that tokens become the opposite of that which they were meant to express.

Peter, impetuous as ever, takes a sword and cuts off the ear of a slave. Jesus had to tell him to stop this, and he healed the slave's ear, as we know from another Gospel. We read: *"Am I leading a rebellion," said Jesus, "that you come out with swords and clubs to capture me? Every day I was with you, teaching in the temple courts, and you did not arrest me"* (Mark 14:48 f., *NIV*). He is rebuking those who came to arrest him, accusing them of being cowards. They could have taken him any time in Jerusalem and they did not. The disciples must have felt terribly ashamed of themselves at that point. They all forsook him and fled. James ran, John ran, Peter ran, Thomas ran, they all ran. When it came to the push, when it came to the decisive moment when they could either stay or run and save their lives, they all ran, and so would we. Not one of them was man enough to stay, and nor would we have been. This is human nature; the spirit is willing but the flesh is terribly weak, and self-preservation took over in this moment.

Now comes a most interesting little detail. Hiding behind some trees in that garden was a youth. He had nothing on but a bed sheet. He ran when the others ran. A soldier spotted him and grabbed the sheet, pulling it off him. He ran away naked in the night and that is all we know about this young man. Who was he? We do not know for certain, but we can guess. Putting two and two together we can say it was a young man called John Mark — a man in whose home the early church met, a young man whose home was probably the home used for the upper room and the Last Supper, a young man who, lying awake that night in his bed, heard the disciples go out from the upper room and decided to follow, a young man who hid among the trees and listened breathless to that prayer of our Lord as he sweated drops of blood, someone was there to record it for us — a young man who wrote this Gospel down. It was his way of saying he was there — he does not even name himself. It is as if he just wanted to put something into this Gospel to say that he was involved too. He could never forget that night trying to find his way home without any clothes and trying to get up to his room. He could not forget what he had seen and what he had heard as he was there. John Mark is telling us that he had been to Gethsemane, he had seen it all; they nearly caught him, but he got away. It is as though he is asking: 'Have you been in Gethsemane and seen it all? I have.'

18

TRIAL AND EXECUTION
14:53 – 15:47

Our Lord had two trials, a Jewish and a Roman one, and both of them were rigged. Both of them were rank injustice. Fifteen things about the Jewish trial before the priests were illegal:

1. Jesus was arrested without a charge being made. Even in those days if anyone was arrested they had to be told at the time why they were being arrested, but no charge was laid against Jesus.

2. The arrest was organised by his judges, who thus became accomplices to the arrest.

3. The trial was held at an illegal time. Such trials had to be held during daylight hours and this was held at night.

4. It was held at an illegal place in someone's home and it should have been held in the public law courts.

5. The trial began without a charge.

6. The witnesses for the prosecution had no consistent story, so there was no case.

7. The witnesses who disagreed with each other were not punished for perjury, and the prisoner was not released as he should have been when the witnesses did not agree.

8. The judge became a witness for the prosecution and therefore partial.

9. The judge asked a leading question of the prisoner.

10. The judge condemned him on his own confession.

11. He called no witnesses for the defence and made no examination of our Lord's claim.

12. He condemned the prisoner for speaking the truth by calling him a liar.

13. No vote was taken from the members.

14. A full quorum of the council was not present. Some members were not there.

15. The execution was organised for the same day, not allowing the normal time for a legal appeal to be made against the sentence.

Fifteen things that make the first trial rank injustice — this was judicial murder. The one thing that I would draw from this is that the priests were desperate men. Desperate men do dreadful things, and they were doing dreadful things to our Lord and Saviour Jesus Christ.

Let me underline our Lord's words on which they incriminated him. They asked a direct question, *"Are you the Christ, the Son of the Blessed One?"* (Mark 14:61, *NIV*). And his reply was an astonishing one. He said, *"I am"*, which is the name of God himself, as revealed to Moses. As soon as the high priest heard that, he tore his clothes and said, *"Why do we need any more witnesses? You have heard the blasphemy"* (Mark 14: 63f., *NIV*). They had heard from his own mouth that Jesus claimed to be God. But the high priest never stopped to ask whether it was true. For a man to have said this was seen as being blasphemy, the worst crime in the Jewish book. If any human being had said such a thing he deserved to die straight away, but this was not just a human being speaking, and our Lord was telling the truth. But they rushed through toward the execution. And Jesus added, *". . you will see the Son of Man sitting at the right hand of the Mighty One and coming on the clouds of heaven."* He was claiming to be the fulfilment of one of the predictions in Daniel.

The next incident is out in the courtyard, Peter's denial. It is so human. You and I have done exactly the same thing in the school, in the office. There has been an opportunity when we could have said openly that we belong to Jesus and we flunked it, so let us not throw stones at poor old Peter. But let us notice four things.

First of all, at least he got as far as the courtyard, which the others did not. I am not trying to whitewash him, I am just trying to put it in balance and remind you that at least he followed and at least he was there. But when it came to the push he could not go through with it.

Secondly, he did deny Jesus. Both his face and his speech gave him away, and our face and our speech should give away that we belong to Jesus.

Thirdly, he did weep. It broke this man's heart. Judas could not have wept, except for himself, but Peter wept. It is all in that word. There is something very cleansing about tears, especially when a man weeps over something he has done.

Fourthly, Peter himself must have told this story to John Mark or we would not have it in the Gospel of Mark. So the man who did this was the man who wanted us to know about it, which tells us of his humility. He wanted to encourage us by telling us that he failed and that he let the Lord down, and that the Lord picked him up again, as we learn elsewhere.

We turn to the Roman trial. It is now six o'clock in the

morning. Peter had denied Christ at three in the morning. At three o'clock every morning a Roman bugler blew his trumpet. It was the change of the guard, the end of the first watch of the day (from midnight until three). And it is interesting that the bugle blown at three o'clock was called the 'cock crow'. It may be that this was what our Lord was referring to.

Pilate has had to be dragged from his bed early, and the trial is now shifting from a religious to a political one, and the charges have been changed. The Jews condemned Jesus for blasphemy, but now when they come to Pilate they indicate it is a political crime, not a religious one. Claiming to be the king is a challenge to Roman authority. See how they twist the truth again and again, changing the charge on which Jesus is tried. Pilate would not be interested in blasphemy so they present a political charge.

Pilate tried a number of things to get out of this dilemma and evade what they were trying to get him to do. At least he tried.

First of all, he demanded that the case be re-opened and re-tried, and he demanded to know the charge. He was not going to take their word for it.

Secondly, he could have taken the easy way out and simply rubber-stamped their decision, but instead he examined the prisoner himself, by a direct question — again, incidentally, it was a leading question. Pilate said, *"Are you the king of the Jews?"* and Jesus simply replied, *"Yes, it is as you say."* In other words, they should not be asking him, they should be examining the evidence. You do not ask a defendant, 'Did you do this? Right, you're condemned.' Even if he pleads guilty you must examine the evidence.

Thirdly, Pilate did give Jesus a chance to defend himself, which the others had not done. *He said, "Aren't you going to answer?"* But our Lord would not defend himself.

Fourthly, Pilate passed Jesus to Herod, hoping that that would be a way of getting out of this dilemma, but Herod sent him back again.

Fifthly, Pilate had a brainwave. At every Feast when there were so many hundreds of thousands of Jews in Jerusalem, it was a very tense situation. To keep the crowd happy he always used to give them a sop or favour at this time, and agree to set loose from the prison any prisoner they named, and it kept them reasonably happy. So here was a ready-made prisoner to hand back to them. He asked them, *"Do you want me to release the king of the Jews?"* (Mark 15:9, *NIV*). They were not having any of that, they wanted another man. It is very interesting that the man they asked for was called Jesus Barabbas — the same name. 'Bar' means son and 'abba' means father, so they were saying that they wanted Jesus, son of the father. It could hardly have been more pointed. They were saying this man is called Jesus and says he is Son of the Father; we want another man called Jesus, son of the father — release Barabbas. Barabbas was a political resistance leader, an insurrectionist, and the crowd that welcomed Jesus on Palm Sunday, thinking he was going to fight for them and set them free, are so disappointed with Jesus now because instead of going to tackle the Roman garrison he simply cleansed the temple. That crowd is now saying: we'll have this man; away with that man, he is not going to give us what we want; give us Barabbas, he will do it. It is an amazing choice. So Pilate could not escape that way.

Sixth, he tried to stand there on the steps of his house and ask them why. What crime had Jesus committed? But they shouted all the louder, *"Crucify him!"*

Seventh, he decided to have Jesus flogged to within an inch of his life. That was a very naughty thing for Pilate to do. He had no right to condemn an innocent man to a flogging like that. Again he was trying to give them a sop to buy them off. But they were not going to let him off. Whipping Jesus was not enough for them, they demanded that he be crucified.

In handing over Jesus to be crucified Pilate ensured that for two thousand years at least his name would be forever linked with the death of Jesus. For wherever Christians have recited the Creed they have included one man apart from Jesus, and it is Pilate: he 'suffered under Pontius Pilate'.

Many people ask, 'How could Pilate have come to do such a terrible thing?' The real problem however is precisely the opposite: how could Pilate ever try to get out of it? Why do I say that? Because of Pilate's history. He started life as a slave. He was the first slave ever to be a Roman governor and he was the last, and he was no good at the job. This was a man with a petty mind, a bully. When he came to Palestine in the year AD 26 he did certain things that were the blunders of a bully. For example, he set up a Roman eagle in the temple and caused such a riot that he ended up ordering soldiers to go in dressed in civilian clothes with their swords under their cloaks and kill the rioters. We are told that the blood of Galileans mingled with sacrifices in the temple. That was one major blunder.

Another time, he was building a water supply into Jerusalem, an aqueduct from the pools of Hebron. You can still see it today —a wonderful construction. It cost a lot of money, and Pilate was very short of money, so he thought about how they were getting good collections at the temple at that time, and he decided to borrow a bit from the treasury, only he forgot to tell them that he had borrowed it, and it started another riot. Again he sent Roman soldiers in among the rioters with swords inside cloaks and killed the rioters — again, the act of a bully.

Word of these two blunders had got back to Rome and Caesar sent a warning letter to Pilate. One more blunder like that and he would be finished. Pilate knew that if he were to cause another riot among the Jews, that was the end of Pontius Pilate the governor. So the mystery is not why he let them crucify Christ — you would have expected that, knowing his background — the mystery is why he tried to stop it. The reason is that his wife had a dream, and Romans were superstitious, setting great store by dreams. We learn from Matthew that his wife sent him a warning: *"Don't have anything to do with that innocent man, for I have suffered a great deal today in a dream because of him"* (Matthew 27:19, *NIV*). We can see Pilate's dilemma — caught between Caesar and his wife; caught between the Romans and the Jews; caught in this dilemma: if I let Jesus go it will cause a riot; if I don't, I have betrayed justice, and that dream will certainly bring disaster to me. Disaster faced him both ways, and Pilate, caught in that dilemma, did what every one of us would have done in such a dilemma and tried desperately to save his own skin. Pilate was a man caught between his past and his future. We have been caught like that, and we have behaved like this — maybe without such far-reaching consequences, but haven't we done this? It is instinctive in us to behave this way.

COME WITH ME THROUGH MARK

It was not Jesus who was on trial that morning. The people who were really on trial were Annas and Caiaphas, and Herod, and the soldiers who spat on Jesus, and Pontius Pilate and his wife, and Caesar and everybody else. It seems to me, as I look at this trial, that Jesus stands there as judge and that all the others were on trial that day. The other thing that strikes me is if anyone ever suffered for the sins of others it was Jesus. You can see the sin even of Peter, of Pilate, of the priest, and all that sin seems to come onto him so that the one who suffers for their envy, their cowardice, their cruelty is Jesus, and so he is led away to be crucified.

Two things strike me about this part of the account. One is the restraint of the writer. You could paint a terrible picture of crucifixion, you could play on the emotions, you could really touch the feelings, and yet it is stated in simple fact. There is no attempt to move our feelings, the facts are presented to us. We are not here to pity Jesus, we are not here to dwell on the gory details. I am going to give you some of those to try and help it to be fresh to you, but not in any way to play on your feelings. Jesus said, *"Daughters of Jerusalem, do not weep for me; weep for yourselves and for your children"* (Luke 23:28, *NIV*).

The other thing that strikes me is the restraint of Jesus. I say it reverently, but he could have blasted them off the face of the earth. They spat at him, but with one word he could have just blasted them to eternity, and he is so restrained, he does not lift a finger against them. Let us just go through the five things they did to him.

They scourged him. This was totally unnecessary. A man who was crucified was never made to suffer beforehand — this was totally wrong, but Pilate did it and allowed it. The scourge was a terrible thing. It was a long leather thong with pieces of bone and metal fastened to it at intervals. A man who was flogged with that not only had his back torn to ribbons but he could be blinded very easily, he could be paralysed, or even killed, by a flogging. It explains why Jesus could not carry his cross more than a few hundred yards; he must have been half dead before he ever set out on that journey.

I remember a preacher once saying something which I found to be a remarkable insight. He pointed out that in all the sacrifices of the Old Testament, in all the hundreds and thousands of lambs that had been killed up to that point, not one had been made to suffer — a quick, clean cut with a knife and it was all over; not one lamb offered to God as a sacrifice for sins had ever been tortured first. But when the Lamb of God came, men added to the sufferings that God had ordained for him. God did not ordain this scourging — man added that — and we see that something of the suffering of Jesus was added by the cruelty and malice of human nature.

They also mocked him. It was a bit of barrack room buffoonery and they dressed him up. They took his clothes off him, they plaited that crown of thorns, they put a purple robe on him, and they said, *"Hail, king of the Jews!"* Still to this day in the place where they did it, you can see scratched on the floor the games of the soldiers, and one of the games they played was 'Mock King'. They would cast lots and one of their number would be chosen as 'king', and they would dress him up and make him 'king' for the day and bow down to him and take orders from him. They decided, this day, to laugh at Jesus. I remember going to see a lady who had been offended because of something that happened in church. Somebody had said or done something to her and off she went, she was never going to that church again, and so on. She told me the whole story in detail even though it had happened many years ago. I asked, 'Did they spit at you?' And she replied, 'I should think not.' I said, 'Well, they did spit at Jesus and he said, "forgive them, for they know not what they do."' They spat on the Lord of Glory, they mocked him, the Son of God who made the universe.

They marched Jesus through the streets and made an exhibition of him. Picture the scene. The crime was written on a board, and a soldier walked in front carrying the board so that everybody might learn the lesson of Roman justice. Pilate had wondered what to write on this board because he knew that Jesus was going to be led through the streets and the people would want to know why he was being crucified. So he wrote down in language that everybody could understand — the last burst of courage he ever showed — THE KING OF THE JEWS. So in spite of Jewish protests Pilate's board was carried. Then behind the board came a ring of soldiers, and in the middle of the ring was the prisoner, carrying the heavy wooden beam that was to be the crosspiece of the cross. Jesus could not even carry it.

They did not go straight from Pilate's house to the place of crucifixion. They used to go round and round the town, making the procession as long as possible so that everybody might learn their lesson and never do anything against Roman law. A short way round this tortuous route Jesus fell, and the Roman centurion (regimental sergeant major would be the equivalent rank) was in a dilemma. No Roman would carry a cross, it was beneath his dignity. He knew that he dare not ask a Jew to carry the cross because that would render him unclean for the Passover the next day and would start a riot. What was he to do? He picked on a man because of the colour of his skin, to carry the load for the Europeans. He got hold of Simon and made him carry the beam. It was an African who carried the cross of Jesus up to Golgotha. Reading between the lines in the rest of the New Testament, I can tell you what happened to that man. As he carried that heavy cross, he saw Jesus, his flesh torn to ribbons, staggering along in front, and he must have wondered who it was, becoming interested in him. He began to ask questions, and he became a leading Christian in the first Gentile church at Antioch. Even in Mark's Gospel he is so well known now to the Christians that Mark can say, *A certain man from Cyrene, Simon, the father of Alexander and Rufus . . .* (Mark 15:21, *NIV*). The readers of this Gospel knew this man, this great African Christian, the first African to be a Christian, and he became a Christian because on this day he had to think about the cross of Christ.

Then they crucified Jesus. They came to a hill called Golgotha, which means not the face of the skull but the cranium, the dome. As it happens there is a hill outside the city wall where you can see the sunken hollows of the eyes, the nose and the mouth of a skull carved out by the wind and the erosion of centuries in the cliff. But on that day they came to the top of it which they called the dome, the 'brow' of the hill, so we use the same word. There they crucified him.

They did four things. They gave him wine to get him drunk and to deaden his sensitivity a bit. He would not take it —why not? Partly because he was going to go through with it all, and partly because he had said the previous night, *"I will not drink again of the fruit of the vine until that day when I drink it anew in the kingdom of God"* (Mark 14:25, *NIV*) — he is keeping to his word and he did not take it. It had myrrh in it which would have helped to deaden the pain, but he did not take it. If he had taken it we should never have had the wonderful words from the cross that came, he would have been too drunk to give them. It was normal to make a criminal drunk to help him through the dreadful pain.

They took his clothes off him. By the way, in spite of every picture you have ever seen, a person crucified was naked, it was part of the public shame. Then they gambled for his clothes. It was part of the execution party's right that they could have anything that the prisoner had on him at the time of execution. They did not want to split his clothes so they cast lots for them. If ever gambling was condemned it is there. Six feet below the cross they gambled, and they missed the most important thing that was happening in the universe. They drove the nails through him at nine o'clock in the morning. They pinned the board above his head, the board they had carried through the streets. THE KING OF THE JEWS, and only one person in that vast crowd believed it. They put criminals on either side — the last jest. Hundreds of years before this, the prophet Isaiah had said, *. . . he poured out his life unto death, and was numbered with the transgressors. For he bore the sin of many, and made intercession for the transgressors* (Isaiah 53:12b, *NIV*). That night as the regimental sergeant major filled up the day book he would write down: 9 a.m. — three criminals executed. And somewhere in a Roman record that may be lost now, Jesus was 'numbered' with transgressors.

Then came the reviling. You would think they had done enough to him, wouldn't you? You would think that they had done all they could do. But no, they had to add to all the pain and the suffering their mockery. The passers-by reviled him and said, *"So! You who are going to destroy the temple and build it in three days, come down from the cross and save yourself!"* (Mark 15:29 f., *NIV*) And he could have done, as easily as I write these words; it was not the nails that held him to the cross, it was something else. Then the priests came by in all their gorgeous robes: *"He saved others,"* they said, *"but he can't save himself! Let this Christ, this King of Israel, come down now from the cross, that we may see and believe"* (Mark 15:31f, *NIV*). They wanted the people to see them as the real religious leaders of the nation. They mocked. And even one of the thieves crucified with him had enough breath left (maybe he had taken that wine), and he began to mock too.

Six things happen so quickly now — the final climax has come. At midday, when the sun should have been so bright that there were no shadows on the ground, when the sun should have been overhead, it was as dark as midnight. It was not just a human conflict, the powers of darkness were there. But the reason the sky went dark was that God is light and God had gone. *"My God, my God, why have you forsaken me?"* (Mark 15:34, *NIV*) God is light, and where God is there is light. There had been a star in the sky at Jesus' birth, and when he comes back again there will be lightning in the sky from east to west, but now the sky goes absolutely black. The Saviour dies after two loud cries, recorded here. The first proved that Jesus went to hell for a few hours. To be in hell is to be so far away from God that you cannot get through to him. *"My God, my God, why have you forsaken me?"* It was the first time in all eternity that Jesus and his

Father had been away from each other. If that is a sorrowful experience for a little child, think what it must have been to the eternal Son of God — to be separated from his Father.

Then there had been Jesus' final cry. It was finished. Everybody was saying that — the disciples, Pilate — but when Jesus' time on the cross was finished it was only just the beginning. He had done all that he came to do, and the effects of it would now begin. He expired at three o'clock, and in fact he would not have been expected to die then, even though he was in a very weak physical condition. A man usually took two to seven days to die on a cross. If they wanted to hurry the death they broke the legs with a spear so that the one crucified then suffocated because they could not support their own weight to breathe. When they came to do this to Jesus, he was dead. Jesus chose to die; Jesus decided to die; he had done it — it was finished, there was nothing more to do, and it was Jesus who laid down his life. He had said that no-one would take his life from him, he would lay it down of himself. If he had not laid it down he would have survived perhaps two or three days longer, except that they would probably have hastened his death before the Passover. He died at three o'clock, at the very moment when thousands of lambs were being killed for the Passover.

The next thing that happened was that the screen divided. In the heart of the temple was a huge, beautiful curtain maybe forty feet high, embroidered all over, keeping people out of the holy place where God lived. The moment Jesus died it was ripped in two from the top to the bottom. It was so high that no man could have done that. Man would have ripped it from the bottom to the top — this was God saying: finished. The temple, priests, vestments, altars, incense, sacrifices

— all that is finished. No Christian needs priests, temples, sacrifices — none of us needs any of these things. God has ripped them out. When they looked in, there was nothing there. God was no longer to be found in a temple made with hands — he had gone.

The fourth thing that happened was that this tough centurion, when he saw how Jesus died, how he breathed his last, felt blood on his hands. He said, *"Surely this man was the Son of God!"* (Mark 15:39, *NIV*). You can see him turning to the other soldiers in the execution party with the realisation that they had just killed the Son of God. A pagan Roman was the first to realise who was hanging on the cross that day.

Then the sad depart. The men were still running, but the women were there. They were last at the cross and the first at the tomb. They saw him die, they cared for the body, they came to find it on Easter morning. I have noticed again and again at funerals it is the women who know what to do with a body, it is the women who stay up and watch, it is the women who see it through. Finally, bewildered and broken, they had nothing to stay for, so they went too.

The final thing that happened that day was that a man who had kept his light under a bushel for many months, a man who was a secret believer who really believed that Jesus was right but had not dared to say so, now that he was dead took courage and went to Pilate. He could not bear to think of Jesus' body being left on the cross for the vultures or thrown out with rubbish, and he came right out and went boldly to Pilate to ask for the body so that he could give Jesus a proper burial. Here was Joseph of Arimathea, a man who until this moment had been afraid to stand for Jesus, afraid to acknowledge that he really thought he was right, a man who had a lot to lose by giving him this burial, a man who was part of the very council, a man who had not consented to the death of Jesus, who even if he had not consented did nothing to protest — this man at last came out. He was trying to make up for the fact that he did not openly accept Christ when he believed in him. It seemed too late, but Joseph was to find out it was not. The tragedy is that there are many who will one day come right out and say, 'He was right.' In fact, everybody will one day acknowledge that Jesus is the Lord; one day it will be popular to say that Jesus is Lord. It is wonderful when people can get over their inhibitions and say: 'I belong to him now; I believe in him now, whatever it costs.'

So they buried Jesus, they laid the body in the tomb. But if that was the end of the story, if that was all I could preach, we would have to close our churches now. If this was all we had to celebrate at Easter wouldn't it be terrible? It finishes in utter gloom and tragedy, it finishes in a grave — the death of all our hopes and all our dreams, and the disciples crept away, shattered men. If that were the end of the story there would be nothing left. It would mean that all our hopes for the future are dashed by death. It would mean that however wonderful Jesus' teaching may be, it is impracticable and idealistic and it does not work in this world. It would mean that Jesus was deluded. But that is not the end of the story. We will pick up the story in the next chapter and we will shout 'Hallelujah!' because the story did not end there. Even while we were yet sinners Christ died for us and he went through all this for each one of us as if we were the only person in the world.

19

RESURRECTION AND ASCENSION
16:1–20

Every time I read this passage I find something in it that I never saw before. It is always fresh and new and wonderful. The thought that comes to me as I look at it again is what a remarkable likeness there is between the beginning and the end of the life of our Lord. Have you ever noticed that the names Joseph and Mary both appear at the beginning and at the end — at the womb and the tomb? There was Joseph his foster father and Mary his mother. At the other end of his life there is Joseph who gave him the tomb and there are at least two Marys who come to the tomb to find his body, so there is a link.

There is something more than that. Both the womb and the tomb belonged to a man called Joseph and was freely given to God for his purposes. Mary was betrothed to Joseph, her body belonged to him. But when Joseph knew what it was needed for, he gladly accepted that the womb of his wife should be the home of the Son of God. Joseph of Arimathea had a tomb, it belonged to him, he had prepared it for himself no doubt at the bottom of his garden — a lovely tomb — but when he knew that he could use it for the Lord Jesus it became his. If I could say it reverently, Jesus left both the womb and the tomb. Everybody knew that a baby is only in the womb for nine months but nobody expected a corpse to come out of a tomb after three days. Jesus came out of the womb to live his life on earth; out of the tomb to begin an even greater ministry. And therefore both the womb and the tomb were back as the property, as it were, of the owners — Joseph in both cases. We know that Mary's womb was used again — there were other children, brothers and sisters. Whether the tomb was ever used again I do not know. I question whether, it having been used for the Lord Jesus, anybody would ever use it again.

But there is something even more wonderful that links the womb and the tomb. In both, hidden from the eyes of men, the Holy Spirit was doing something wonderful, creative, powerful. In the womb of Mary, the Holy Spirit, having caused the conception, was preparing a body for thirty-three years' ministry. But in the tomb, shut off from the eyes of men, the same Holy Spirit was raising up Jesus from the dead, giving him a glorious body that would not grow any older. So the Holy Spirit was working in both. It is interesting that the psalmist says,

> *When I was woven together in the*
> *depths of the earth,*
> *your eyes saw my unformed body.*
>
> Psalm 139:15f., *NIV*

He was referring to his mother's womb, but the tomb was literally in the depths of the earth, the place where the Holy Spirit was creating the glorious body of Jesus. So there is a wonderful parallel.

The interesting thing is that there were two Marys who were not at the tomb on Easter Sunday morning. One was

Mary the mother of Jesus (John was looking after her in his own home), but the other was the Mary who had anointed his body beforehand for burial. She did not come because, as we saw, she knew that there would probably be no opportunity afterwards to anoint the body, which was why she did it before he died.

The women were the last at the cross and the first at the tomb. This is quite typical. Men would be sitting silently or talking aimlessly behind locked doors, but women get on with things pretty quickly. They get over their grief by doing something practical. So the women came first thing in the morning to the tomb. They passed through two experiences — one of fear, and one of faith. What caused the fear was the evidence of the resurrection, and what caused the faith was the experience of the risen Jesus. These are the two stages through which we need to pass. The evidence considered impartially by anybody should convince them that something supernatural happened on the first Easter Sunday, but that does not lead to faith. Faith comes when you meet the risen Jesus and have an experience of him. The evidence will convince but it could lead to no more than fear — it is the experience that leads to faith.

Remember that they were tired and sad, and remember it was early, in the first light of morning. Remember that they had come to perform a rather distasteful task, especially after three days and three nights, and you will realise that their nerves must have been very much on edge. Then they saw three things, any one of which at first sight could be assumed to be a human event, but when looked at more closely became a divine event — at first sight a surprising thing, at second sight a supernatural thing and it was this that caused their fear. When people first meet the supernatural and realise that something has been happening that no human being could have done, they are invariably afraid.

We look at the three things. First of all, the rolled stone which may have weighed over a ton. Had they forgotten about it? Did they think the guards would let them in? Did they think there would be somebody around to roll it away for them? I do not know. But imagine: they came, and they had forgotten until they got to the garden about the stone. Perhaps in their grief they had not thought it through. But they looked down into the garden and there they could see the stone was rolled away. It was not just rolled away sideways. I think from the scripture it was lying flat because an angel rolled it away and sat on it. I love that phrase. The contempt of an angel for a huge block of stone — he just flicked it away and sat on it, as much as to say that is nothing to heaven, it is a pebble. At first sight it must have seemed like a human act. We know that it was a supernatural act. No man rolled that stone away — indeed, there were guards there to see that they could not.

The second thing they saw was what appeared to be a young man dressed in white. Who was it? At first sight again it seems to be a human event, yet we know that it was a supernatural event — they had not expected to see this.

The third thing was the empty tomb itself, and the young man, whom we know to be a supernatural visitor, an angel, told them to come and see, then go and tell. Here is Christian mission in a nutshell: make sure in your own experience that Jesus is alive, then go and share that blessing with somebody else. But you notice that they did not go, and they did not go and tell. Why? Because three supernatural things before breakfast was more than the three women could take, and they were afraid so they ran.

At that point Mark's Gospel finishes in the middle of a sentence. We do not know why it finishes at that point. But if the gospel itself finished at that point we would never have heard it. Fear does not make you go and witness; a taste of the supernatural does not make you a burning messenger, wanting to share it all. If they had got no further than the evidence and fear, the silence would have stayed until this time. But the evidence prepared their minds for the experience. There has to be a certain amount of the truth grasped by a person before they can meet Christ. A certain amount of the evidence must be presented. But evidence alone does not convince anyone of the need to go out and tell others about Jesus. An empty tomb alone would not have been sufficient. So somebody, realising that Mark's Gospel was incomplete, wrote an ending to it. That does not mean that we can dismiss the ending and say, 'Ah well, it's not the Word of God' —far from it. Everything that is added in this other ending that somebody has rightly added can be checked elsewhere in the Bible. Some of the things can be checked in Matthew, some in Luke, some in John, some in the book of Acts. Now there was experience and evidence. The empty tomb gave way to a full upper room. He appeared to one woman in the garden, to two disciples as they went into the country along the road to Emmaus, and to eleven in the upper room as they sat at the table. They were full of joy, they believed; the fear with the evidence had changed to faith with the experience. I say again: anybody who will examine the evidence for the resurrection with an open mind and with an honest, scientific, historical approach, must be convinced by the evidence, which is better for this event than any other in ancient history. The disciples had to be convinced that something supernatural had happened in that garden two thousand years ago. But to go out and preach, something more was needed: experience. They got that in the appearances of the risen Lord Jesus.

Jesus said, *"Go into all the world and preach the good news to all creation. Whoever believes and is baptised will be saved"* (Mark 16:15f., *NIV*). Notice he did not say if somebody is not baptised they will be lost; he said, *"but whoever does not believe will be condemned"*. So if you do believe, baptism is the next step.

Someone who does not believe in the risen Jesus is lost, so believing is a matter of life and death. That is why we preach, and that is why we baptise. The disciples were witnesses but not intellectuals, they were ordinary men and women going out with hearts full of experience, and the risen Lord went with them everywhere they went. He is everywhere his people are. Everywhere people who believe in him gather, there he is in the middle of them —our living, risen Saviour and Lord, Jesus Christ.

Note on Mark's 'Lost ending'

It is noticeable that the earliest manuscripts of Mark's Gospel end so abruptly and with the extraordinary phrase: 'for they feared', almost in the middle of a sentence (verse 8 in our Bibles).

The most obvious explanation is that the original scroll was damaged, the final part torn off and lost. Was this accidental or deliberate? If the latter, who would have done such a thing and why? I can think of one possible answer, but emphasise that it is my own speculation.

Tradition tells us that Mark wrote in Rome and based his account on Peter's reminiscences, told in his preaching. We know from other scriptures that Peter was specially singled out for a personal meeting with the risen Jesus (1 Corinthians 15:5). But we have no record of where or when this happened, much less what was said (though there might be a clue in 1 Peter 3:18-20 and 4:6). Was this encounter so personal, so sacred to Peter himself that he did not want it made public for posterity? Did he tear a strip off Mark's scroll when he read it? Did he fear it would give him undue prominence over the other apostles (which happened in Rome anyway)?

Whatever, early Christians recognised the incompleteness of Mark's version and compiled a 'Shorter' and a 'Longer' Ending, the latter usually used to complete the story.

*For the benefit of preachers and teachers, here are
the outlines of these studies, originally given to listeners:*

1. MARK 1:1–13 Book and baptism
A. THE BOOK
i. Certainly the shortest ii. Probably the earliest iii. Easily the liveliest
1. WHAT IT IS ABOUT
a. Not a biography b. But a Gospel
2. WHO IT IS ABOUT
a. Jesus b. Christ c. Son of God
B. THE BAPTIST (1–8)
1. THE MAN
a. Fulfilment of prophecy
        i. Challenge (Malachi 3) ii. Comfort (Isaiah 40:1)
b. Revival of prophecy
        i. District ii. Diet iii. Dress
2. THE MISSION
a. Repentance b. Baptism
3. THE MESSAGE
a. Second person of the Trinity b. Third person of the Trinity
C. THE BEGINNING (9–13)
1. THE VISION
2. THE VOICE
a. Psalm 2:7 b. Isaiah 42:1
3. THE VIGIL
a. Spirit b. Satan c. Beasts d. Angels

2. MARK 1:14–45 Disciples and Demons
A. THE PATTERN (14–15)
1. PREACHING FOR THE SPIRIT
a. Gospel b. God c. Time d. Kingdom e. Hand f. Repent g. Believe
 2. TEACHING FOR THE MIND
a. Place — synagogue b. Power — authority
3. HEALING FOR THE BODY
B. THE PARTNERS (16–20)
1. HUMAN — EARTHLY
a. What they were   b. What he said
        i. Demand ii. Offer
2. DIVINE — HEAVENLY
C. THE PROBLEM (21 – 45)
1. DEMONS
a. Supernatural b. Messiah
2. DISEASES
a. Natural b. Healer
        i. The leper's need ii. The leper's faith iii. The leper's disobedience

3. MARK 2:1–3:6 Hostility and authority
A. WHEN? (1–17, 1–6)
1. MAN WITH PALSY CURED (sins!)
a. Faith b. Forgiveness
2. MAN AT CUSTOMS CALLED (sinners!)
a. Publicans b. Sinners
3. MAN WITH HANDICAP HEALED (Sabbath!)
a. Their question: urgency b. His question: mercy
B. WHO?
1. SCRIBES 2. PHARISEES 3. HERODIANS
C. HOW?
1. THOUGHT 2. WORD 3. DEED
D. WHY? (18–28)
1. HIS CHALLENGE TO THEIR AUTHORITY
a. Sabbath b. Fasting
2. HIS CLAIM TO HIS AUTHORITY
a. Forgiver of sin b. Physician of sinners Bridegroom of Israel.
d. Lord of Sabbath e. Son of Man
      i. Human (Ezekiel 2:1, 3, 8) ii. Divine (Daniel 7:13)

4. MARK 3:7–35 Friends and foes
A. HIS FAME: 'A MIRACLE WORKER' (7–12)
1. DISEASES —natural   a. Danger b. Distraction
2. DEMONS —supernatural   a. Danger b. Deception
B. HIS FOLLOWERS: 'A MASTER' (13–19)
1. WHY DID JESUS CHOOSE THE TWELVE?
a. Communion: disciples b. Commission: apostles
2. WHY DID JESUS CHOOSE TWELVE?
a. Convenient b. Significant
3. WHY DID JESUS CHOOSE THESE TWELVE?
i. Temperament? ii. Politics? iii. Education? iv. Occupation?
v. Background? vi. Blood?
a. His call b. His choice
C. HIS FRIENDS: 'A MANIAC' (20–21)
1. PRESSURE: multitude 2. PROTECTION: solitude
D. HIS FOES: 'A MAGICIAN' (22–30)
1. BLINDNESS: good 2. BLASPHEMY: evil
E. HIS FAMILY: 'A MAN' (31–35)
1. EARTHLY RELATIVES 2. HEAVENLY RELATIONS

Appendix: Study Guide

5. MARK 4:1–34 Parables and pointers

Parables: stories with a . . .   i. Moral ii. Meaning iii. mirror iv. mystery
A. THE SOIL — NO LASTING EFFECT? (1–28)
1. THE FAULT LIES IN THE SOIL
a. Wayside — hardened — no result
b. Rocky — shallow — quick result
c. Thorny — choked — slow result
2. THE FRUIT COMES FROM THE SOIL
d. Good — receptive — huge result
B. THE SEED — NO VISIBLE EFFECT? (26–29)
1. ACTIVE — patience 2. PRODUCTIVE — confidence
C. THE SHRUB — NO GREAT EFFECT? (30–34)
1. COLOSSAL
2. UNIVERSAL i. Light must be revealed ii. Truth must be received

6. MARK 4:35–5:43 Fear and faith

A. DANGER — from fear to fear (35–41)
1. DISCIPLES REBUKE JESUS
2. JESUS REBUKES THE STORM
3. JESUS REBUKES THE DISCIPLES
B. DEMONS — from faith to fear (1–20)
1. ACTIONS a. Resisted b. Retorted c. Retreated
2. REACTIONS a. They asked Jesus to go. b. He asked to go with Jesus.
C. DISEASE — from fear to faith (21–34)
1. THE CONTACT 2. THE CONVERSATION
D. DEATH — from faith to faith (35–43)
1. TO JAIRUS: comfort 2. TO MOURNERS: challenge
3. TO GIRL: command 4. TO PARENTS: care

7. MARK 6:1–56 Actions and reactions

A. HOSTILITY — Nazareth (1–6a)
1. FAMILIARITY 2. FAITHLESSNESS
B. HELP — Galilee (6b–13)
1. AUSTERITY 2. AUTHORITY
C. HORROR — Machaerus (14–29)
1. SUPERSTITION 2. SENSUALITY
D. HUNGER — Tabgha (30–44)
1. COMPASSION 2. CONSIDERATION
E. HARDNESS — Bethsaida (45–52)
1. ANXIETY 2. ASTONISHMENT
F. HELPLESSNESS — Genessaret (53–56)
1. FAMILIARITY 2. FAITH

8. MARK 7:1–8:26 Places and people
A. GENESSARET — RITUAL (1–23)
1. EXTERNAL TRADITION (1–13)
a. Outside rather than inside b. Human rather than divine
c. Physical rather than spiritual
2. INTERNAL TRUTH (14–23)
a. Not into stomach b. But out of heart
B. TYRE — RACE (24–30)
1. JEWISH PRIORITY (24–27) 1. GENTILE PERSISTENCE (28–30)
C. DECAPOLIS — RELIEF (31–10)
1. PRIVATE FACULTIES (31–37) 2. PUBLIC FEEDING (1–10)
D. DALMANUTHA — REASON (11–21)
1. HOSTILE CRITICISM (11–13) 2. FRIENDLY STUPIDITY (14–21)
E. BETHSAIDA — RELIEF (22–26)
1. OBSCURE SHADOWS (22–24) 2. CLEAR SIGHT (25–26)

9. MARK 8:27–9:13 Testing and transfiguration
A. THE GREAT CONFESSION (27–33)
1. THE QUESTION a. Others' opinion b. Own observation
2. THE QUALIFICATION a. Silence b. Suffering
3. THE QUARREL a. Peter b. Satan
B. THE GREAT COMMISSION (34–1)
1. SELF DENIED
2. SAFETY DENOUNCED
3. SUCCESS DEVALUED
4. SHAME DEFEATED
C. THE GREAT CONFIRMATION (2–13)
1. THE INSIGHT
a. The vision   i. Jesus ii. Moses and Elijah
b. The voice   i. This is my beloved Son ii. Listen to him
2. THE INJUNCTION
3. THE INQUIRY
a. Messenger has spoken b. Messenger has suffered

10. MARK 9:14–50 Lessons and life
A. IMPOTENT — faith (14–29)
1. DOUBTING — FATHER   2. CONFIDENT — DISCIPLES
B. IGNORANT — knowledge (30–32)
1. HUMAN — DEATH   2. DIVINE — RESURRECTION
C. IMPORTANT — humility (33–37)
1. GREATEST — SERVANT   2. LEAST — CHILD
D. INTOLERANT — love (38–42)
1. DIFFICULT — DEMON   2. EASY — CUP
E. INDULGENT — holiness (43–50)
1. NEGATIVE — FIRE   ˎ   2. POSITIVE — SALT

11. MARK 10:1–52 Tough and tender
A. DIVORCE (1–12)
1. PUBLIC CONTROVERSY
a. Moses — divorce permitted b. God — Marriage permanent
2. PRIVATE CONVERSATION
a. Disciples — marriage is alarming
b. Jesus — remarriage is adultery
B. CHILDREN (13–16)
1. ALWAYS ROOM FOR CHILDREN 2. ONLY ROOM FOR CHILDREN
C. POSSESSIONS (17–22)
1. HIS CHECK 2. HIS CHALLENGE 3. HIS CHARM
4. HIS CHANCE HIS CHOICE
D. STATUS (23–52)
1. SACRIFICE 2. SERVICE

12. MARK 11:1–11 Colt and crowd
A. HIS INTENTION: PRINCE OF PEACE (1–7)
1. COLT FOR THE LORD (Zechariah 9:9)
2. CLOAKS FOR A SADDLE
B. THEIR IMPRESSION: FREEDOM FIGHTER (8–11)
1. WHAT THEY DID
a. Garments (2 Kings 9:13) b. Palms (1 Maccabees 13:51)
2. WHAT THEY SAID
a. Hosanna = save us now b. Blessed is he... (Psalm 118:26; note v. 10).
c. Kingdom of David

13. MARK 11:12–12:2 Jesus and Jews
A. CURSING OF THE TREE (12–14)
1. NO FRUIT 2. NO FUTURE
B. CLEANSING OF THE TEMPLE (15–19)
1. EXPEDIENT THOROUGHFARE 2. EXPLOITING BUSINESS
3. EXCLUSIVE CLUB 4. EXPOSED HIDEOUT
C. CONDITION OF THE TREE (20–25)
1. FAITH 2. FORGIVENESS
D. COURT OF THE TEMPLE (27–33)
1. AUTHORITY OF JESUS? 2. AUTHORITY OF JOHN?
E. CRIME OF THE TENANTS (1–12)
1. VINEYARD — Israel 2. OWNER — God 3. TENANTS — priests
4. SERVANTS — prophets 5. SON — Jesus

14. MARK 12:13–44 Cut and thrust

A. DEFENCE (13–34)
1. POLITICAL (13–17) a. The bait b. The trap
2. PHILOSOPHICAL (18–27) a. Negative b. Positive
3. SCRIPTURAL (28–34)
a. Love of God (Deuteronomy 6:4f) b. Love of neighbour (Leviticus 19:18)
B. ATTACK (35–44)
1. SPIRITUAL (35–37) a. David's son b. David's lord
2. ECCLESIASTICAL (38–40) a. Greed b. Pride c. Hypocrisy
3. PERSONAL (40–44) a. Not what gift would buy b. But what gift had cost

15. MARK 13:1–37 Tragedy and triumph

A. GENERAL PREPARATION
1. THEIR MINDS TESTED BY FALSE PROPHETS
2. THEIR HEARTS TESTED BY FREQUENT PERILS
3. THEIR WILLS TESTED BY FIERCE PERSECUTIONS
B. PARTICULAR PREDICTION
1. THE END OF THE JEWS (14–23; 28–30)
a. The sign — abomination of desolation b. The time — soon
c. The advice — watch and flee
2. THE END OF THE AGE (24–27; 32–37)
a. The sign — shaking of heavens b. The time — sudden
c. The advice — watch and pray

16. MARK 14:1–11 Anointing and betrayal

A. TWO FEASTS (1–2)
1. HISTORICAL (Passover)
2. AGRICULTURAL (Unleavened bread)
B. TWO FOLLOWERS (3–11)
1. MARY AND HER TIMELY ACT (3–9)
a. The meal b. The murmur c. The meaning
i. Lovely ii. Opportune iii. Discerning iv. Memorable
2. JUDAS AND HIS TREACHEROUS PACT (10–11)
a. His need b. His greed c. His deed

17. MARK 14:12–52 Indoors and outdoors

A. INDOORS — THE UPPER ROOM (12–31)
1. THE SUPPER (12–16)
2. THE BETRAYAL FORETOLD (17–21)
3. THE SACRAMENT (22–26)
4. THE DESERTION FORETOLD (27–31)
B. OUTDOORS — THE GETHSEMANE GARDEN (32–52)
1. THE AGONY (32–42)
2. THE BETRAYAL FULFILLED (43–45)
3. THE ARREST (46–49)
3. THE DESERTION FULFILLED (50–52)

18. MARK 14:53–15:47 Trial and execution

A. EXAMINATION (54–15)

1. JEWISH TRIAL — Annas and Caiaphas
2. ROMAN TRIAL — Pontius Pilate

B. EXHIBITION (16–32)

1. FLOGGED
2. MOCKED
3. MARCHED
4. CRUCIFIED

a. Clothes off him b. Nails through him c. Wine for him
d. Accusation above him e. Thieves beside him

5. REVILED

a. Bystanders b. Priests c. Criminals

C. EXECUTION (33–47)

1. SKY DARKENS
2. SAVIOUR DIES
3. SCREEN DIVIDES
4. SOLDIER DISCERNS
5. SORROWING DEPART
6. SCHOLAR DECIDES

19. MARK 16:1–20 Resurrection and ascension

A. EVIDENCE (1–8)

1. ROLLED STONE

a. To let the Saviour out? b. To let the world in!

2. YOUNG MAN

a. He has risen b. He is not here

3. EMPTY TOMB

a. Come and see b. Go and tell

> *NOTE: vv. 9-20 = an added ending to replace Mark's incomplete*

B. EXPERIENCE (9–14)

1. TO ONE IN THE GARDEN (cf. John)

Thought he was just a gardener

2. TO TWO IN THE COUNTRY (cf. Luke)

Thought he was just a guest

3. TO ELEVEN IN THE HOUSE (cf. Luke)

Thought he was just a ghost

C. ELOQUENCE (15–20)

1. THE WORDS OF JESUS (cf. Matthew)

a. Universal mission b. Urgent message c. Unique miracles

2. THE WORKS OF JESUS (cf. Acts)

a. The finish of his material body b. The beginning of his mystical body

3206089R00169

Printed in Great Britain
by Amazon.co.uk, Ltd.,
Marston Gate.